S0-BIE-322
ST JOSEPH PUB LIBRA

Great Lakes Ships We Remember III

A Photo-History of Selected Great Lakes Ships

GREAT LAKES SHIPS WE REMEMBER III

Rev. Peter J. Van der Linden
Author & Editor

IN COOPERATION WITH

Jay N. Bascom
John H. Bascom
Ronald F. Beaupre
Rev. Edward J. Dowling, S.J.
E.B. (Skip) Gillham
David T. Glick
Wesley R. Harkins
James H. Jackson
M. Karl Kuttruff
C. Patrick Labadie
Robert J. MacDonald
Daniel C. McCormick
Michael J. Nicholls
Rudi Rabe
Ralph K. Roberts
The Marine Historical Society of Detroit, Inc.

Published by
FRESHWATER PRESS, INC.
1700 E. 13th Street, Suite 3 R-E
Cleveland, Ohio 44114
U.S.A.

Library of Congress Card Catalog # 79-112286

Presented by

Alice Thornycroft
Lou MacFarlane

In Memory of

Barbara Troost

Maud Preston Palenske Memorial Library
St. Joseph, Michigan

Eternal Father, strong to save,
Whose power can still the restless wave,
Who formed our mighty Lakes so deep,
In whom we trust our souls to keep,
O, hear us when we pray to thee,
For those who sail the troubled sea.

Based on the Navy Hymn

FIFTIETH ANNIVERSARY EDITION

This Third Edition in the Series "Great Lakes Ships We Remember" commemorates the 50th anniversary of the founding of The Marine Historical Society of Detroit, Inc. The following is the account of that beginning as described by Roy Bates, one of the four-man group whose imagination and energy were responsible for the creation of the society.

Early in 1943 I visited the Detroit Historical Museum in the Barlum Tower in Cadillac Square, Detroit, and made the acquaintance of the Curator of the Museum, Mr. Robert H. Larson. Having common interests and friendships Larson and I discussed the possibility of getting together a group of people interested in lake shipping, to meet occasionally at the museum or elsewhere and talk boats, look at pictures, and eventually work out a program of meetings along marine lines. At the same time a Museum Shipping Committee was appointed to design models and to plan an annual museum shipping exhibit. Among the members of this committee were Mr. William A. McDonald and Mr. John M. O'Brien, both of whom I contacted at these committee meetings and both of whom became enthusiastic backers of the idea of a ship lovers organization. Mr. O'Brien contacted me frequently thereafter. His enthusiasm and insistence did as much as anything to bring the plans to a head. So Messrs. Larson, O'Brien and I began work in earnest to organize what is presently The Marine Historical Society of Detroit. Mr. Larson persuaded Mr. George W. Stark of the Detroit News to mention the proposal and announce the first meeting date of July 13 in his "Town Talk" column in the News on July 9, 1944.

On that eventful evening, high in the Barlum Tower, the following persons appeared: Roy M. Bates, Robert H. Larson, William A. McDonald, Norbert K. Neff, John M. O'Brien, Kenneth E. Smith, Captain William J. Taylor and Alastair J. Weir. I called the meeting to order and briefly announced what was intended to be done and turned the meeting over to O'Brien. A temporary organization was set up with Kenneth E. Smith as chairman and John M. O'Brien as secretary. A committee of Constitution and By Laws was appointed comprising of McDonald, Neff and me. This group completed its work in a later meeting at the old BOB-LO Club at the foot of Woodward Avenue.

The next meeting of the organization was held on July 27, with Captain William J. Taylor as the first speaker to appear on our program. His subject was "The Lighthouse Service." The organization was, at this time, named "Marine Historical Society of Detroit."

At the August 31st meeting the Constitution and By Laws were discussed and adopted and the charter membership closed with the addition of the following names; Rev. Edward J. Dowling, S.J., Gerald Holland, Miss Louisa Butler, John G. Ivers, Lowell Johnson, Thomas K. Weber, making a total of 14 Charter Members.

On September 28, another meeting was held at which Mr. Smith led a brief discussion on the history and ships of the White Star Line, after which permanent officers were elected, as follows: President, Kenneth E. Smith; Vice President, Roy M. Bates; Secretary, John M. O'Brien; Treasurer, Robert H. Larson.Thus the organization brought into being by a Swede (Larson), an Irishman (O'Brien) and a Hoosier (Bates) was on its way. That which has followed is a matter of secretarial record.

Roy M. Bates

Fort Wayne, Indiana (June, 1955)

The fourteen charter members in alphabetical order were:

Roy M. Bates (Founder)
Miss Louisa Butler
Rev. Edward J. Dowling, S.J.
Gerald Holland
John G. Ivers
Lowell Johnson
Robert H. Larson (Founder)
William A. McDonald
Norbert K. Neff
John M. O'Brien (Founder)
Kenneth E. Smith
Capt. Thomas J. Taylor
Thomas K. Weber
Alastair J. Weir

WE REMEMBER...

Down through the ages, the fascination and romance of ships has captivated the thousands who have watched the leviathans plow through calm or troubled global waters. Great Lakes ships, as well as the men who have labored aboard them, have had their enthusiasts since La Salle's GRIFFON first sailed these inland waters. We remember these ships, old and new, and now recall in story and pictures some of the fascination we have felt for them.

This volume is a sequel to the first and second books authored by members of The Marine Historical Society of Detroit and feature entirely new vessels and photographs from various sources listed below. Again, we have selected these vessels as a representative group. Not all the ships that have sailed these Great Lakes can be included. We hope that these are familiar to many enthusiasts and fascinating to those uninitiated.

We dedicate this volume especially to Peter B. Worden, Sr. and to the many historians and ship buffs who have led the way to a more comprehensive study of the vessels which sailed and still sail our "Inland Seas." These dedicated men have now passed to their eternal reward, but we would like to remember them for giving us the incentive and the fruits of their research. We remember Roy Bates, Dana Thomas Bowen, Dwight Boyer, Al Bradley, Milton Brown, Dyke Cobb, Eugene Cote, Frank Crevier, Tom Dancey, Fred and Lucy Frederickson, Captain Frank Hamilton, Curt Hazeltine, Erik Heyl, Alan Howard, Captain H. C. Inches, Hal Jackson, Ted Jones, Jim Kidd, Fred Landon, Roy Larson, Robert E. Lee, Bill MacDonald, Peirce McLouth, Edward Middleton, Neil Morrison, John Poole, Herman Runge, Rev. Franklin C. St.Clair, Kenneth and Keith Smith, Captain William Taylor, Elmer Treloar, Stoddard White, Edwin Wilson, Loudon Wilson, Tom and Nels Wilson, Harry Wolf, Scott Worden, Rick Wright, Bob Zeleznik and others who have been the forerunners of the many historians of today.

Our thanks go to those who have been so instrumental in putting this third volume to press. Our co-authors have been especially helpful. These are: John H. and Jay N. Bascom of Toronto, whose specialty is the Canadian old-timers; Father Edward J. Dowling, S.J., without whose help hardly any of us would be where we are now as Great Lakes ship enthusiasts; C. Patrick Labadie, whose fascination with older ships prior to 1900 has greatly enhanced the stories in this volume; and also to Ronald Beaupre of Port Elgin, E. B. (Skip) Gillham of Vineland, Ontario, David Glick of Lakeside, Ohio, Wesley Harkins of Duluth, James Jackson of Dearborn, Karl Kuttruff of Sterling Heights, Robert MacDonald of Erie, Daniel McCormick of Massena, Michael Nicholls of Allen Park, Rudi Rabe of Wyandotte, Ralph Roberts of Saginaw all of whom contributed to the success of this book...my personal thanks.

Our special thanks go to those who supplied the photographs for this new volume: Abass Studio, Stephens Adamson, Barry Andersen, George Ayoub, J.W. Bald (late), Jim Bartke Collection, Jay N. Bascom, John H. Bascom, Ron Beaupre, Richard Bibby, R.S. Blakeslee, Blue Water Studio, Duff Brace, Bill Bruce, Buffalo Dry Dock Co., Canadian Forces of Ottawa, Canal Park Museum at Duluth, Detroit Photographic, Rev. Raymond M. Donahue, Dossin Marine Museum, Rev. Edward J. Dowling, S.J., Firefighters' Museum of Nova Scotia, Freshwater Press, Brian Gamula, Skip Gillham, Dave Glick, Great Lakes Graphics, Wes Harkins, R.V. Inness, Jim Jackson, Mr. Jacoby, Ted Jones (late), Jim Kidd (late), Rudy Kleyn of Rozenburg, Holland, Knudsen Bro. S/Y Photo, Elmer Kremkow, M.K. Kuttruff Collection, C. Patrick Labadie Collection, Wm. Lafferty, Jr., Paul C. LaMarre, Jr., Library of Congress, Claude Lockwood, William J. Luke, R.J. MacDonald, Emory Massman, Materna Studios, Gordon McCauley, Dan McCormick, William A. McDonald (late), McKenzie (late), Scott McLellan, McNutt Photo, Charles Mensing (late), Nelson Merrifield, Rowley W. Murphy (late), National Archives of Canada, Mike Nicholls, Nipigon Transports, J. Michael O'Brien, Frank T. Patyk (late), Pesha Photo, Rudi Rabe Collection, Ralph Roberts, The Royal Gazette (Bermuda), Russ Sawyer, William A. Schell, A. Scrimali, Paul Sherlock (late), Paul H. Silvestone, Kenneth E. Smith (late), Walt Smith, Steamship Historical Society of America Collection, Capt. Ron Tackaberry, Capt. Wm. J. Taylor (late), Elmer Treloar (late), Tugboat Photos & Research, US Army Military History Institute, U.S. Navy Photo, Fr. Peter Van der Linden, John Vournakis, Edwin Wilson (late), Loudon Wilson (late), Peter B. Worden, Sr. (late), A.E. Young (late). Others including "Lake Log Chips", the "Scanner" of the Toronto Marine Historical Society, the VALLEY CAMP Museum at Sault Ste. Marie, the Canal Park Museum at Duluth, the Dossin Great Lakes Museum at Belle Isle and the Great Lakes Museum at Vermilion, Ohio have been most helpful in promoting this third volume.

Special thanks go to the Steamship Historical Society of America, the Library of Congress, the Mariners Museum in Norfolk, Virginia and the U.S. Naval Institute for use of their photographs. The staff of Freshwater Press and that of the Great Lakes Research Center of Bowling Green State University, the Center for Archival Collections, have been exceedingly helpful in making this work a success.

Lastly, to Wayne Garrett who transcribed the manuscript onto the computer and to Bill Luke who helped and added many suggestions, many thanks.

Rev. Peter J. Van der Linden
Editor/Author

EXPLANATION

The ships depicted in this book were creations of engineering art. The following explanations about the dimensions and statistics of these vessels should be understood to follow accurately the chronology of each individual ship story.

Unless otherwise noted, the length of the vessel is that length found in the official documents of the country in which the vessel was constructed. The length dimension nearly universally used in these documents is "length between perpendiculars". This is defined as "the length of the vessel as measured on the Summer load line from the foreside of the stem to the afterside of the rudder post." Other lengths which apply to vessel statistics and which typically are used in the maritime field are: 1) "keel length", which is the length of the vessel measured along the keel plate, and 2) "overall length", which is the extreme length of the vessel as measured from its forward most to aftermost perpendicular extensions. The beam and depth of the vessel as shown refer to the greatest breadth measured over the frames and the moulded vertical hold depth measured on the center line of the vessel amidships, respectively. **IN ALL CASES, THE TECHNICAL INFORMATION SHOWN WITH EACH VESSEL STORY IS THE ORIGINAL STATISTICAL DATA WHEN THE SHIP WAS PUT INTO SERVICE WITH THE EXCEPTION OF ANY SUBSEQUENT OFFICIAL NUMBERS. ANY SALIENT SUBSEQUENT CHANGES TO THIS ARE NOTED IN THE TEXT.**

Each ship is given an official number when first documented in a country. The vessel might have many different names in its lifetime, but the official number rarely changes unless she is transferred to another nation, in which case she is given a new official number according to the system used in that particular country.

The types of engines used in various steam and diesel vessels have particular significance to an enthusiast of the shipping world. Each engine is a little different than the next. The dimensions of each engine are given for sake of completeness. The diameter of cylinders used can vary during a ship's lifetime. The engine can be re-bored to make it more economical, thus changing the diameter. The stroke is the vertical distance that a piston takes to make one up or down movement. If an engine is a "triple expansion" (the most popular) type, it will have three cylinders, the low pressure, the intermediate, and the high pressure. The steam flows from the high pressure cylinder to the low, giving added power with each stroke. Propulsion machinery data are, of course, not shown in this book for non-self-propelled vessels such as barges and schooners.

The hull numbers are noted because they are a means of determining just how many ships a shipyard built during its lifetime. The numbering will differ from one firm to another, but most keep an accurate record of the ships they have built. Although uncommon, some yards preferred not to assign hull numbers.

Gross registered tonnage (GRT) applies to vessels, not to cargo. It is determined by dividing by 100 the contents, in cubic feet, of the vessel's closed-in spaces. A vessel ton is 100 cubic feet. This tonnage is determined by hull inspectors of the classification society for each ship. This may change from time to time in a ship's life according to the measurement system and governing rules under which the calculation is made. GRT is included in the statistical record of each vessel. The tonnages listed are taken from the American and Canadian records found in the annual reports issued by these nations. The American vessels will be in the "Merchant Vessels of the United States," the Canadian in the "List of Shipping."

Launch dates, when available, have usually come from articles appearing in daily newspapers when the vessel was christened. Specifications of the engines and other dimensions were traced back through the various classification society records such as "Lloyds Register of Shipping," "The Record" of the American Bureau of Shipping , older issues of "Inland Lloyds," "Beeson's Marine Directory" and "Underwriters Insurance" records. Today, such statistics may be found in "Greenwood's Guide to Great Lakes Shipping," an annual publication by the publishers of this volume.

To any enthusiast or "Boat Collector," everything about a ship is of utmost importance. So that the reader may see the effort of pleasureful research that goes into a hobby such as this, we have attempted to share herein all we know about any given vessel's history. Particularly interesting sidelights have been added whenever possible.

Renaming of ships often causes difficulty. To make it easier to understand the time sequence and order in which the ship was given various names, the first name a ship is given in official records is listed as the "a" name. Each successive name and the date it is changed are mentioned. The second name, therefore, becomes the "b" name, etc. Some ships were originally destined to be named one way but were given a name change before the official records were made. These cases were noted wherever possible.

B.F. AFFLECK

The B.F. AFFLECK was built for the Pittsburgh Steamship Company by the Toledo Shipbuilding Company and was launched June 25, 1927. She cleared Toledo on her first trip August 28, 1927.

In 1952, her ownership changed to the U.S. Steel Corporation of Cleveland, Ohio. On December 17, 1955, in heavy fog, she collided head-on with her fleetmate HENRY PHIPPS in the Straits of Mackinac. Both vessels were damaged but were able to sail under their own power for repairs.

The AFFLECK last operated in the 1979 season and then laid up at Duluth, Minnesota. She was sold for scrapping to Western Metals in Thunder Bay, Ontario in October, 1983, and then resold to Hyman-Michaels Company of Duluth for scrapping in June, 1984. On October 31, 1986, the B.F. AFFLECK parted her lines at Azcon/Hyman Michaels scrap dock in Duluth, blew across the bay and grounded near the U.S. Coast Guard Station on Minnesota Point. Her final resting place was just 30 feet astern of the U.S. Coast Guard Cutter SUNDEW. Tugs pulled the AFFLECK back to the dock within five hours.

On November 6, 1986, the tug THUNDER CAPE towed the AFFLECK out of Duluth bound for Port Colborne, Ontario. On November 8, during a storm on Lake Superior, the tug THUNDER CAPE lost power. Due to hazardous conditions caused by winds over 40 knots and seas over 20 feet high, the AFFLECK was cut adrift off the Keweenaw Peninsula. The THUNDER CAPE was towed to Thunder Bay by the tanker EASTERN SHELL and the tug AVENGER IV, based at the Canadian Soo, was dispatched to pick up the B.F. AFFLECK. The AVENGER IV brought the AFFLECK into the Soo on November 11.

When she finally arrived at Port Colborne on November 25, 1986, the AFFLECK was placed in the section of the old canal north of Humberstone. On October 17, 1987, the tugs THUNDER CAPE and MICHAEL D. MISNER moved her to the scrap berth in Port Colborne harbor ahead of the WILLIAM P. SNYDER, JR. She was then scrapped by International Marine Salvage shortly thereafter.

B.F. AFFLECK downbound in the Detroit River 1938

B.F. AFFLECK upbound after leaving the Locks at the Soo in 1950

BUILT:	1927 Toledo Shipbuilding Co. Toledo, Ohio	*DEPTH:*	27.9
		GRT:	7,964
		REGISTRY NUMBER:	US. 226895
HULL NUMBER:	178	*ENGINES:*	24 1/2", 41", 65" Diameter x 42" Stroke Triple Expansion
LENGTH:	587.9		
BREADTH:	60.2	*ENGINE BUILDER:*	Shipyard 1927

B.F. AFFLECK downbound in lower Lake Huron September 14, 1960

ANN ARBOR No. 2

Four years after the wooden car ferry ST. IGNACE was put into service at the Straits of Mackinac and proved that open lake operation of car ferries could be successful, the Toledo, Ann Arbor and North Michigan Railroad reached the shores of Lake Michigan at Frankfort. The Ann Arbor Railroad chartered break bulk boats initially to transport through freight for southern and eastern markets. The principal freight was grain and flour which was loaded and unloaded with costly hand labor. Car ferry operation at the Straits had shown this type of service to be practical, which influenced the decision to try a similar operation from Frankfort to the west shore of Lake Michigan.

The railroad ordered a pair of wooden car ferries from the Craig Shipbuilding Company of Toledo. They were designed by Frank E. Kirby who had designed the successful ST. IGNACE and SAINTE MARIE (1). They were twin screw steamers with an additional propeller at the under-cut bow to aid in breaking ice. The ANN ARBOR No. 2 was the second of the pair, and was launched on December 7, 1892. The delivery trip through the rivers demonstrated her ice breaking capabilities. The Ann Arbor car ferry operation across Lake Michigan proved that car ferries, in fact, could be used in all seasons on the open lake. The ANN ARBOR No. 2 could carry 24 cars on four tracks arranged on the car deck. In 1896, the bow propeller and forward boiler and machinery were removed as it was felt they were not much use in windrowed ice typically encountered at Frankfort. The design worked well for sheet ice, but was ineffective in the windrowed ice. The space gained in the forward hull was sometimes used for carrying bulk grain. In the mid 1890's, both boats had their superstructures aft cut away for about 60 feet to allow easier loading. These modifications altered the vessel's appearance considerably, although they never were considered very handsome vessels.

The ANN ARBOR No. 2 continued year after year in profitable operations for the railroad. The company began to operate steel-hulled car ferries with the addition of ANN ARBOR No. 3 to the fleet in 1898. The ANN ARBOR No. 4 was delivered in 1906. With the addition of ANN ARBOR No. 5 in 1910, the ANN ARBOR No. 2 was semi-retired to serve as a spare boat, being used only in times of peak traffic or, when one of the steel boats was laid up for repairs. Her last revenue trip was made on September 29, 1912, after which she was laid up for good at Frankfort.

She was sold to the Manistee Iron Works in December, 1913 and towed to Manistee by the ANN ARBOR No. 4.

ANN ARBOR No.2 in the ice off Ludington, Michigan

There her machinery was removed and the boilers were installed in two other steamboats for further service. In 1916, she was sold to United Fuel and Supply Company and converted to a sand barge and renamed b) WHALE. The WHALE was purchased by William Nicholson in 1924 and operated as a sand barge until 1927, when she was involved in a collision with the steamer WILLIAM E. COREY. The results of the collision damage inspection, considering her advanced age and overall condition, brought about the decision to abandon her. This spelled the end for one of the earliest open-lake car ferries.

a) ANN ARBOR NO. 2 b) Whale

BUILT:	1892 Craig Shipbuilding Co. Toledo, Ohio
HULL NUMBER:	56
LENGTH:	264.2
BREADTH:	53.0
DEPTH:	14.2
GRT:	1145
REGISTRY NUMBER:	US. 106984
3 ENGINES:	20", 40" Diameter x 36" Stroke Fore & Aft Compound
ENGINE BUILDER:	S.F. Hodge & Co., Detroit, Michigan, 1892

ANN ARBOR No.2 with a load of iron tubing

ANN ARBOR No.2 at Northport under charter to the Manistique, Marquette & Northern R.R.

WHALE as a sand dredge in the early 1920's

ARIZONA

ARIZONA, built by Quayle & Martin at Cleveland, Ohio, was launched on August 19, 1868, for F.B. Gardner of Chicago, reportedly for the Lake Michigan lumber trade. Since she was built with two decks and passenger cabins, she was chartered to run in the Grand Trunk Line between Buffalo and Green Bay.

In April 1872, she was bought by J.C. and E.T. Evans of Buffalo, who ran her as a freight boat in their Anchor Line between Buffalo, Milwaukee and Chicago. In 1878, the Evans' cut down the ship to a single decked steam barge, (870 GRT), and she ran in the Saginaw lumber trade for the next two seasons.

In 1879, the ship was rebuilt again as a package freighter, (924 GRT), and chartered to Lake Superior Transit Company. She ran from Buffalo to Marquette, Portage and Duluth, carrying railroad iron, general merchandise, and acids, oils and kerosene for the mining industry. Down-bound cargoes were invariably grain and barreled flour.

On May 8, 1873, ARIZONA was sunk above the St. Clair Flats by the B.W. BLANCHARD, but was raised and repaired soon after. On October 12, 1882, she was damaged when casks of nitric acid broke during a storm on Lake Superior, but again was repaired.

On November 17, 1887, ARIZONA burst into flames off Marquette when several casks of acid broke, and she ran into the harbor ablaze. The crew jumped onto the pier as she raced past into a slip, and the ship burned for the next 24 hours. She was raised by Tom Reid in June 1888 and taken to Port Huron, where she was rebuilt as a steam barge, (684 GRT), in the Dunford & Alverson yard. She and the barge PLYMOUTH were run in the lumber trade for the next 14 years by Walter D. Young of Bay City. She was rebuilt again at Bay City in 1893, (765 GRT), when she was also given a new Marine Iron Works steeple compound engine of the same dimensions.

Between 1902 and 1920, ARIZONA changed hands three times more, 1) for the White Transportation Company, 1906-1918; 2) for the Twin City Transit Company, 1918-1920; and 3) for McDonald & Griffin, of Ogdensburg, New York, 1920-1922. She was run in the lower lakes coal and lumber trades until she was destroyed by fire at Cape Vincent, New York on December 1, 1922. Her wreckage was removed in June, 1923.

ARIZONA at her dock in her early years as a package and passenger freighter at Duluth

BUILT:	1868 Quayle & Martin Cleveland, Ohio
HULL NUMBER:	None
LENGTH:	187.3
BREADTH:	32.4
DEPTH:	12.0
GRT:	924
REGISTRY NUMBER:	US. 1768
ENGINES:	22", 40" Diameter x 30" Stroke Steeple Compound
ENGINE BUILDER:	Shepard Iron Works, Buffalo, New York, 1868

ARIZONA downbound in the St. Marys River

ARIZONA upbound in the St. Clair River

ARIZONA downbound with lumber in the St. Clair River

ASHCROFT

GLENIFFER upbound at Mission Point, St. Marys River in 1926

a) Gleniffer b) ASHCROFT

BUILT:	1925 Midland Ship Building Co. Midland, Ontario
HULL NUMBER:	12
LENGTH:	546.0
BREADTH:	60.0
DEPTH:	32.0
GRT:	7726
REGISTRY NUMBER:	C. 152641
ENGINES:	24 1/2", 41 1/2", 72" Diameter x 48" Stroke Triple Expansion
ENGINE BUILDER:	Hoover, Owens, Renschler Hamilton, Ohio, 1918

GLENIFFER at an elevator in Georgian Bay

The ASHCROFT spent forty-four years in the Canada Steamship Lines fleet. She was built as a) GLENIFFER and launched at Midland, Ontario, on November 18, 1924, for the Great Lakes Transportation Company.

Canada Steamship Lines acquired this vessel in 1926 and applied the name b) ASHCROFT, in honor of a county in the province of British Columbia.

In the years that followed, this bulk carrier hauled ore, grain and coal. Her early years were concentrated on the upper four Great Lakes but on July 6, 1932, ASHCROFT made her first trip down the newly enlarged Welland Canal. She was bound from Fort William to Kingston at the time and was the largest vessel to use the new waterway to that point.

On April 27, 1944, ASHCROFT was upbound on foggy Lake Erie when she was in a collision with the ore laden JAMES H. REED of the Interlake Steamship Company. The accident occurred off Port Burwell, Ontario, where the JAMES H. REED sank quickly with the loss of twelve lives.

ASHCROFT usually hauled ore in her later years and regularly discharged at the Algoma Steel dock at Sault Ste. Marie, Ontario. In 1950, for example, she took 26 of her 35 loads of ore to that port plus five of her shipments of coal. ASHCROFT loaded a total of 48 cargoes that year.

ASHCROFT operated into 1969 and passed down the Welland Canal for the last time on June 17. She cleared Quebec City a month later under tow of the Polish tug JANTAR, and arrived at Castellon, Spain, on August 9th to be broken up for scrap.

ASHCROFT at Ashtabula after the collision with JAMES H. REED in Lake Erie April 27, 1944

ASHCROFT at Algoma Steel, Sault Ste. Marie, Ontario with T.R. McLAGAN and BRITAMLUBE

ASHCROFT downbound light at Mission Point, St. Marys River August 17, 1958

ASHLAND

The ASHLAND, one of sixteen "Maritime Class" freighters built for Great Lakes service, lasted forty-five years. However, she barely made it to the scrapyard at Mamonal, Colombia, and was almost lost at sea on several occasions in 1988.

This vessel was built by the Great Lakes Engineering Works and was launched at Ashtabula, Ohio, on December 19, 1942. The United States Maritime Commission traded her to Pioneer Steamship Company in exchange for some of its aging tonnage. The latter firm named her a) CLARENCE B. RANDALL (1) and on July 19, 1943, she set out for Two Harbors and her first load of iron ore.

The 9,057 gross ton bulk carrier hauled large quantities of ore for Pioneer but, when that firm ceased operations, CLARENCE B. RANDALL was acquired by Columbia Transportation Division, Oglebay Norton Company, which renamed her b) ASHLAND in 1962.

ASHLAND continued to operate primarily in the ore trade. In 1978, all thirty-three of her cargoes were of that commodity. Thirteen of these loads came from Duluth and seven from Silver Bay. She also took on cargo at Superior, Marquette and Taconite Harbor on Lake Superior, as well as three shipments from Escanaba on Lake Michigan.

Ashtabula received eleven cargoes of ASHLAND's ore in 1978; the ship also discharged at Toledo, Cleveland, Indiana Harbor, Lorain, Conneaut and South Chicago.

The next year was to be her last. On May 9, ASHLAND hit the north pier while outbound from Duluth in blowing snow. A hole was punched in the port bow and an anchor was lost. Then, in December ASHLAND suffered an electrical problem and lost power on Lake Superior. The vessel was caught in the trough of the waves and required the assistance of the U.S. Coast Guard to get under way.

ASHLAND tied up at Toledo on December 19, 1979, and did not leave port until September 14, 1987, after she had been sold for scrap. The tugs TUSKER and THUNDER CAPE pulled her from the lakes and they arrived at Lauzon, Quebec, on September 23.

Then, on December 21, the Liberian tug OSA RAVENSTURM took her in tow, bound for a scrapyard in Taiwan. ASHLAND, and the other lake freighter in the tow, her former fleetmate THOMAS WILSON(3), broke loose in the Atlantic on December 30. The WILSON was lost, and when ASHLAND was recovered on January 2, 1988, she had hull fractures and had been blown 300 miles off course.

The tug REMBERTITURM took her to an anchorage off Bermuda but, on January 16, she dragged her anchors and was swept onto rocks close inshore. ASHLAND was refloated January 20, but had massive bottom damage.

ASHLAND was not permitted to remain at Bermuda, and was towed to Santo Domingo, Dominican Republic. She was not wanted there either, and the tow had to continue despite the fact that ASHLAND was in a badly leaking condition. The vessel barely made Colombia on February 5, and scrapping of the hull began at Mamonal in July, 1988.

CLARENCE B. RANDALL downbound in the St. Clair River August 19, 1950

ASHLAND downbound in the St. Clair River August 6, 1965

a) Clarence B. Randall (1) b) ASHLAND

BUILT:	1943 Great Lakes Engineering Works,Ashtabula, Ohio
HULL NUMBER:	523
LENGTH:	603.8
BREADTH:	60.2
DEPTH:	30.2
GRT:	9057
REGISTRY NUMBER:	US. 243412
ENGINES:	24½", 41", 68" Diameter x 42" Stroke Triple Expansion
ENGINE BUILDER:	Shipyard, 1943

ASHLAND aground at Bermuda January 20, 1988 The (Bermuda) Royal Gazette photo

ASHTABULA

The steel car ferry ASHTABULA was built at St. Clair, Michigan by the Great Lakes Engineering Works and launched on May 12, 1906. She was to enter service as the JAMES W. ELLSWORTH to be operated by the Ellsworth Transportation Company, but she serviced the Ashtabula to Port Burwell route her entire life as ASHTABULA managed by the Pennsylvania-Ontario Transportation Company.

Until her end, she had her original open pilot house, whereas other ships had a rebuild of some kind to their pilot houses. Her double bottom was fitted with an extensive ballast tank system.

On September 18, 1958, the ASHTABULA was involved in a collision with the steamer BEN MOREELL in the outer harbor at Ashtabula. The car ferry sank but, fortunately, no casualties were involved and the hull was subsequently raised and removed to the shipyard facilities. The judge hearing the case came to the conclusion that the evidence was too conflicting. He then ruled, in a rare case, "that neither party is entitled to recover". As a result, the car ferry was scrapped and the service to Port Burwell was abandoned.

Launching of ASHTABULA at St. Clair, Michigan May 12, 1906

ASHTABULA outbound at Ashtabula for Port Burwell,

ASHTABULA turning for her dock at Ashtabula, Ohio 1913

ASHTABULA inbound at Ashtabula

BUILT:	1906 Great Lakes Engineering Works St. Clair, Michigan	*DEPTH:*	21.5
		GRT:	2670
		REGISTRY NUMBER:	US. 203071
HULL NUMBER:	19	*2 ENGINES:*	19 1/2", 31", 52" Diameter x 36" stroke Triple Expansion
LENGTH:	338.0		
BREADTH:	56.0	*ENGINE BUILDER:*	Great Lakes Engineering Works, 1906

ATLANTA

Built at Cleveland in 1890 by the short-lived Cleveland Dry Dock Company for the Goodrich Transportation Company, of Chicago, ATLANTA was a typical Goodrich wooden passenger and freight propeller. Very similar in size and appearance were the Lake Michigan built Goodrich propellers GEORGIA (ex CITY OF LUDINGTON), ARIZONA (ex CITY OF RACINE), IOWA (ex MENOMINEE) and INDIANA. All had a length of about 200 feet.

These ships sailed on the two main Goodrich routes - one along the west shore of Lake Michigan from Chicago to Green Bay - and the other across Lake Michigan to Grand Haven and Muskegon.

ATLANTA's career came to a sudden end while the vessel was downbound from Green Bay ports to Chicago. On March 18th of 1906, fire was discovered in the hold, when the ship was abreast of Port Washington, Wisconsin, which is about 25 miles north of Milwaukee. All on board, with one exception, were rescued by the steam fish tug TESSLER. One crew member jumped overboard and was drowned. The ATLANTA burned to the water's edge.

BUILT:	1891 Cleveland Dry Dock Co. Cleveland, Ohio	*GRT:*	1129
HULL NUMBER:	unknown	*REGISTRY NUMBER:*	US. 106823
LENGTH:	200.1	*ENGINES:*	24", 44" Diameter x 36" Stroke Fore and Aft Compound
BREADTH:	32.2	*ENGINE BUILDER:*	Globe Iron Works, Cleveland, 1891
DEPTH:	13.6		

ATLANTA at her Goodrich Dock

AUBE

The steel-hulled bulk carrier ROSEMOUNT (1) was built in 1896 at Bill Quay, Newcastle, England, by Wood, Skinner & Company, and was launched on October 6, 1896. Constructed to the order of the Montreal Transportation Company Ltd., Montreal, she was almost a duplicate of the ill-fated BANNOCKBURN, which was lost without a trace on Lake Superior during the night of November 21, 1902.

ROSEMOUNT was the first vessel in the M.T.Co. fleet to be given a name ending with the suffix "mount", and many such names subsequently were chosen for the company's vessels. The steamer's early years in the M.T.Co. fleet were largely uneventful. However, she stranded some twelve miles below DeTour Light in Lake Huron on September 12, 1906, when upbound with coal for the Lakehead. The accident was caused by poor visibility resulting from nearby forest fires which cast a thick pall of smoke over the lake.

ROSEMOUNT continued in the lake trade until 1915, when World War I conditions led her to be chartered to the Nova Scotia Steel and Coal Company, of Sydney, Nova Scotia, for service on the east coast. In 1916, she was sold to the French Government Marine and, at this time, she was renamed b) AUBE and operated in the French coastal waters under the management of Compagnie Generale Trans- atlantique, Le Havre, France.

At the war's end, she was laid up at St. Nazaire, France and remained there until 1922 when Capt. J.W. Norcross, of Canada Steamship Lines Ltd., Montreal, arranged for her return to Canada athrough the firm of Anderson & Company of Canada. In order to facilitate her re-entry into Canadian registry, C.S.L. gave her back her original name of ROSEMOUNT. Upon her return, she was sold to Mapes and Ferdon Ltd., Montreal, and was renamed d) AUBE under the ownership of the Aube Steamship Company, Montreal.

In the early part of the 1926 season, AUBE was engaged in carrying rails from Sydney, Nova Scotia, to Fort William, Ontario, and in the later portion of the season, she was employed in the grain trade. Very late in that same season, AUBE stranded in the Brockville Narrows section of the St. Lawrence River and, as a result, spent the winter of 1926-1927 in the drydock at Kingston undergoing the necessary repairs. AUBE was back in the Kingston drydock during the winter of 1928-1929 for repairs required after a collision with a scow in the Welland Canal.

In 1930, the ship was severely pounded in a June storm on Lake Superior while downbound with a cargo of grain. Once again, it was necessary that AUBE visit the drydock at Kingston for repairs.

Her last year of operation was 1931. Late that autumn, while downbound with grain, AUBE ran aground in the St. Clair River due to a jammed rudder. She managed to get herself off the mud bank and proceeded on her way to Montreal, but en route, she ran aground below the Morrisburg Canal in the St. Lawrence. She was freed and finally laid up at Lachine, Quebec, in December of 1931.

In the spring of 1932, the Aube Steamship Company found itself under the trusteeship of the Montreal Trust Company as a result of unpaid accounts. As a consequence, the AUBE was sold on June 6, 1932, to Sinmac Lines Ltd. for $2,800 and, in August, she was towed from Lachine to Sorel, Quebec.

Finally, in 1937, AUBE was cut up for scrap at Sorel by Les Chantiers Manseau, Ltee.

AUBE in the old St. Lawrence Canals

AUBE upbound at Mission Point, St. Marys River in 1926

a) Rosemount (1) b) AUBE c) Rosemount (1) d) AUBE

BUILT:	1896 Wood, Skinner & Co. Bill Quay, Newcastle, England
HULL NUMBER:	63
LENGTH:	244.3
BREADTH:	40.2
DEPTH:	18.5
GRT:	1580
REGISTRY NUMBER:	C. 103565
ENGINES:	20", 34", 57" Diameter x 39" Stroke Triple Expansion
ENGINE BUILDER:	North Eastern Marine Engineering Co. Ltd. Newcastle, England,1896

ROSEMOUNT (1) downbound in the St. Marys River

AURORA

The wooden-hulled steamer AURORA was built at Cleveland, Ohio, by the Murphy & Miller Company and launched on August 23, 1887. She ran for John Corrigan until 1898 when an accident occurred that changed her entire life. On Monday December 12, 1898, the AURORA was fast in the ice at Amherstburg, Ontario, when a watchman smelled smoke. The crew tried to put out the fire, but to no avail. They were taken off the burning vessel by the tug C.A. LORMAN. The ship burned to the water's edge.

The following year, the remains were raised and taken to Alex Anderson's shipyard at Marine City. The engine was removed and placed in the barge AUSTRALIA in 1902 and the hull of the AURORA was rebuilt into a tow barge in 1900. E.D. Carter of Erie, Pennsylvania, owned the vessel in 1901 and sold her the following year to Henry Wineman, Jr. He operated the ship until 1915 when he sold her to the Morton Salt Company to run in the salt trade, mostly on Lake Michigan. The Construction Materials Company was owner of the vessel at the end of her career in 1927. She was placed in lay-up but was never used thereafter. Her bones were removed at Marine City in the 1930's.

When she was a steamer, a Port Huron newspaper article said she "was probably the strongest built and most powerful on the lakes." Her engine was certainly powerful enough to tow two barges in the fall of 1889, the ADAMS and the DAVID DOWS. The engine lasted until the S.B. COOLIDGE, ex AUSTRALIA, was scrapped in 1952.

BUILT:	1887 Murphy & Miller Co. Cleveland, Ohio
HULL NUMBER:	none
LENGTH:	290.0
BREADTH:	41.0
DEPTH:	22.4
GRT:	2282.24
REGISTRY NUMBER:	US. 106493
ENGINES:	19", 33 1/2", 56" Diameter x 42" Stroke Triple expansion
ENGINE BUILDER:	Cleveland Shipbuilding Co., 1887

AURORA upbound at Mission Point, St. Marys River

As a barge, AURORA upbound in the upper St. Marys River

AURORA upbound at Mission Point, St. Marys River in 1914

AZOV

In 1886, William Buntin of Wellington Square, Ontario had the two-masted schooner AZOV built for himself at the shipyard operated by John Potter and John Simpson. John Simpson was the accredited master builder. Buntin and his business associates operated their schooner mostly on Lake Ontario during the first eighteen seasons of her career.

John Shaw and John Forest, of Port Lambton, Ontario, owned AZOV in 1884 and she ran in the salt and lumber trades. Salt was the northbound cargo for Owen Sound, Ontario and other Georgian Bay ports. From there she would run light to a North Channel port or Manitoulin Island for lumber or cedar shingles. In May of 1894, AZOV collided with the Canadian Government fisheries cruiser PETREL near Amherstburg.

At the turn of the century, AZOV was owned by W.F. Lawrence, of Hamilton. By 1903, he had sold her to H.P. Laurence, of Watford, Ontario, who in turn sold her to Captain John McDonald, of Goderich. About 1906, Captain McDonald sold his schooner JOHN G. KOLFAGE in order to pay for purchasing the AZOV and also to have her rebuilt at Sarnia.

Sailing the AZOV on Lake Huron became a family affair as Captain McDonald's son, Dan, was the mate and his daughter, Etta, was in charge of the galley. The McDonalds painted their schooner white with green trim.

On October 22, 1911, AZOV was southbound on Lake Huron loaded with lumber and shingles for Chatham, Ontario. She was working her way across the mouth of Saginaw Bay in heavy weather when she began to leak. The crew exhausted themselves at the pumps and the AZOV began to settle and became unmanageable.

The yawl boat was lowered and crew abandoned AZOV about nine miles east by south of Point Aux Barques. The abandoned schooner quickly broached to and capsized. Captain McDonald and his crew of five, including his son and daughter, were driven away from the Michigan shore by the westerly winds. They rowed and bailed as the little yawl boat sailed across the heaving lake. Sometimes a wave would break over them and half fill the boat.

The crew were in a state of exhaustion, cold and wet, and all became very drowsy. The Captain had to prod someone occasionally with his steering oar in order to keep them going. The crossing took eighteen hours and they came ashore six miles north of Goderich. A farmer took them to his house, where they recovered sufficiently to make the stage coach ride to Goderich.

The AZOV drifted across the lake and was found by the tug McGAW about five miles off Kincardine. An attempt was made to tow her but she would not follow. She eventually came ashore near McGregor Point, about four miles south of Port Elgin, Ontario. The elements broke her to pieces where she lay.

AZOV in the St. Clair river under tow

AZOV with a load of lumber in the St. Clair River

BUILT:	1866 John Potter/John Simpson Wellington Square, Ontario
HULL NUMBER:	none
LENGTH:	108.4
BREADTH:	23.7
DEPTH:	10.0
GRT:	195
REGISTRY NUMBER:	none issued

AZOV upbound light

GEORGE F. BAKER

At Superior, Wisconsin, one of the largest steel boats ever built by the Superior Shipbuilding Company, was the bulk freighter GEORGE F. BAKER. She was launched on June 15, 1907, for the Pittsburgh Steamship Company. (The other was the EDWARD Y. TOWNSEND.) She was one of the first of many 580 footers to grace the lakes and give many years of excellent service to her fleet. She was the first vessel to use the West Neebish Channel of the St. Marys River, when it opened on August 16, 1908.

The BAKER sailed for many years for the "Steel Trust" fleet. In 1965, she was sold to the Kinsman Marine Transit Company which promptly renamed her b) HENRY STEINBRENNER (3).

On the morning of May 23, 1974, the HENRY STEINBRENNER collided with the Hall Corporation Shipping Ltd.'s tanker CARDINAL in Pelee Passage, Lake Erie. Although there was no loss of life or vessel in this incident, CARDINAL did not continue in service thereafter, and was subsequently sold for scrap at Hamilton, Ontario in 1974. United Metals Ltd. completed the scrapping in 1975.

Through a reorganization of the fleet, Kinsman became S & E Shipping in 1976. The STEINBRENNER's cargoes included grain as well as iron ore, sailing mainly from Duluth, Minnesota to lower lake ports.

In 1979, HENRY STEINBRENNER was retired and was scrapped at Ashtabula, Ohio later the same year.

a) GEORGE F. BAKER, b) Henry Steinbrenner (3)

BUILT:	1907 Superior Shipbuilding Co. Superior, Wisconsin
HULL NUMBER:	517
LENGTH:	586.0
BREADTH:	58.0
DEPTH:	25.5
GRT:	7210
REGISTRY NUMBER:	US. 204225
ENGINES:	24", 39", 65" Diameter x 42" Stroke
ENGINE BUILDER:	American Shipbuilding Co. Cleveland, Ohio, 1907

GEORGE F. BAKER in an early photo upbound in the St. Clair River off Marine City

GEORGE F. BAKER upbound in the Detroit River July 18, 1950

GEORGE F. BAKER upbound at Mission Point, St. Marys River June 28, 1953

GEORGE F. BAKER downbound West Neebish cut, St. Marys River August 20, 1960

HENRY STEINBRENNER (3) downbound St. Clair River at Port Huron July 23, 1977

BURT BARNES

Launched at Manitowoc, Wisconsin in 1882 by master shipbuilder Green S. Rand, BURT BARNES was delivered to her owner J.W. Barnes, of Manitowoc. The three-masted, wooden-hulled schooner was engaged in the Lake Michigan lumber trade to Chicago.

Caught in a storm on October 11, 1895, she was driven onto a shoal in Lake Michigan near Jacksonport, Wisconsin and severely wrecked. She was deemed worth salvaging, however, and was refloated and rebuilt at the shipyard in Manitowoc.

The BARNES was acquired by Oliver Oberg, of Manitowoc, in 1896 and he sold her to Thomas E. Torrison, of the same city, in 1899.

In 1904, she was purchased by the Graham Brothers, of Kincardine, Ontario. (C. 130489) They used her to haul cargoes of lumber from Johnston Harbor, on the Bruce Peninsula, or from Manitoulin Island to the cities on the St. Clair and Detroit Rivers. The Grahams owned her until 1924, and it was during that time that she was partially dismasted in a storm on Lake Huron. The BARNES managed to reachKincardine safely after the main and mizzen masts had gone over the side.

The James Swift Coal Company, of Kingston, bought the BURT BARNES in 1924. She paid her way with coal cargoes from the south shore of Lake Ontario to Kingston and Bay of Quinte ports.

The schooner left Big Sodus, New York, on September 1, 1926, with 210 tons of coal for Kingston. The wind changed to the northeast and began to blow hard as she neared Prince Edward Point. Captain McManus began to tack onto a new course, but the foremast came crashing down. Then the mainmast was toppled back and it took down the mizzen, which fell over the stern and badly damaged the yawl boat.

After a long night of rolling in the trough of the seas, the schooner began to leak and the work of pumping out the water exhausted the crew. They patched the yawl boat and abandoned the schooner off Point Petre at 4:00 p.m. on September 2nd. The wind drove the yawl boat across Lake Ontario, and 12 hours later, the crew landed safely at Braddock Point, 12 miles west of Rochester, New York. BURT BARNES was last seen low in the water off Point Petre.

BURT BARNES of Southampton leaving the harbor

BURT BARNES dismasted, entering Kincardine Harbour in the 1920's

BUILT:	1882 Green S. Rand Manitowoc, Wisconsin
HULL NUMBER:	none
LENGTH:	95.5
BREADTH:	24.5
DEPTH:	7.3
GRT:	134
REGISTRY NUMBER:	US. 3193

M/S JULIUS H. BARNES

The Erie & St. Lawrence Corporation, of New York, was a firm that was in the shipping business between the Great Lakes and coastal ports for many years. Its ships were specially designed to negotiate the New York State Barge Canal and trade directly between Great Lake ports and the Coast. During winter months the ships traded coastwise and to various West Indies ports and were renowned for their wide ranging ports-of-call and odd cargoes. In 1956, the firm sold the last three ships of the fleet and withdrew from business. Newest and largest of the ships owned by the firm was the a) JULIUS H. BARNES, named for the president of the company, who was a noted Duluth, Minnesota, industrialist and financier. The JULIUS H. BARNES was built in 1940 at Charleston Shipbuilding & Dry Dock Company of South Carolina. It was powered by twin-screw diesel engines that developed a speed of 9 mph. These original Fairbanks Morse engines were replaced by Caterpillars in 1963.

The other two ships remaining in the fleet when it sold out in 1956 were RICHARD J. BARNES and ROBERT BARNES FIERTZ. These were sister ships, 242 feet in length and beam of 36 feet, that had been built at MacDougall-Duluth (later Barnes-Duluth) Shipyard in 1921. All of Erie & St. Lawrence ships were low profile canal boats (*nicknamed "bridge-skinners"*) with hinged masts and a minimum of topside structure.

The versatile Barnes ships were the last of the general cargo carriers operating between the Great Lakes and the Coast and their cargoes were often quite unique. For example, in 1953, JULIUS H. BARNES carried general merchandise to Havana, Cuba, and returned to the Great Lakes with sugar destined for Hershey Candy Company, for offloading at Cleveland. A number of cargoes of Chilean copper ingots were transferred from ocean ships in New York harbor and moved into the Great Lakes to Cleveland and Detroit. Some of these cargoes were valued at over a million dollars. The ships carried packaged chemicals from Freeport, Texas, to New York; fertilizer from Baltimore to Toronto; finished steel products from Cleveland to New York; coal from Lake Erie to the head of the lakes; wheat from Richmond, Virginia, to Albany, New York; grain from Superior, Wisconsin to Toledo; and grain from Toledo to various East Coast ports.

An especially "odd-ball" cargo was loaded by the JULIUS H. BARNES in 1952. An old French Monastery in The Bronx, New York, was being torn down, and the JULIUS was engaged to haul the carefully dismantled and marked limestone blocks from New York to Port Everglades, Florida, where the new owner reassembled them as a real estate development. It took many trips over several months to complete the building's transfer to the new site.

Erie & St. Lawrence transferred JULIUS H. BARNES to Powerbarge Corp., New York, in 1957, and this company refitted the ship for work in connection with the St. Lawrence Seaway construction program. Subsequently the ship was sold to Toth Motorships, Inc., of Toledo, Ohio, in 1958, and it continued to operate under the name JULIUS H. BARNES in this company's Great Lakes/Coastal trades.

In 1963, the ship was sold foreign to Bamar Marine Co. Ltd., of Nassau, Bahamas, and given Bahamian registry No. 316334. A new name, b) ABOCOL, was given to the ship in 1966 and it continued to operate primarily in ocean trades. The ship was reported to have run aground entering Cartagena harbor, Spain, on November 17, 1973, and it was subsequently towed back to the U.S., arriving at New Orleans for lay-up in February, 1974. It was used for a time in 1976 and 1977 as a barge, but dropped from the 1978-79 edition of Lloyds Register of Shipping.

A word about Mr. Julius H. Barnes - a Duluthian who was a nationally known financier who made millions in the grain, shipping and business world. From a humble start as an office boy in the Ward Ames grain brokerage firm in Duluth, he rose to become the world's largest exporter of grain. During World War I, he headed the government's Food Administration Grain Corporation, for which he was decorated by several countries. He served as president and chairman of the board of the U.S. Chamber of Commerce over several terms. Mr. Barnes was among the first men of national prominence to give active support to the St. Lawrence Seaway and was often called "Grandfather of the Seaway". During his lifetime he built and lost several fortunes, headed a shipping firm that launched 45 ships, was elected to Duluth's Hall of Fame, and was honored as one of "Minnesota's 100 Living Giants". Mr. Barnes passed away in Duluth in 1959 at age 86, but his philanthropic endeavors have had a lasting mark on Duluth and the country.

a) JULIUS H. BARNES b) Abocol

BUILT:	1940 Charleston Shipbuilding & Dry Dock Co. Charleston, South Carolina
HULL NUMBER:	5500
LENGTH:	281.3
BREADTH:	42.2
DEPTH:	16.0
GRT:	1623
REGISTRY NUMBER:	US. 239491
2 ENGINES:	12" Diameter x 15" Stroke 5 cylinder diesels
ENGINE BUILDER:	Fairbanks Morse, Beloit, Wisconsin, 1940

JULIUS H. BARNES downbound at Mission Point, St. Marys River

JULIUS H. BARNES aground, high and dry, at Point Edward, Ontario, August 23, 1941

JULIUS H. BARNES loading a 90,000 bushel cargo of grain at Osborn-MacMillan elevator, Superior, Wisconsin in 1957

BELLECHASSE

The steel-hulled tug BELLECHASSE was built in 1912 at Kingston, Ontario, by the Kingston Shipbuilding Company Ltd. for the Canadian Government. Especially designed for service in the channels of the lower St. Lawrence River, she was launched on May 15, 1912, and was christened by the 90-year-old Mrs. E. Grimason.

A very handsome steamer fitted with two tall stacks in tandem, BELLECHASSE was especially designed as a survey and inspection vessel, with light ice breaking capabilities. She was an oil-burner, and her large capacity bunkers gave her a cruising range of 2,000 miles.

BELLECHASSE saw some thirty years of service for the federal government, primarily for the Department of Marine and Fisheries, but latterly for the Department of Transport.

She was sold in 1942 to the United Towing and Salvage Company Ltd., an affiliate of Sinmac Lines Ltd., Montreal, and Marine Industries Ltd., Sorel, Quebec. Her new owners refitted her as a salvage vessel, with GRT of 389.

BELLECHASSE remained in service until 1948, when she was laid up at Sorel. After six years of inactivity, she was dismantled at Sorel in 1954 by Marine Industries Ltd.

BUILT:	1912 Kingston Shipbuilding Co. Kingston, Ontario
HULL NUMBER:	3
LENGTH:	142.2
BREADTH:	27.0
DEPTH:	12.0
GRT:	417
REGISTRY NUMBER:	C. 133935
2 ENGINES:	12 1/2", 21", 34" Diameter x 21" Stroke Triple Expansion
ENGINE BUILDER:	Collingwood Shipbuilding Co., 1912

BELLECHASSE at Owen Sound in 1942

BETHLEHEM

The first of five similar and very fine appearing steel-hulled package freighters built for the Lehigh Valley Transit Company was the E.P. WILBUR of 1889, soon to be renamed b) BETHLEHEM in 1904. The other four were CAYUGA, SARANAC, SENECA and TUSCARORA. All were built by the Globe Iron Works of Cleveland, Ohio. The vessels carried four tall masts and had their machinery positioned a little aft of amidships.

The CAYUGA was lost in a collision on May 10, 1895. The other four sailed for their owner until World War I, when they were sold to the U.S. Shipping Board for salt water service and were cut apart and bulkheaded through the Welland and St. Lawrence Canals. After the war, BETHLEHEM was renamed c) BARBARA and operated under the British flag (Br. 151279) until she was eventually scrapped in 1924.

The Lehigh Valley package freighters operated out of Buffalo to the Lake Michigan ports of Milwaukee and Chicago with occasional voyages to Lake Superior. The company's services came to an end after the Panama Canal Act of 1916 decreed that U.S. railroads could not simultaneously operate lake shipping fleets, and the various U.S. package freight fleets were joined into the new Great Lakes Transit Corporation. The Lehigh Valley fleet was the last holdout against the legislation.

a) E.P. Wilbur, b) BETHLEHEM, c) Barbara

BUILT:	1888 Globe Iron Works Cleveland, Ohio
HULL NUMBER:	16
LENGTH:	290.0
BREADTH:	40.8
DEPTH:	13.6
GRT:	2633
REGISTRY NUMBER:	US. 135984
ENGINES:	24", 38", 61" Diameter x 42" Stroke Triple Expansion
ENGINE BUILDER:	Globe Iron Works, Cleveland, Ohio, 1888

E.P. WILBUR at the dock at Chicago

BETHLEHEM downbound in the Detroit River

BETHLEHEM upbound in the St. Clair River off Marine City

BETHLEHEM after being cut in two at Buffalo November 3, 1917

BIRCHGLEN

American Ship Building Company launched its newest vessel at Lorain, Ohio, on October 7, 1926. She was built for the Interlake Steamship Company and was christened a) WILLIAM McLAUCHLAN. She was delivered in the spring of 1927, along with her sister, ROBERT HOBSON, to Interlake. American Ship Building also delivered the sister steamer GEORGE M. HUMPHREY (1) to the Kinsman Transit Company during April, 1927.

The McLAUCHLAN remained in Interlake ownership, operated by Pickands Mather & Company, until 1975, with the only change being a rename to b) SAMUEL MATHER (5) in 1966. She became the fifth vessel of the Interlake fleet to be so named.

In 1971, the SAMUEL MATHER (5) delivered a test load of 5,040 tons of Montana low-sulfur coal to the Erie Mining Company at Taconite Harbor, Minnesota. She loaded the coal on July 19, 1971, at Superior's Burlington Northern Ore Dock. This was the first coal cargo to be shipped from the Head of the Lakes and was test-burned at Erie Mining's steam electric generating facility. As they say, the rest is history, for now there are millions of tons of low-sulfur coal shipped from Duluth-Superior every year.

In 1975, SAMUEL MATHER (5) was sold into Canadian registry (C. 370162) to Robert Pierson Holdings Ltd., to be managed (at first) by Westdale Shipping Ltd. She was towed on December 20, 1975, from Ashtabula to Port Colborne, converted to oil firing by Herb Fraser & Associates andrenamed c) JOAN M. McCULLOUGH. In 1977, her ownership was changed to Pierson Steamships Ltd., but she continued to operate under the name of the Soo River Company. On Friday, August 6, 1982, the Pierson fleet was placed in receivership and the entire fleet was purchased by P & H Shipping Division, Parrish & Heimbecker Ltd. The new owner renamed the steamer d) BIRCHGLEN.

On June 8, 1986, she arrived in Toronto for lay-up and was towed to Hamilton on August 15. She was fitted out and sailed briefly in 1987, but soon was laid up again at Midland, Ontario. On October 11, 1987, BIRCHGLEN was towed past Detroit by the tugs MICHAEL D. MISNER and GLENADA en route to Toronto for use as a storage barge.

On April 21, 1988, tugs ELMORE M. MISNER and ATOMIC towed BIRCHGLEN from Toronto. The tug THUNDER CAPE replaced ATOMIC in the Seaway and the tow cleared the Snell Lock on April 23. The WILLIAM McLAUCHLAN/BIRCHGLEN, which never had suffered a major mishap since she was built in 1927, experienced her first on April 23, 1988. While downbound near the entrance to the St. Lawrence Seaway near Caughnawaga, Quebec, she collided with the QUEDOC (3), a) BEAVERCLIFFE HALL.

The QUEDOC began taking on water and had to make temporary repairs before clearing for Port Weller Dry Docks. The BIRCHGLEN continued on and was turned over the next day at Orleans Island to the tug ORION EXPEDITOR which cleared on April 26 with BIRCHGLEN bound for Halifax, Nova Scotia, for scrapping.

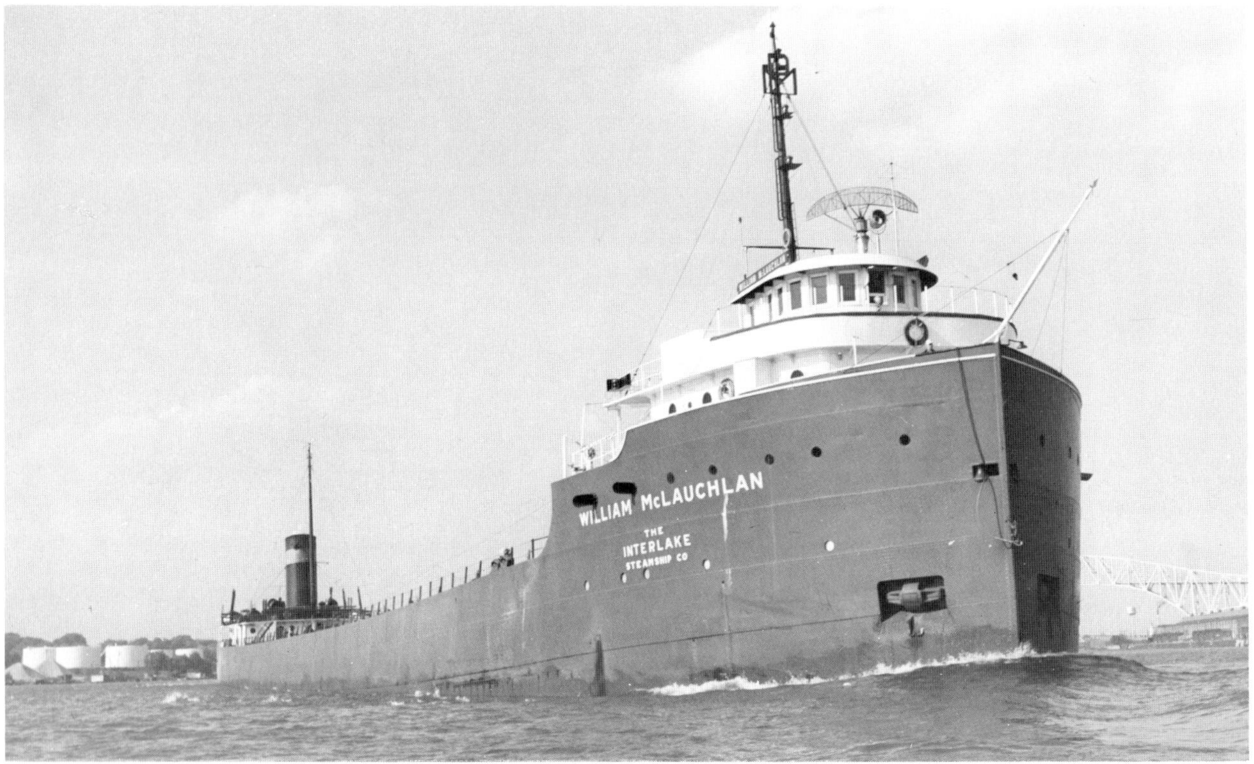

WILLIAM McLAUCHLAN downbound in the St. Clair River at Port Huron September 29, 1960

SAMUEL MATHER (5) downbound in the St. Marys River August 15, 1973

JOAN M. McCULLOUGH upbound in the St. Clair River April 20, 1976

JOAN M. McCULLOUGH
upbound in the St. Marys River
July 18, 1981

a) William McLauchlan b) Samuel Mather (5)
c) Joan M. McCullough d) BIRCHGLEN

BUILT:	1927 American Ship Building Co. Lorain, Ohio	*DEPTH:*	27.9
HULL NUMBER:	793	*GRT:*	8024
LENGTH:	586.3	*REGISTRY NUMBER:*	US. 226176
BREADTH:	60.2	*ENGINES:*	24", 41", 65" Diameter x 42" Stroke Triple Expansion
		ENGINE BUILDER:	Shipyard, 1927

BIRCHGLEN upbound in the Middle Neebish cut, St. Marys River July 16, 1983

B.W. BLANCHARD

The wooden package freighter B.W. BLANCHARD was built by the shipyard of Quayle & Martin at Cleveland, Ohio, in 1870 for the Union Steamboat Company of Buffalo, New York, and sailed in this capacity for sixteen years.

In 1887, her ownership was registered in the name of A.A. Parker and others of Detroit, Michigan, and she continued her duties as a package freighter. From 1892 to 1895, records show that the BLANCHARD was chartered from A.A. Parker by the Clover Leaf Steamboat Line.

In 1902, the steamer's owner was shown as Charles W. Kotcher of Detroit, Michigan, at which time the vessel was cut down to a lumber hooker. Her new dimensions were 221.3 x 32.4 x 12.2; GRT 919. During her conversion to a lumber hooker, the vessel's hogging arches were left in place, giving the steamer a look of sturdiness. The arches also helped to contain any lumber that was placed on her main deck, but certainly must have caused problems for the loaders and dock workers when loading and unloading the BLANCHARD's deck cargo.

The B.W. BLANCHARD's career was not without incident. In October of 1878, she collided with the scow schooner MARY GARRETT, severely damaging the schooner. In October of 1884, the steamer was greatly damaged by fire at Milwaukee, Wisconsin. On June 28, 1885, the vessel again caught fire and sank when fire-fighters poured excessive amounts of water into her while extinguishing the blaze.

On June 10, 1887, while on a trip from Milwaukee, Wisconsin, to Ogdensburg, New York, the crown sheet in the boiler burned through and dropped two inches, stranding the vessel off South Manitou Island, Lake Michigan, and causing $15,000 worth of damage.

On November 25th, 1904, the aging B.W. BLANCHARD, towing the consort schooners JOHN T. JOHNSON and JOHN KELDERHOUSE, all laden with lumber and making a run from Cheboygan, Michigan, to Detroit, was caught in a strong south-south east gale. The steamer became unmanageable in the heavy seas and stranded on the North Point Reef, Lake Huron, and broke up. The two schooners also stranded at this time, the JOHNSON also going to pieces and becoming a total loss. The KELDERHOUSE, however, was later salvaged.

B.W. BLANCHARD downbound in the St. Marys River

B.W. BLANCHARD on North Point Reef, Lake Huron November 25, 1904

BUILT:	1870 Quayle & Martin Cleveland, Ohio	*GRT:*	1142
HULL NUMBER:	none	*REGISTRY NUMBER:*	US. 2806
LENGTH:	221.0	*ENGINES:*	24", 54" Diameter x 36" Stroke Steeple Compound
BREADTH:	32.4	*ENGINE BUILDER:*	Shepard Iron Works, Buffalo, New York, 1870
DEPTH:	11.8		

E.J. BLOCK

The W.R. WOODFORD, built at West Bay City, Michigan, by the West Bay City Shipbuilding Company for W.A. and A.H. Hawgood, was launched on May 16, 1908. In 1911, she was purchased by the Inland Steamship Company (Hutchinson & Company, Managers) and renamed b) N.F. LEOPOLD. She was taken over by Inland Steel in 1936.

In 1943, she was renamed c) E.J. BLOCK. By 1946, the vessel was in need of repowering and, she was outfitted with a General Motors diesel-electric drive by the American Ship Building Company, Lorain. She was the first Great Lakes vessel to be so equipped. The BLOCK was reconstructed to the following dimensions; 539.1 x 56.3 x 27.3; 6,933 gross tons.

She operated in limited service during 1984-85, being used primarily to shuttle raw materials between Inland Steel's Plants Number 2 & 3 at Indiana Harbor. In 1986, Inland Steel began using the tug CINDY B. and four barges to shuttle the iron ore with great savings in crew costs. With this development, the E.J. BLOCK's days were numbered. She was sold to Marine Salvage in May, 1987, and was downbound past Detroit on August 18, 1987, towed by the tugs TUSKER and GLENADA. She arrived at Ramey's Bend, Humberstone on August 20. Scrapping began there on January 25, 1988. Part of her was still visible in November of 1989.

W.R. WOODFORD upbound above the Soo Locks in 1909

a) W.R. Woodford, b) N.F. Leopold, c) E.J. BLOCK

BUILT:	1908 West Bay City Shipbuilding Co. West Bay City, Michigan	*DEPTH:*	27.3
HULL NUMBER:	626	*GRT:*	6,929
LENGTH:	532.0	*REGISTRY NUMBER:*	US. 205250
BREADTH:	56.0	*ENGINES:*	23 1/2", 38", 63" Diameter x 42" Stroke Triple Expansion
		ENGINE BUILDER:	Detroit Shipbuilding Co., 1908

N.F. LEOPOLD upbound at Mission Point, St. Marys River in 1928

E.J. BLOCK downbound at Neebish Island, Rock Cut in 1950

E.J. BLOCK upbound light in the St. Marys River August 20, 1960

E.J. BLOCK on way to the scrapyard in tow of the tug TUSKER

PHILIP D. BLOCK

The PHILIP D. BLOCK spent most of her career carrying iron ore to Indiana Harbor. In the early years, she hauled about a half-million tons per season, and most of the cargoes were loaded at Lake Superior ports, with Superior the most common loading port. On occasion, this bulk carrier brought stone to the Inland Steel docks.

In later years, PHILIP D. BLOCK spent more time on the shorter run between Escanaba and Indiana Harbor. She topped one million tons for the first time in 1964 carrying seventy-four loads of ore, of which fifty-six originated at Escanaba, while ten came aboard at Superior and eight at Port Arthur.

Her busiest season proved to be 1970 when the vessel carried 1,131,676 tons of cargo which included a single, rare shipment of coal.

PHILIP D. BLOCK was launched at Lorain, Ohio, by American Ship Building on January 17, 1925. She entered service for the Pioneer Steamship Company April 11, loading coal at Huron, Ohio, for Indiana Harbor. The ship moved to the Inland Steel fleet in 1936 and served them until final lay-up on September 12, 1981.

Originally this vessel measured 586.3 feet long but in 1953 she was lengthened to 672 feet, which changed her gross tonnage from 7,931 to 9,149. A year later, in 1954, a 4,950 horsepower Westinghouse steam turbine engine replaced her old triple expansion power plant.

Lengthening the ship increased her capacity and as a result in 1955, PHILIP D. BLOCK carried a season total of 670,415 tons. This was based on forty-six cargoes, all ore, as the vessel traveled 58,611 miles for the year.

PHILIP D. BLOCK was sold to Marine Salvage in 1985 and arrived at their Port Colborne, Ontario, scrapyard November 13, 1985, under tow of the tug OHIO. She was resold and towed down the Welland Canal August 22, 1986, en route to Brazil.

The Polish tug JANTAR left Quebec City September 16, 1986, taking PHILIP D. BLOCK and W.W. HOLLOWAY to Recife, Brazil. They arrived October 24, and Siderurgica Aco Notre S.A. began scrapping PHILIP D. BLOCK the next month.

PHILIP D. BLOCK upbound at the Soo Locks early in her career

PHILIP D. BLOCK upbound at Mission Point, St. Marys River

PHILIP D. BLOCK downbound in the St. Marys River August 17, 1958

BUILT:	1925 American Ship Building Co. Lorain, Ohio	*GRT:*	7931
HULL NUMBER:	789	*REGISTRY NUMBER:*	US. 224508
LENGTH:	586.3	*ENGINES:*	24 1/2", 41", 65" Diameter x 42" Stroke Triple Expansion
BREADTH:	60.2	*ENGINE BUILDER:*	Shipyard, 1925
DEPTH:	28.0		

PHILIP D. BLOCK in the Welland Canal, August, 1986 in tow of the tug SALVAGE MONARCH

C. L. BOYNTON

The wooden tug C.L. BOYNTON was typical of the hundreds of river and harbor tugs that were built during the late 1800's and early 1900's. She was built at Port Huron, Michigan, in 1894 by James Mason for the Thompson Tug Line, also of Port Huron, and was named after the company's secretary and treasurer.

In 1899, the Great Lakes Towing Company was formed for economic reasons, by combining many of the independent tug companies around the Great Lakes into one operating company. It was during this time that the tug's ownership came under Great Lakes Towing. She continued to operate for this firm until she was sold to the Nicholson Transit Company in 1916. At this time her GRT was reduced to 96.

The tug remained under Nicholson's ownership until 1919 when she lay idle at the dock. In September of 1919, she was abandoned and dismantled at Detroit. The machinery and part of the hull were then used in the building of the tug UFASCO for the United Fuel & Supply Company of Detroit, Michigan.

BUILT:	1894 James Mason Port Huron, Michigan
HULL NUMBER:	none
LENGTH:	86.7
BREADTH:	21.6
DEPTH:	12.1
GRT:	103
REGISTRY NUMBER:	US. 127037
ENGINES:	17", 34" Diameter x 30" Stroke Fore and Aft Compound
ENGINE BUILDER:	S.F. Hodge & Co., Detroit, Michigan #236, 1894

C.L. BOYNTON early in her career on Lake Huron

C.L. BOYNTON at the Soo in 1908

C.L. BOYNTON downbound in the St. Clair River

C.L. BOYNTON and ONTARIO in an east Lake Huron harbor

UFASCO at the dock at Detroit after her rebuild from the hull of C.L. BOYNTON

BURLINGTON

BURLINGTON was built by Daniel O'Connor at Buffalo, New York and was a duplicate of the propellers DUBUQUE, QUINCY and CITY OF MADISON, all canallers built for the second Welland Canal and owned by Fitzhugh, Littlejohn & Company's "Old Oswego Line". They all ran between Oswego and Chicago.

Due to the 1857 financial panic, the four new boats found few cargoes, and they were idle during most of 1857 and 1858. BURLINGTON was auctioned off for $8,000 in June 1859, and she and QUINCY changed hands again in the spring of 1860. In November 1861, BURLINGTON and KENTUCKY were bought by C.C. Blodgett of Detroit, who chartered both to the Erie Railway Line to run from Buffalo to Dunkirk, Cleveland, Sandusky, Toledo and Detroit. In 1868, BURLINGTON, CITY OF DETROIT (1) and GUIDING STAR were chartered to the New York Central Line.

BURLINGTON was made a steam barge, 137.0 x 25.3 x 12.0, 276 GRT, in 1869, towing the barge KENTUCKY. She was holed and sunk in the Pelee Passage in late November, 1872, and sold on the spot to Captain Robert Hackett.

She was raised and repaired at Detroit and employed in Hackett's Western Coal & Dock Company hauling lumber and coal. In the spring of 1879, she was sold to William Jenkinson of Port Huron and rebuilt again at the Wheeler Shipyard in West Bay City. She was sold again in 1881 to the Port Huron Transportation Company for whom she towed the consorts O.J. HALE, A.C. KEATING and H.F. CHURCH for several years. In April, 1885, BURLINGTON and the barges CHURCH and HALE were torn from their moorings in the Black River in Port Huron by a spring freshet and swept downstream to the Military Street Bridge, where they blocked the river for several days.

In 1887, the steamer was acquired by C.H. Bradley of West Bay City, and in 1894, by G.K. Jackson of Bay City. On April 16, 1894, she was badly damaged by fire in the Detroit River, but again she was repaired and returned to service. She burned to the water's edge in Mississauga Strait near Manitoulin Island on August 24, 1895. She was owned at the time by Stephen B. Grummond of Detroit, who had salvaged her the previous summer.

BUILT:	1857 Daniel O'Connor Buffalo, New York	*GRT:*	460
HULL NUMBER:	none	*REGISTRY NUMBER:*	US. 2157
LENGTH:	144.0	*ENGINES:*	24" Diameter x 36" Stroke Direct Acting
BREADTH:	25.4	*ENGINE BUILDER:*	Swartz Foundry, Buffalo, New York, 1857
DEPTH:	11.1		

BURLINGTON, H.F. CHURCH and A.C. KEATING caught up in the Military Street Bridge, Port Huron

BURLINGTON entering port in her early years as a package and passenger freighter

BURLINGTON and one of her barges in another view in April of 1885 at Port Huron

CADILLAC (4)

Built in River Rouge, Michigan, by Great Lakes Engineering Works, LAKE ANGELINA was launched on October 31, 1942. She was one of 16 vessels built by the United States Maritime Commission. Shortly after launching, LAKE ANGELINA was acquired by Cleveland Cliffs Steamship Company and renamed b) CADILLAC (4). As payment for both LAKE ANGELINA and BELLE ISLE (later renamed CHAMPLAIN), Cliffs traded five of its older vessels — CADILLAC (2), COLONEL, MUNISING, NEGAUNEE and YOSEMITE.

CADILLAC departed River Rouge on June 19, 1943, on her maiden voyage, bound for Superior, Wisconsin, to load iron ore. On April 9, 1944, CADILLAC won annual honors for being the first ship from the lower lakes to reach Duluth-Superior Harbor. On April 17, 1966, CADILLAC unloaded a shipment of coal destined for the Upper Peninsula Generating Company to mark the first coal receipt of 1966 at the port of Marquette, Michigan.

In 1969, CADILLAC became the first Maritime vessel to be converted from coal to oil firing. She was simultaneously equipped with automated boilers, each with a single burner. The automation system, which reduced the size of the boiler room crew from twelve to eight, was installed by the Manitowoc Shipbuilding Company in its Manitowoc, Wisconsin yard.

Bound for Cleveland from Duluth on July 15, 1977, loaded with taconite, CADILLAC ran aground because of fog in the St. Marys River, approximately twenty miles northwest of Sault Ste. Marie. CADILLAC was freed the next day after receiving assistance from three tugs.

On September 7, 1981, CADILLAC was laid up for the final time in Toledo, Ohio. On December 31, 1982, Cleveland Cliffs transferred her to Craig Maritime, Inc., in preparation for converting her to a container carrier, to be used in a proposed service between Chicago, Detroit and Quebec City. However, these plans never materialized. CADILLAC was sold in 1985, to Pai Marine of Jacksonville, Florida. As a result of prolonged litigation in the U.S. District Court for the Northern District of Ohio, CADILLAC was ordered sold in 1987, through Jacques Pierot, Jr. & Sons of New York. On July 30, 1987, the U.S. Maritime Commission was asked to approve the sale of CADILLAC to Corostel Trading Ltd. in Montreal, Quebec, for scrapping overseas.

On August 17, 1987, CADILLAC was towed by the tugs GLENADA and ELMORE M. MISNER, from Toledo's Frog Pond to Quebec City, arriving on August 31. On September 8, 1987, the Dutch-flag tug/supply vessel THOMAS DE GAUWDIEF cleared Quebec City with CADILLAC and her former fleetmate CHAMPLAIN. Both vessels arrived on October 30, 1987, at the Turkish port of Aliaga to be scrapped.

CADILLAC downbound on Lake St. Clair

CADILLAC upbound light in lower Lake Huron, June 1, 1960

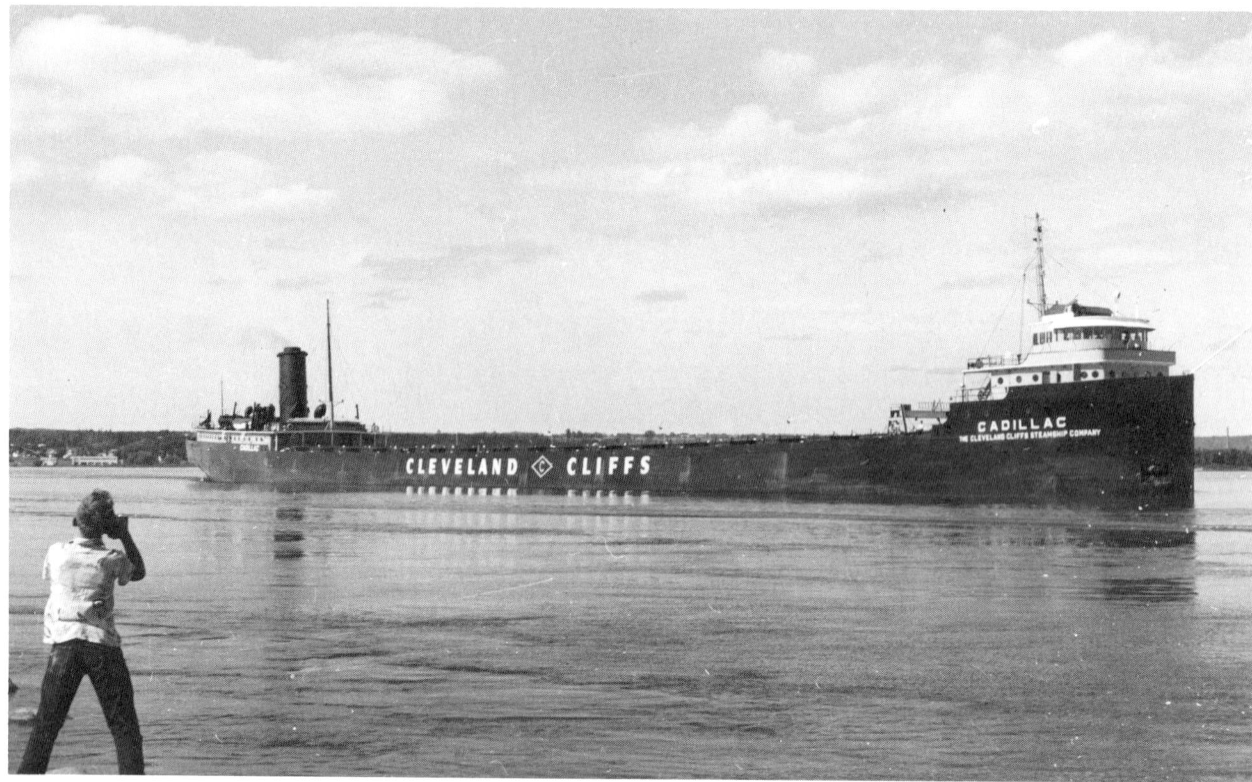

CADILLAC downbound at Mission Point, St. Marys River, being photographed by a young Peter B. Worden, August 12, 1951

CADILLAC on her way to the scrappers. Tug GLENADA at her bow

a) Lake Angelina, b) CADILLAC (4)

BUILT:	1943 Great Lakes Engineering Works River Rouge, Michigan
HULL NUMBER:	291
LENGTH:	603.8
BREADTH:	60.2
DEPTH:	30.2
GRT:	9057
REGISTRY NUMBER:	US. 243423
ENGINES:	24", 41", 68" Diameter x 42" Stroke Triple Expansion
ENGINE BUILDER:	Shipyard, 1943

CANADA

Captain J.B. Fairgrieve took delivery of the propeller CANADA at Hamilton, Ontario in 1872. The wooden ship had been built to the maximum Welland Canal dimensions by A.M. Robertson. Fairgrieve's daughter christened the new ship when she was launched on June 5,1872. Captain Fairgrieve and his partners, Hugh Fairgrieve, D. Butters and T. Howard, ran their ship from Montreal to Chicago in the passenger and package freight trades.

In 1878, they formed the New England Transportation Company, operating CANADA, COLUMBIA, CALIFORNIA and LAKE ERIE on the run from Collingwood, Ontario to Chicago. The vessels often carried barrels of salt pork and bulk cargoes of corn.

In 1886 and 1887, CANADA was chartered to the Canadian Department of Marine to carry supplies to the lighthouses on the Great Lakes. While in this service, she ran aground near Goulais Point, west of the Soo. She was pulled off without injury to either ship or crew.

While docked at Port Huron, Michigan, near the Grand Trunk Bridge on October 18, 1892, her upper cabin was found to be on fire. She was heavily damaged; however, she was rebuilt into a schooner at Port Huron. She measured 135.2 x 24.2 x 11.5; 557 GRT. The ship's engine was removed and replaced in the new steamer ARABIAN being built at Hamilton, Ontario. At the time of the fire, CANADA was owned by John Nisbet, of Sarnia.

On July 7, 1893, she was enrolled at Detroit as the schooner b) SCHILDE (US. 116578); when placed on the U.S. Register, she measured 140.0 x 26.0 x 11.8; 338.14 GRT. Thomas Murphy, who was the managing owner, sold her to Jane E. Leonard, of Port Huron, in January of 1896, and the schooner was renamed c) EUREKA; her register being transferred to Port Huron. Captain George Bennet bought her in March of 1897, sailed her for a part of that season and sold her to George W. Allen in September. In October 1897, Allen sold her to Elizabeth Rogan, of Port Huron.

EUREKA was under tow of the Canadian steamer ONTARIO on Lake Superior August 11, 1899 in heavy fog. The ONTARIO ran ashore and was wrecked near Rossport. A tug managed to rescue EUREKA, while her consort, WAWANOSH, reached Rossport on her own.

On the night of September 11, 1900, EUREKA sank at Jenkinson's coal Dock at Port Huron. Lightered of her coal cargo, she was pumped out and refloated. It most likely was after this occurrence that EUREKA was reconverted into a steamer. She was fitted with a high-pressure, non-condensing engine which had one cylinder of 24 inches in diameter and a stroke of 28 inches. This engine had been built by Pusey, Jones & Company of Wilmington, Delaware.

EUREKA was caught out on Lake Huron in heavy weather on November 7, 1901. Loaded with lumber from Tawas for Lorain, she became waterlogged after her steam pump broke down. The crew abandoned ship on a raft about 20 miles W.S.W. of Kincardine, Ontario. Driven by a south west wind, they drifted all night and several times the raft overturned. At 6 a.m. the next day, they came ashore two miles north of Kincardine. The ship's cook, who was married to the mate, drowned in the surf as the exhausted crew crawled ashore. The EUREKA broke up and sank out in Lake Huron.

a) CANADA, b) Schilde, c) Eureka

BUILT:	1872 A.M. Robertson Hamilton, Ontario
HULL NUMBER:	none
LENGTH:	142.1
BREADTH:	23.9
DEPTH:	13.0
GRT:	392
REGISTRY NUMBER:	C. 100392
ENGINES:	20 1/4", 40" Diameter x 34" Stroke Steeple Compound
ENGINE BUILDER:	F.G. Beckett & Co., 1872

CANADA at Kincardine, Ontario

PAUL H. CARNAHAN

HONEY HILL was built in 1945 by the Sun Shipbuilding & Dry Dock Company in Chester, Pennsylvania for the U.S. Maritime Administration. She was built as a 504-foot, turbo-electric, T-2 Class tanker and was launched on July 5, 1945.

HONEY HILL was sold in 1946 to the Atlantic Refining Company and was renamed b) ATLANTIC DEALER; she sailed twelve years for Atlantic Refining before being decommissioned in 1958 at the Mobile yards of the Alabama Shipbuilding & Dry Dock Company.

In 1960, the Skar-Ore Steamship Corporation purchased ATLANTIC DEALER for conversion to Great Lakes service. Brought out of retirement, ATLANTIC DEALER was towed up the Atlantic Coast and through the Seaway to the American Ship Building's Buffalo, New York yard, where her stern and bow were sandblasted. During August, 1960, ATLANTIC DEALER was moved to the Company's Lorain, Ohio yard for the conversion.

A 530 foot mid-section, equipped with 21 hatches, was built by Schlieker Werft in Hamburg, Germany and towed 5,250 miles to Lorain. The tow across the Atlantic, began on April 6, 1961. The Dutch tug ZEELAND was 500 miles off St. Johns, Newfoundland when, due to numerous course changes resulting from bad weather, the tug ran low on fuel. Once the captain realized his predicament, he cut loose the mid-body to drift, manned only with a skeleton crew and radio while he headed north to St. John's for fuel. Returning almost three days later, radio contact was made, the mid-body made fast and the tow headed for Cabot Straits at the entrance to the Gulf of St. Lawrence. At Montreal, the tugs GRAEME STEWART and HELEN McALLISTER took over the tow, arriving at Lorain on June 9, 1961, more than 64 days after leaving Hamburg.

Dry docked at Lorain, the stern of the ATLANTIC DEALER was removed, floated out and moved stern first into an adjacent dry dock. The German-built mid-section was floated in and secured to the stern of the tanker. With the pilot house moved to its new location forward, the bow of the ATLANTIC DEALER was removed and attached to the new mid-section, creating a 730 foot ship. Her new dimensions were: 707.6 x 75.0 x 39.0; 12,626 GRT. The old mid-section of the ATLANTIC DEALER was taken to Ashtabula, Ohio for scrapping.

Renamed c) PAUL H. CARNAHAN in honor of the president of the National Steel Corporation, she sailed from Lorain on October 15, 1961, bound for Superior, Wisconsin. Arriving there on October 17, she loaded 19,252 gross tons of iron ore at the Great Northern Railroad Docks. She departed the same day, and arrived at C & P in Cleveland on October 20.

In 1961, PAUL H. CARNAHAN was transferred from Skar-Ore Steamship Company to the National Steel Corporation. On April 23, 1972, PAUL H. CARNAHAN arrived at the Burlington Northern Docks at Superior, Wisconsin to load 22,402 gross tons of iron ore bound for Detroit, opening the 1972 shipping season at Superior. On January 1, 1973, the CARNAHAN arrived back at Superior to load the final cargo of the 1972 season and also established a record for the latest closing date at the ore docks at that port. She loaded 17,651 gross tons of iron ore bound for Hanna Furnace Corporation's plant in Detroit.

On December 22, 1984, PAUL H. CARNAHAN arrived at Duluth with a storage load of cement for the St. Lawrence Cement Company Ltd. The bulk cement cargo amounted to 20,175 metric tons which had been loaded at the St. Lawrence Cement Company's Clarkson dock in Mississauga, Ontario.

On August 24, 1985, PAUL H. CARNAHAN arrived for her final lay-up at Nicholson's in Ecorse, Michigan. Ironically, only a few hours later, her near sister LEON FALK, JR. departed the same slip on her final trip bound for Quebec City and overseas scrapping.

National Steel sold PAUL H. CARNAHAN in 1986 to Shiong Yek Steel Corporation of Taiwan. The CARNAHAN departed Ecorse on August 21, 1986, under her own power, bound for Lauzon, where she arrived on August 24. PAUL H. CARNAHAN and her former fleetmate, GEORGE M. HUMPHREY (2), departed Lauzon on September 3, 1986, under tow of the Dutch tug SMIT LLOYD 109, for Taiwan. To accommodate the long tow, the CARNAHAN's fuel tanks were filled sufficiently to allow her to bunker the Dutch tug. The tow arrived safely at Kaosiung, Taiwan on December 10, 1986.

a) Honey Hill, b) Atlantic Dealer, c) PAUL H. CARNAHAN

BUILT:	1945 Sun Shipbuilding & Dry Dock Co. Chester, Pennsylvania	*DEPTH:*	39.2
HULL NUMBER:	481	*GRT:*	10636
LENGTH:	504.0	*REGISTRY NUMBER:*	US. 248208
BREADTH:	68.2	*ENGINES:*	Steam Turbine/Generator and Electric Drive Motor
		ENGINE BUILDER:	Westinghouse, 1945

HONEY HILL as a tanker in the 1940's

ATLANTIC DEALER c.1945

ATLANTIC DEALER upbound at Homer Bridge with tug MARION MORAN, June 16, 1960

PAUL H. CARNAHAN upbound under the Blue Water Bridge, October 15, 1961

PAUL H. CARNAHAN downbound in lower Lake Huron at full speed in 1962

PAUL H. CARNAHAN on her last trip down the Welland Canal, August 22, 1985

CEDARBRANCH (2)

The tanker CEDARBRANCH (2) served Branch Lines Limited from 1951 to 1978. The vessel was built by the fleet's parent company, Marine Industries Limited, and launched at Sorel, Quebec, in September 1951.

CEDARBRANCH was used to haul the petroleum needs of residents of the north shore of Quebec. She made many trips to that region on charter to British-American Oil and later Gulf Canada, but she also found time for voyages into the Great Lakes.

CEDARBRANCH was constructed to dimensions suitable for trading through the old St. Lawrence Canals. She was lengthened following an engine room fire at Montreal on July 31, 1965. The accident left one sailor dead, three injured and the vessel on the bottom of the St. Lawrence. When refloated, CEDARBRANCH was sent to Sorel for repairs and the insertion of a thirty foot section. This brought her length to 284 feet, 5 inches and it raised her carrying capacity from 27,350 barrels to 29,900 barrels of product. Her gross tonnage was increased to 2,439.

A year later, on November 10, 1966, the crew of CEDARBRANCH rescued eighteen sailors from the burning motor vessel CAP DIAMANT on the Gulf of St. Lawrence.

CEDARBRANCH usually worked a full season. She was noted as opening the Welland Canal in 1961. Then, on January 10, 1967, she was first of the year into the port of Toronto. The vessel had been in lay up only to be recalled for short-haul work on Lake Ontario.

In 1978, CEDARBRANCH was sold to the Secola Shipping Company and renamed b) SECOLA. She spent two years in this firm's colors before laying up at Sorel. Her Canadian registry was closed on November 29, 1979.

Naviera Cerralvo, S.A. purchased this tanker and she cleared Sorel on December 5, 1979, as c) KITO MARU. She was registered in Mexico and sailed on the Caribbean and Gulf of Mexico.

In 1985, her career came to an end with her sale to Gulmar, Inc. KITO MARU arrived at the company's scrapyard in Brownsville, Texas, on February 24 and demolition began the next month.

a) CEDARBRANCH (2), b) Secola, c) Kito Maru

BUILT:	1951 Marine Industries Limited Sorel, Quebec
HULL NUMBER:	197
LENGTH:	252.6
BREADTH:	43.6
DEPTH:	20.0
GRT:	2,144
REGISTRY NUMBER:	C. 192529
ENGINES:	8" Diameter x 10" Stroke Diesel
ENGINE BUILDER:	Fairbanks Morse 1944

CEDARBRANCH upbound in the St. Clair River

CEDARBRANCH on fire at Montreal East August 1, 1965

SECOLA in the Welland Canal in 1978

SECOLA leaving Lock 7, Welland Canal
October 9, 1978

KITO MARU at Sorel December 2, 1979

CHINA

The iron-hulled package freight and passenger vessel CHINA was built at Buffalo, New York by Gibson and Craig and launched on September 19, 1871. She and her identical sisterships, INDIA and JAPAN, were the backbone of the Anchor Line fleet (the Pennsylvania Railroad) for many years, 1871 - 1904. Toward the end of her career in this fleet, a person could reserve one of her 43 cabins and go round trip from Buffalo to Duluth for $50.00. Stops were made at Erie, Cleveland, Detroit, Mackinac Island, the Soo, Marquette and Houghton/Hancock.

The Merchants Montreal Line Ltd., bought the vessel in 1904 and transferred her registry to Canadian (C. 117073). In 1905, she was renamed b) CITY OF MONTREAL. Her engines were rebuilt by the Bertram Iron Works, Toronto in 1906 and made a fore and aft compound of 22", 44" diameter x 36" stroke.

In 1908, she was owned by the Montreal & Lake Erie Steamship Company who sold her to the Western Transportation Company Ltd. in 1913. At this time the CITY OF MONTREAL was renamed c) WESTERIAN. She was converted to bulk freight at Kingston, Ontario in 1913-14 after she had been damaged considerably by a fire at Montreal in late 1913. Her new dimensions were: 218 x 32.6 x 14.2; 988 gross tons.

In 1918, WESTERIAN was purchased by the Montreal Transportation Company Ltd., who sold her in 1919 to James H. Hall. In 1922, she was renamed d) SULA to operate in the banana trade in the Caribbean. Her last dimensions were 219 x 32.0 x 15.2; 977 gross tons. In 1923, she was again renamed e) WESTERIAN and owned by the International Waterways Navigation Company Ltd. From then until the end of her career, WESTERIAN again saw lakes service but, after being used as a storage barge, was abandoned and scuttled at St. Johns, Newfoundland on November 9, 1935.

CHINA in the Lock at the Soo very early in her career

CHINA upbound above the Locks at Sault Ste. Marie, Michigan

CITY OF MONTREAL at her dock, ready to depart

WESTERIAN upbound at Nine Mile Point in 1915

a) CHINA, b) City of Montreal, c) Westerian, d) Sula, e) Westerian

BUILT:	1871 Gibson and Craig Buffalo, New York
HULL NUMBER:	6
LENGTH:	210.0
BREADTH:	32.6
DEPTH:	14.0
GRT:	1239.46
REGISTRY NUMBER:	US. 5972
ENGINES:	36" Diameter x 36" Stroke Double Acting Low Pressure
ENGINE BUILDER:	H.G. Trout, Buffalo, New York, 1871

SULA in 1922

CIBOLA

The sidewheel passenger steamer CIBOLA was the first vessel built especially for the excursion service of the Niagara Navigation Company Limited between Toronto and ports of the lower Niagara River. The company had been operating the former blockade runner CHICORA on the route, but by 1886, the traffic on the cross-lake service had exceeded CHICORA's capacity. Accordingly, the N.N. Co. placed an order with E.W. Rathbun & Co., Deseronto, Ontario, for a new steamer. The vessel was designed by Robert Morton, a noted Glasgow designer of Clyde River steamers. The hull was built at the Rathbun shipyard by W.C. White, of Montreal, using Dalzell steel shipped from Scotland.

Construction began on May 24, 1887, and the hull was launched into the Bay of Quinte on November 1st of that year. Miss Constance Cumberland, daughter of the N.N. Company's vice-president, Barlow Cumberland, christened the steamer CIBOLA, an Indian name meaning "Buffalo". The engines, designed by Archie Rankin, were then put into the hull and Rathbun's foreman carpenter, J. Whalen, began work on the superstructure. The interior mahogany trim and decorations were done by the William Wright Company, of Detroit, Michigan while the Edison Company, of New York, supplied the electric lighting.

CIBOLA's first revenue run was on June 10, 1888, when she carried a load of troops to summer camp at Niagara-on-the-Lake. However, her cabins had not been completed when it came time to leave the builder's yard, and the carpenters stayed aboard and finished the superstructure during the course of the delivery trip from Deseronto to Toronto.

CIBOLA entered service as scheduled and proved to be a great success. Her first commander was Captain J. McCorquodale, who was succeeded at the time of his death in 1891, by Captain J. McGiffin, who in turn left to take over as master of the flagship CHIPPEWA upon her completion in 1893. CIBOLA's third master was Captain W.H. Solmes, who commanded her for the rest of her career.

Unhappily, the handsome and popular CIBOLA was not to serve the Niagara route for long. While tied up for the night at Lewiston, New York, on July 15, 1895, the steamer caught fire and burned to the main deck with the loss of one life. Third Engineer William Hammond was trapped below and was unable to escape through a porthole out of which he had attempted to crawl. Meanwhile, the burning steamer had floated free of the Lewiston dock and was carried downstream by the current. The burned-out hull finally was captured and was towed to a wharf at Youngstown, New York, near the mouth of the Niagara River.

When the wreck had finally cooled, it was towed across the lake to Toronto, where her engines and boilers were removed by the Bertram Engine & Shipbuilding Company. They were eventually placed in the new steamer CORONA, which was built by Bertram for the Niagara Navigation Company in 1896. The hull of CIBOLA then lay forgotten for nearly thirty years and, although it has never been verified by the finding of the remains, it is believed that she simply was covered over with fill during the reshaping of Toronto's waterfront during the early 1920s.

CIBOLA at Toronto. Notice the auxiliary sail on her head stay.

BUILT:	1887 E.W. Rathbun & Co. Deseronto, Ontario	*GRT:*	962
HULL NUMBER:	none	*REGISTRY NUMBER:*	C. 92732
LENGTH:	252.0	*ENGINES:*	57", 85" Diameter x 66" Stroke Inclined Compound
BREADTH:	28.4	*ENGINE BUILDER:*	Rankin, Blackmore & Co., Greenock, Scotland, 1887
DEPTH:	10.7		

CIBOLA in the Niagara River

CITY OF KINGSTON

Canada Steamship Line's steel package freighter, CITY OF KINGSTON, was built by Davie Shipbuilding Company Ltd. and was launched in November, 1925. The ship was of the same configuration as the ubiquitous St. Lawrence canaller, but was a bit shorter, some 238.5 feet overall, and she was blessed with somewhat finer lines. This meant higher speed in the open river and on the lakes than the true canaller. Distinctive features extended to the vessel's side ports and deck mounted-elevator frames.

Like the others utilized on CSL's package freight service between Montreal and Toronto, CITY OF KINGSTON bore the name of a community served by the line. She was joined on that run by the CITY OF TORONTO, built by Davie in 1926, CITY OF HAMILTON and CITY OF MONTREAL, built at Midland in 1927, and by CITY OF WINDSOR, last and largest (GRT 1905) of the group, launched by Davie in 1929.

The year 1952 proved a hard one for the doughty veteran. On August 27, while docked at Montreal, a fire broke out aboard which was confined and extinguished within an hour. Only ten tons of her sugar cargo were damaged. Then, in November, CITY OF KINGSTON went aground on Stone Shoal, on the American side of Gooseneck Island. Following lightering by Pyke Salvage Company vessels, the package freighter worked herself off on Sunday, November 14.

On April 28, 1954, CITY OF KINGSTON was the first ship of the season to make a downbound transit of the St. Lawrence canals and took the same honors on April 16, 1956. In the second case, she contended with very heavy ice in the canals all the way to Montreal, where she was the season's first downbound ship. When the 1958 season opened, it was evident that the handwriting was on the wall. While the seaway would open in its entirety in 1959, the flooding of Lake St. Lawrence took place in July, 1958, allowing the use of the new American locks, Eisenhower and Snell. But, CITY OF KINGSTON and her cohorts, with the exception of CITY OF WINDSOR, would not trade through the completed waterway. CITY OF KINGSTON, CITY OF TORONTO, CITY OF HAMILTON and CITY OF MONTREAL were laid up at Canada Steamship Line's Kingston dock at the conclusion of the 1958 season. Late in November, 1959, CITY OF KINGSTON was towed from this site, by Pyke's SALVAGE PRINCE, to the Kingston elevator on Little Cataraqui Bay.

When these boats were removed from service, the 36 hour fast freight runs between Montreal and Toronto ended. The priority granted the CSL package freighters at the locks on the old St. Lawrence Canals was not extended to the new seaway system. In 1961, CITY OF KINGSTON went to Steel Factors, Limited and she was scrapped at Lauzon.

CITY OF KINGSTON downbound in the St. Clair River at Point Edward in 1950

CITY OF KINGSTON upbound in the Detroit River

BUILT:	1925 Davie Shipbuilding Co. Lauzon, Quebec	*GRT:*	1690
HULL NUMBER:	490	*REGISTRY NUMBER:*	C. 152837
LENGTH:	230.3	*ENGINES:*	18", 30", 50" Diameter x 36" Stroke Triple Expansion
BREADTH:	38.1	*ENGINE BUILDER:*	Richardson Westgarth & Co. Ltd., Hartepool, England, 1925
DEPTH:	23.2		

CITY OF KINGSTON in the Cornwall Canal, Lock 21 November 22, 1952

CITY OF PARIS

The wooden-hulled steamer CITY OF PARIS, built at West Bay City, Michigan by the renowned wooden shipbuilder James Davidson, was launched on May 21, 1891. After other shipbuilders were already turning to steel hulls, James Davidson continued to build wooden ships, most of them to his own account as the Davidson Steamship Company. He built no less than seven ships whose names started with CITY OF. He built the VENICE, GENOA, NAPLES, BERLIN, LONDON, GLASGOW and PARIS. The smallest were LONDON and GLASGOW and the largest were the VENICE, GENOA and NAPLES.

Thomas Cranage's McGraw Transportation Company bought the CITY OF PARIS in 1893 and operated her until 1914, meanwhile chartering her to the Edward Smith Lumber Company from 1894 to 1905. In 1915, she was sold to the Jacob & Evans Transportation Company and renamed b) C.W. JACOB. In 1919, the Hammermill Paper Company bought her and used her in the pulp trade.

While as a steamer for the Hammermill Company, C.W. JACOB towed the barge CRETE. She was renamed c) ISOLDE in 1929 when her engine was removed. On her first trip, being towed by the steamer TRISTAN, the towline broke and she went aground at Four Mile Beach, east of Erie Harbor on May 1, 1933. This proved to be the end of the ISOLDE since it was too difficult and expensive to remove her from her precarious position on the beach. Her bones rotted on the spot.

a) CITY OF PARIS, b) C.W. Jacob, c) Isolde

BUILT:	1891 James Davidson West Bay City, Michigan
HULL NUMBER:	41
LENGTH:	298.0
BREADTH:	41.0
DEPTH:	21.0
GRT:	2062.55
REGISTRY NUMBER:	US. 126722
ENGINES:	20", 32", 54" Diameter x 42" Stroke Triple Expansion
ENGINE BUILDER:	Samuel F. Hodge, Detroit, Michigan, 1891

CITY OF PARIS downbound after leaving the Soo Locks

C.W. JACOB downbound with pulpwood at Mission Point, St. Marys River in 1924

ISOLDE at the dock at Erie, Pennsylvania

CLARK BROS.

The wooden-hulled, Toronto Island ferry steamer CLARK BROS. was built in 1889-1890 by D.W. Murphy at the Medlar & Arnot Shipyard, Toronto, to the order of the Clark Family (T.J. Clark, Joseph Clark and Margaret A. Clark), of Toronto. She was a single decker, with an open foredeck, and was employed by her owners in the freight service to the Toronto Islands, where a thriving summer community had developed. Her high pressure, non-condensing engine, with steam supplied by a fire-box boiler, 4 feet by 7 feet, developed 125 indicated horse power.

In 1896, CLARK BROS. was rebuilt at Toronto and enlarged to 51.0 x 11.0 x 3.4; 33 GRT, but she remained a single decked vessel. About 1900, the Toronto Ferry Company Ltd. and the Clarks entered into an operating arrangement, and in 1901 CLARK BROS. was taken to the Andrews Shipyard at Oakville, where she was given a further rebuild and was enlarged to 80.0 x 16.2 x 5.5; 92 GRT. At this time, her ownership was registered in the name of Mary (Margaret?) Clark, but on August 28, 1906, Lawrence Solman, the proprietor of the Toronto Ferry Company, purchased the steamer.

In 1910, CLARK BROS. was rebuilt as a double deck passenger ferry, licensed to carry 216 passengers. Quite possibly, it was at this time that her engine was rebuilt as a steeple compound, condensing power plant.

During much of her time as a double decker, CLARK BROS. regularly served the ferry route to Ward's Island. On Thursday, April 21, 1921, her upper works were badly damaged in a fire which broke out shortly after the steamer completed her last trip from the Island about 6:00 p.m. Fortunately, the fire was extinguished, and the CLARK BROS. was reconstructed by the Toronto Dry Dock Company Ltd. At this time, she was fitted with electric lighting to replace her old oil lamps, and she returned to service in 1922.

Late in 1926, the fleet of the Toronto Ferry Company Ltd. (including CLARK BROS., which still was registered to Lawrence Solman), was acquired by the Corporation of the City of Toronto, and in 1927 the operation of the ferry service was placed in the hands of the Toronto Transportation Commission, which also operated the city's street railways.

CLARK BROS. continued in operation during 1927, 1928 and 1929, but the condition of her wooden hull and superstructure had deteriorated to such an extent that, in the Autumn of 1929, passengers were not allowed to use the upper deck. The steamer was laid up at the close of the 1929 season and did not fit out in 1930.

The old ferry was turned over to the Toronto Harbour Commission and was burned as a spectacle at Toronto's Sunnyside Amusement Park during the celebrations that began on the evening of June 30 and extended into the early morning hours of the Dominion Day Holiday, July 1st, 1930. (Several other vessels, including two other Island ferries - JOHN HANLAN and JASMINE - also were burned at various times in spectacles off Sunnyside Beach.) The registry of CLARK BROS. was closed on July 9, 1930.

BUILT:	1889-90 Medlar & Arnot Shipyard Toronto, Ontario
HULL NUMBER:	none
LENGTH:	40.0
BREADTH:	8.9
DEPTH:	3.4
GRT:	5
REGISTRY NUMBER:	C. 94984
ENGINES:	9" Diameter x 9" Stroke High Pressure Non-condensing
ENGINE BUILDER:	H.W. Petrie, Toronto, 1890

CLARK BROS...a drawing of the vessel in her early years

CLARK BROS. backing away from Toronto city docks June 6, 1927

CLARK BROS. Toronto City ferry docks. Left to right; T.J. CLARK, JOHN HANLAN, CLARK BROS., LUELLA April 6, 1928

CLARK BROS. Ward's Island Docks...high water conditions May 22, 1929

CLARK BROS. in Toronto Harbour

R.G. COBURN

The wooden passenger and freight vessel R.G. COBURN was launched from Thomas Arnold's shipyard at Marine City, Michigan, on the 9th of April in 1870 for Eber Brock Ward's Lake Superior Line to carry freight and passengers to the burgeoning Lake Superior country. The exploding populace in the eastern states and the thousands of new immigrants fled westward in the 1860's and 70's and E.B. Ward was there to transport them through the new (1855) locks at Sault Ste. Marie, Michigan, on his fast propellers. The R.G. COBURN was one of these.

Unexpectedly, however, the life of this fine vessel was short. On October 15, 1871, while downbound in Lake Huron from Duluth, Minnesota, to Buffalo, New York, carrying a general cargo and wheat, the R.G. COBURN met tragedy. Off Saginaw Bay in Lake Huron a furious southwest gale struck the vessel. Very soon she became unmanageable in the tremendous waves. Her rudder was torn off, she drifted into the trough of the seas, her cargo shifted and she was helpless. Crewmen tried to save her by jettisoning as much of her cargo as possible but to no avail. The winds shrieked through her rigging, and in combination with the frothing waves, tore off her smokestack, ripped her lifeboats from their davits and turned them bottom side up.

The second mate, 12 crewmen and six passengers took to the yawl boat and were saved. The entire texas deck floated off the vessel when she foundered. Captain Demont, 15 crewmen and 16 passengers aboard this portion of the ship were never seen again. The angry waves of Lake Huron had claimed another unfortunate vessel, its passengers and crew.

R.G. COBURN in center at Duluth. Schooner COMMERCE is astern; Steamer NORMAN ahead

BUILT:	1870 Thomas Arnold Shipyard Marine City, Michigan
HULL NUMBER:	none
LENGTH:	193.4
BREADTH:	30.8
DEPTH:	12.0
GRT:	867
REGISTRY NUMBER:	US. 21954
ENGINES:	45" Diameter x 40" Stroke High Pressure Non-condensing
ENGINE BUILDER:	Samuel F. Hodge Detroit, Michigan, 1870

R.G. COBURN at her Duluth dock

CONSUMERS POWER (3)

Completed in 1927 by the American Ship Building Company at Lorain, Ohio for the Kinsman Transit Company, the GEORGE M. HUMPHREY (1) was christened on December 29, 1926. She was named for the executive vice-president of the M.A. Hanna Company of Cleveland, who was later to become Secretary of the Treasury.

GEORGE M. HUMPHREY spent seventeen uneventful seasons for Kinsman before becoming the focus of one of the greatest salvage efforts in Great Lakes history. On June 15, 1943, the HUMPHREY was bound for South Chicago with 13,992 tons of iron ore. She was proceeding in heavy fog through the Straits of Mackinac when, at 2:50 a.m., she collided with the Pittsburgh Steamship Company's D.M. CLEMSON (2). Hit hard on her starboard side abreast number three hatch, the HUMPHREY was left with an 18 x 20 foot hole. Sinking almost immediately in 78 feet of water, 1 7/8 miles off Old Point Mackinac light, her entire crew was miraculously saved by both the CLEMSON and the LAGONDA.

The owners of the HUMPHREY abandoned the wreck to underwriters who, in turn, passed the vessel to the United States Engineers for removal as a navigation menace. The Engineers awarded a contract to Captain John Roen, wreckmaster and ship owner from Sturgeon Bay, Wisconsin. The contract was for removal of the obstructive portions of the vessel. However, Captain Roen had an additional objective. His plans included salvaging a large portion of the iron cargo, then salvaging the 600 foot ship with full ownership as the goal. Captain Roen's salvage effort began in September, 1943. Despite the great depth of water from which the ore had to be lifted, 8,000 tons of salable ore was raised by clam bucket before winter set in.

Operations resumed on May 6, 1944. Using the barges MAITLAND and HILDA as pontoons, the HUMPHREY was towed while under water until she was clear of all shipping lanes. To accomplish this, the HUMPHREY was moved along under the MAITLAND until it touched bottom.

Then the MAITLAND was partially submerged and cables connecting the two vessels shortened for the next step toward shallow water. Then the MAITLAND was pumped out which lifted the HUMPHREY off the bottom. This was repeated until the HUMPHREY's deck was lifted close to the MAITLAND's bottom. The HILDA then acted as a pontoon, as both barges took over the lifting and towing on each side of the HUMPHREY.

By September 5, 1944, the HUMPHREY's deck was six feet above water. The forward end of the wreck was tilted and the 18 x 20 foot hole patched. After almost fifteen months submerged in the Straits of Mackinac, the GEORGE M. HUMPHREY was pumped out and back afloat. She limped into Roen's shipyard at Sturgeon Bay, partially under her own power, assisted by Captain Roen's tugs.

After repairs were completed and the HUMPHREY inspected, she returned to service in May, 1945 as b) CAPTAIN JOHN ROEN for the Roen Transportation Company. She was chartered in 1945 to the Pioneer Steamship Company (Hutchinson and Company) and in 1946 to the Interstate Steamship Company (Jones and Laughlin).

In 1947, CAPTAIN JOHN ROEN was sold to Boland and Cornelius. In 1948, she was converted to a self-unloader at Manitowoc Shipbuilding Company. On November 25, 1948, in ceremonies at Manitowoc, she was re-christened c) ADAM E. CORNELIUS (2), honoring one of the founders of the American Steamship Company. Her gross tonnage was increased to 8,217. She was repowered in 1955, with a 5,500 horsepower DeLaval steam turbine engine. In 1958, ADAM E. CORNELIUS was renamed d) CONSUMERS POWER (3), in honor of an important customer of the American Steamship Company. In 1975-76, the Nicholson Terminal and Dock Company of Ecorse, Michigan converted CONSUMERS POWER from coal to oil-firing with automated boilers. In 1980, CONSUMERS POWER was chartered to the Erie Sand Company, for whom she was operating when she was laid up in Erie for the last time on December 6, 1985.

In March, 1988, American Steamship Company requested permission from the U.S. Maritime Administration for approval to sell CONSUMERS POWER to Corostel Trading Ltd. of Montreal for scrapping overseas. CONSUMERS POWER cleared Erie with McKeil Marine's W.N. TWOLAN on May 2, 1988, bound for Quebec City, where she arrived on May 9th. On June 14, 1988, CONSUMERS POWER, with her former fleetmate JOHN T. HUTCHINSON, departed Lauzon in tow of the Panamanian tug/supply ship OMEGA 809, bound for Kaohsiung, Taiwan. CONSUMERS POWER arrived in Kaohsiung on October 2, 1988 and was scrapped shortly afterwards.

a) George M. Humphrey (1), b) Captain John Roen, c) Adam E. Cornelius (2), d) CONSUMERS POWER (3)

BUILT:	1927 American Ship Building Co. Lorain, Ohio
HULL NUMBER:	796
LENGTH:	586.3
BREADTH:	60.2
DEPTH:	27.9
GRT:	8004
REGISTRY NUMBER:	US. 226276
ENGINES:	24 1/2", 41", 65" Diameter x 42" Stroke Triple Expansion
ENGINE BUILDER:	Shipyard, 1927

GEORGE M. HUMPHREY (1) upbound in the Detroit River opposite Belle Isle

GEORGE M. HUMPHREY (1) after being raised from the Straits of Mackinac

GEORGE M. HUMPHREY (1) another view of what damage the ice did to her upper works

CAPTAIN JOHN ROEN downbound in the Detroit River

CAPTAIN JOHN ROEN in Boland & Cornelius colors, upbound at Fort Gratiot Light, Lake Huron

ADAM E. CORNELIUS (2) downbound under the Blue Water Bridge in 1949

CONSUMERS POWER (3) downbound in lower Lake Huron July 13, 1962

CONSUMERS POWER (3) upbound in the St. Clair River near Harsens Island June 17, 1980

JOHN B. COWLE (2)

The steel bulk freighter JOHN B. COWLE (2) was built in 1910 at Lorain, Ohio by the American Ship Building Company for the United States Transportation Company, her operators. She was ordered to replace the JOHN B. COWLE (1) which was sunk in collision with the ISAAC M. SCOTT on July 12, 1909. In 1912, the vessel, along with others of the USTC fleet, went into a new firm called the Great Lakes Steamship Company.

In 1957, this company was purchased by the Wilson Transit Company and the COWLE was sold to the Republic Steel Corporation in a subsequent transaction. In 1969, she was renamed b) HARRY L. ALLEN. In 1970, she was again sold, this time to the Kinsman Marine Transit Company, which became S. & E. Shipping in 1976. While the ALLEN was at winter quarters at Duluth, Minnesota on January 21, 1978, the Capital Grain Elevator #4 caught fire. The flames were so intense that the ALLEN, lying along side, could not be moved; so she also caught fire. Her cabins were gutted by the flames, and her plates were severely buckled because of the intense heat. This caused her to be declared a total loss. Her remains were scrapped at Duluth in 1979, by the scrap firm of Hyman Michaels.

a) JOHN B. COWLE (2), b) Harry L. Allen

BUILT:	1910 American Ship Building Co. Lorain, Ohio
HULL NUMBER:	379
LENGTH:	525.0
BREADTH:	58.0
DEPTH:	31.0
GRT:	6614
REGISTRY NUMBER:	US. 207227
ENGINES:	23 1/2", 38", 63" Diameter x 42" Stroke Triple Expansion
ENGINE BUILDER:	Shipyard, 1910

JOHN B. COWLE (2) downbound leaving the Locks at the Soo

JOHN B. COWLE (2) upbound at Mission Point, St. Marys River

JOHN B. COWLE (2) downbound in St. Marys River September 5, 1960

HARRY L. ALLEN upbound in the St. Marys River August 16, 1969

HARRY L. ALLEN upbound in the St. Marys River in 1976

HARRY L. ALLEN after the fire at Duluth January 21, 1978

CYCLO-CHIEF

The CYCLO-CHIEF was one of a number of similarly designed tankers built in the United Kingdom just before the full effect of the Great Depression struck. This vessel was constructed by the Furness Shipbuilding Company of Haverton Hill-on-Tees, England, with keel laying ceremonies December 17, 1929. CYCLO-CHIEF was launched April 29, 1930, and soon sailed for Canada to work for the McColl-Frontenac Oil Company.

In 1947, the Texaco Oil Company Ltd. purchased McColl-Frontenac interests and thus acquired their Great Lakes fleet of three tankers. This vessel was renamed b) TEXACO CHIEF (1). The ship spent seven years hauling petroleum for Texaco but was laid up at Port Weller in 1954. She was resold to Gayport Shipping of Toronto the following year and resumed trading as c) FUEL TRANSPORTER.

On July 1, 1959, the Hall Corporation took a large step in developing their tanker fleet by purchasing the Gayport vessels. As a result, a fourth name, that of d) FUEL TRANSPORT was given to this ship.

From 1960 to 1963, FUEL TRANSPORT was chartered to the Eagle Oil Company and spent most of her time in Atlantic Coastal trading. She later returned to the Great Lakes but was laid up at Toronto from 1968 to 1970.

West Indies Transport Limited purchased this ship in 1970 and had her registered for new service in the Caribbean. The vessel was renamed e) WITFUEL and reclassified for Caribbean and Pacific Coastal service. She originally carried Panamanian registry, but this was later changed to Guatemalan and then Nicaraguan.

WITFUEL was listed as laid up at St. Thomas, Virgin Islands, with survey overdue in July, 1974 but a 1985 report indicated that the vessel had been renamed f) WITWATER (2) and registered in the Cayman Islands for Challenger Ltd. Though gone from the lakes, it appears that this vessel is still intact.

a) CYCLO-CHIEF, b) Texaco Chief (1), c) Fuel Transporter, d) Fuel Transport, e) Witfuel, f) Witwater (2)

BUILT:	1930 Haverton Hill-on-Tees, U.K.
HULL NUMBER:	177
LENGTH:	250.0
BEADTH:	43.3
DEPTH:	21.8
GRT:	2500
REGISTRY NUMBER:	C. 160729
ENGINES:	19", 33", 54" Diameter x 42" Stroke Triple Expansion
ENGINE BUILDER:	North Eastern Marine Engineering Co. Ltd., 1930

CYCLO-CHIEF upbound light

CYCLO-CHIEF downbound in the Detroit River

TEXACO CHIEF at Port Weller

FUEL TRANSPORTER in the Welland Canal December, 1955

FUEL TRANSPORT downbound in lower Lake Huron in 1965

WITFUEL in the West Indies

CYCLONE

An unusual twin stack steam yacht was built in 1883 by Paul Lohmeyer at Cleveland, Ohio for himself and W.J. Innis. They named her a) CYCLONE and ran her by themselves for their own pleasure in the Lake Erie area. In 1888 and 1889, her owner was Charles W. Laskey, who had her lengthened to the dimensions: 97.6 x 20.8 x 6.7; 122 GRT at Chaumont, New York. The Milwaukee Excursion Company bought her in 1889, and ran the CYCLONE in the excursion trade out of Milwaukee until 1892. Herman Dahlke and Willian R. Kurhle bought the vessel in 1892 and sailed her until 1899.

George B. Massey became her owner in 1899 and sold the CYCLONE in 1900. E.J. Newman was her owner in 1900 and 1901. In 1903, Frank D. Phelps bought the vessel and had her converted to a steam barge whose dimensions now were: 90.5 x 20.0 x 8.1; 83 gross tons. He renamed CYCLONE as b) FRANK D. PHELPS the same year and used her to transport various cargoes around Lake Superior. Her official number became: US. 200234.

In 1908, the Peoples Milling Company, G.H. Herrick, president, bought the PHELPS and converted her to a "bumboat", a supply vessel for ships in the Duluth-Superior area. In 1915, the Northern Fish Company, A. Miller McDougall, president, bought the PHELPS to use as a fish tug and "fish market afloat" in the same general vicinity. The last owner, John Roen of Sturgeon Bay, Wisconsin, purchased the FRANK D. PHELPS in 1920 and operated her in general services until 1929, when she was dismantled and her document surrendered at Grand Haven, Michigan on March 30, 1929. Thus ended the varied career of CYCLONE, b) FRANK D. PHELPS, a yacht, a passenger vessel, a steam barge, a "bum boat" and a fish tug.

a) CYCLONE, b) Frank D. Phelps

BUILT:	1883 Paul Lohmeyer Cleveland, Ohio
HULL NUMBER:	none
LENGTH:	96.6
BREADTH:	20.8
DEPTH:	2.9
GRT:	69
REGISTRY NUMBER:	US. 126155
ENGINES:	12", 36" Diameter x 17" Stroke Fore & Aft Compound
ENGINE BUILDER:	unknown

CYCLONE as a two-stacked passenger vessel

FRANK D. PHELPS as a steam barge

FRANK D. PHELPS as a "bumboat" in Duluth Harbor

FRANK D. PHELPS, a stern view at the dock

DON JUAN de AUSTRIA

This gunboat, built of iron at the Cartagena Dock Yard at Cartagena, Spain, for the Spanish Navy, was launched on January 23, 1887. She was a unit of the Spanish squadron at Manila, Philippine Islands, when the United States Asiatic squadron attacked on May 1, 1898 in the opening engagement of the Spanish American War. The Spanish fleet was anchored under the shore batteries at the naval base at Cavite. In the ensuing action, the DON JUAN de AUSTRIA was damaged and settled to the bottom near shore. Her armament was still in use, thus constituting a threat. She was boarded under cover of darkness that night by small boat parties from the U.S. fleet and set afire.

After the surrender of the Spanish forces, the DON JUAN de AUSTRIA was raised by the U.S. Army and on November 9, 1899 was transferred to the U.S. Navy. She was taken to Hong Kong where she was repaired, refitted and placed in commission on April 11, 1900. Based at Canton, China, from June 5, 1900 to October 18, 1900, she was there to protect American shipping off the China coast. She sailed from Hong Kong November 25, 1900 to Cavite, and based from there, was employed on duties around the islands during the insurgency. She visited Yokohama, Japan from June 1, to July 27, 1902 on a courtesy visit.

She returned to Cavite and performed patrol duties until April 19, 1903, when she departed for Yokohama for repairs which took from April 27 to June 1, 1903, after which she again cruised the coast of China. She departed Hong Kong December 16, 1903 for the United States via Singapore, Ceylon, India, Suez Canal and Mediterranean ports. DON JUAN de AUSTRIA arrived at the Portsmouth, New Hampshire Navy Yard April 21, 1904. She was placed out of commission for repairs from May 5, 1904 to December 10, 1905.

The ship was attached to the Third Squadron, Atlantic Fleet, and sailed from Norfolk, Virginia, February 28, 1906 to patrol off the Dominican Republic. She returned to the Portsmouth Navy Yard on February 21, 1907, where she was placed out of commission on March 7, 1907. The ship was loaned to the Michigan Naval Militia and sailed from Portsmouth on July 28, 1907, via the St. Lawrence River to Detroit, where she served as a training vessel. Recommissioned on April 6, 1917, she departed Detroit on July 17th for Newport, Rhode Island, where she was used to patrol off the east coast until called to New York in August to escort two Army tugs towing barges to Bermuda.

The ship returned to Newport October 1, 1918 and towed the schooner CHARLES WHITEMORE to Charleston, South Carolina, then revisited Bermuda to escort U.S. and French submarines to Newport. After more escort duties, she was decommissioned at Portsmouth on June 18, 1919 and sold to Andrew Olsen of Brooklyn, New York, for commercial use. She was renamed b) DEWEY and given official number US. 220078 in 1920.

After several years, she sank at her dock in New York. Her document was surrendered in 1926, endorsed as "Abandoned for age". Thus ended the career of a much traveled Spanish warship that spent part of her colorful life on the Great Lakes.

DON JUAN de AUSTRIA in the Soo Locks with Naval Reserves on board

DON JUAN de AUSTRIA leaving the Soo Locks

a) DON JUAN de AUSTRIA, b) Dewey

BUILT:	1887 Cartagena Dock Yard Cartagena, Spain
HULL NUMBER:	unknown
LENGTH:	215.6
BREADTH:	32.0
DEPTH:	16.4
DISPLACEMENT TONNAGE:	1130
REGISTRY:	Spanish Navy
ENGINES:	Horizontal Compound
ENGINE BUILDER:	Cartagena Dockyard, 1887

DON JUAN de AUSTRIA anchored in Lake Michigan

CHARLES DICK

The steam sandsucker CHARLES DICK was unique in a number of ways. When she was launched at Collingwood, Ontario on May 27, 1922, she was christened not by a female but by her namesake, a five-year-old lad, the son of David Dick, the owner of the company for which she was built. This was the National Sand & Material Company Ltd. of Welland, Ontario. In later years the firm was acquired by Erie Sand and Gravel of Erie, Pennsylvania and its base of operations moved to Hamilton. Incidentally, Mr. Charles Dick died in 1977, the same year in which his namesake vessel was being cut up at Port Colborne (Humberstone), Ontario.

Another unique feature of the steamer CHARLES DICK was her design, the work of Levi Millen of the Montreal firm of Millen and German. The DICK had two tubes which could be affixed to her bow and lowered to the lake bottom to pump sand or gravel into her open cargo holds where the surplus water was pumped overboard while the sand or gravel settled down. Each of her two holds could contain about 2,000 cubic yards or almost 1,000 tons of material. Above the holds, was an open framework which supported a traveling clamshell bucket which picked up the cargo and deposited it in a hopper which was amidships between the holds. A conveyor, on a short boom affixed to the port side, removed the cargo from the hopper and deposited it on shore.

In order to operate all of this machinery, the DICK had 32 steam engines of various sizes in addition to her main propulsion engine. Although she was not a conventional self-unloader, CHARLES DICK was probably the first vessel built in Canada capable of discharging bulk cargo over a conveyor boom, being ahead of GLENELG which is usually considered the first Canadian-built self-unloader.

The DICK seldom got in trouble but, an exception occurred on August 21, 1971, when she severed two underwater cables in the Maumee River, cutting off power to east Toledo and the Cherry Street Bridge. Massive traffic jams developed on Toledo's streets.

In 1958, the legendary Captain John Leonard assumed command of CHARLES DICK and remained with her until she laid up at Port Colborne at the end of the 1973 season. That winter her pumps and operating gear were overhauled but, before spring arrived, word was received that, because of political opposition, Mersea Township, Ontario, had refused to renew her license to dig sand off Lake Erie's Point Pelee. Thus the DICK did not fit out for the 1974 season but remained cold at Port Colborne until sold to Marine Salvage Ltd. in 1976. Marine Salvage moved her through Lock 8 to their Humberstone scrap yard where they completed the dismantling of CHARLES DICK in 1977—thus removing from the lakes one of its truly unique vessels.

BUILT:	1922 Collingwood Shipbuilding Co. Collingwood, Ontario
HULL NUMBER:	71
LENGTH:	244.0
BREADTH:	43.2
DEPTH:	18.9
GRT:	2015
REGISTRY NUMBER:	C. 141678
ENGINES:	19", 32", 56" Diameter x 36" Stroke Triple Expansion
ENGINE BUILDER:	The Prescott Co., 1922

CHARLES DICK, aerial view from one of the bridges in the Welland Canal

CHARLES DICK at Wallaceburg, Ontario

CHARLES DICK downbound in the Welland Canal

REUBEN DOUD

The three-masted schooner REUBEN DOUD was built in 1873 for the firm of Doud & Vance, Racine, Wisconsin. The hull was built of white oak by C. Gilson at Winneconne, Wisconsin, a town located on the banks of the Wolf River which flows into Lake Michigan's Green Bay. Unfortunately, after the schooner was launched, it was found that there was insufficient depth of water in the river to float her down to Green Bay. The Wolf River had to be dammed in several places to build enough pool water in order that teams of oxen could drag REUBEN DOUD out of the river.

The REUBEN DOUD proved to be a difficult ship to handle, and this problem was only partially solved by the fitting of a concave rudder after she was in service. She was involved in many "incidents" during her career, and truly earned her nickname "Bull of the Woods".

In 1890, REUBEN DOUD was sold to Timothy Hurley, of Detroit, Michigan, who operated her through the 1900 season. That year proved to be a bad one for the schooner. In a late season gale, she lost both her main and mizzen masts, and only barely made port with what sail could be spread on the fore mast.

That would have been her last trip of the season, but freights were so good that autumn that it was decided to postpone repairs so she could make one more trip as a barge in tow of a steamer. She took a load of coal for Detroit from Lake Erie, but broke adrift in heavy weather. Her crew headed the DOUD for Rondeau, running before the wind under the foresail, but the fore sheet post carried away. An effort was made to anchor the vessel, but the anchors would not hold and REUBEN DOUD stranded on the Middle Ground at the western end of Lake Erie. She eventually was pulled free by a salvage tug but, in the process, the schooner left forty feet of her outside keel on the shoal.

REUBEN DOUD was repaired and acquired in 1901 by Albert I. Foster and Captain Alexander Ure, who operated her for the Conger Coal Company, of Toronto. She was brought into Canadian registry and given the Registry Number C. 100305. She was given a most unusual rig, with a new mainmast that was shorter than fore, and with a peculiar, three-cornered "square sail" hung from the yard on the foremast. The rebuilding was done at Windsor.

She had not been in service long when her habit of veering off to windward in a gusty breeze caused her to ground on the weather shore of Lake Ontario off Braddock's Point. She was freed by a tug from Oswego and was towed to Charlotte, where she sank in the Genesee River. She was refloated with the aid of pumps and a cofferdam, after which she went to Port Dalhousie for repairs.

In 1905, Albert I. Foster, of Toronto, became the sole owner of REUBEN DOUD. He was not to have her for long, however, for she was lost in the late summer of the following year.

On the evening of August 23, 1906, REUBEN DOUD was approaching the Eastern Gap entrance to Toronto Harbour, laden with a cargo of coal for Conger's under the command of Captain John Joyce. A strong easterly gale was blowing and the gap was obstructed by the presence of a dredge. As the DOUD attempted to pass the dredge in the early morning hours of August 24, there was a lull in the wind and the schooner lost headway. Her master attempted to head her back into the lake, but she struck the bottom and unshipped her rudder. She then swung off and drove in stern-first on the Ward's Island beach, where she went to pieces about a half-mile west of the piers. The seven-person crew was rescued by the government lifeboat which was commanded by Island resident, Captain William Ward.

BUILT:	1873 C. Gilson Winneconne, Wisconsin
HULL NUMBER:	none
LENGTH:	137.7
BREADTH:	26.0
DEPTH:	11.6
GRT:	324
REGISTRY NUMBER:	US. 110151

REUBEN DOUD, a painting by Seth Arca Whipple

REUBEN DOUD being towed from Toronto by the tug SKYLARK c.1903

REUBEN DOUD wrecked on Ward's Island beach at Toronto

T.L. DUROCHER

The steel tug T.L. DUROCHER was launched by the American Ship Building Company September 22, 1930, for T.L. Durocher, the wrecking master of DeTour Village, Michigan. Unfortunately, she did not last long in Mr. Durocher's employ and was repossessed by the American Ship Building Company for non-payment in 1932. The Independent Steamship Company, a subsidiary for the American Ship Building Company, took her over in 1934, but she lay idle most of the time and was only chartered twice in six years.

In September 1940, the tug was taken to the Atlantic coast. In July 1941, the U.S. Army Quartermaster Department purchased the tug and renamed her b) LT. COL. LAWRENCE O. MATTHEWS. The tug was put into service towing barges with supplies for emergency airfields being built in northern Quebec. On October 28, 1942, at the south end of Ungava Bay on the Koksoak River, the big tug was lost in a severe storm.

a) T.L. DUROCHER, b) Lt. Col. Lawrence O. Matthews

BUILT:	1930 American Ship Building Co. Lorain, Ohio
HULL NUMBER:	807
LENGTH:	117.5
BREADTH:	28.2
DEPTH:	14.9
GRT:	319
REGISTRY NUMBER:	US. 230286
ENGINES:	17", 25", 43" Diameter x 30" Stroke Triple Expansion
ENGINE BUILDER:	Filer & Stowell, Milwaukee, Wisconsin 1930

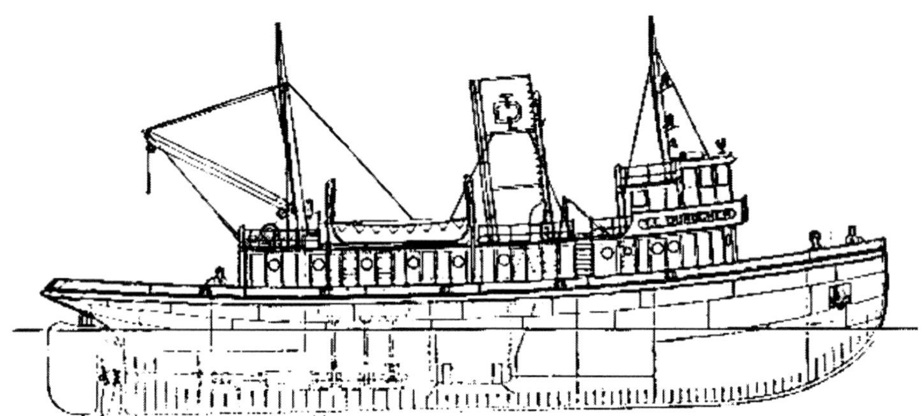

Outboard profile of the tug T.L. DUROCHER

T.L. DUROCHER on the stocks at Lorain, Ohio in 1930

T.L. DUROCHER undergoing trials in Lake Erie

U.S.A.T. LT. COL. LAWRENCE O. MATHEWS at the Brooklyn Army Base at New York in October 1941 US ARMY Signal Corps photo

EASTERN STATES

The steel side-wheel passenger steamer EASTERN STATES was launched on December 7, 1901, by the Detroit Shipbuilding Company for the Detroit and Buffalo Steamship Company. She was to run overnight between the two company namesake cities in conjunction with her sistership WESTERN STATES. On one of her first trips, the high pressure cylinder blew and was destroyed. It took three weeks to replace the cylinder head, causing the loss of use of the ship. In 1909, the Detroit & Cleveland Navigation Company took over the D & B vessels.

On June 19, 1917, the EASTERN STATES collided with the Canadian steamer NATIRONCO near Grassy Island in the Detroit River, sinking the latter vessel. The NATIRONCO was raised and repaired. The EASTERN STATES was repaired and returned to service promptly. No one was seriously injured in the collision.

During World War II, the EASTERN STATES did yeoman service ferrying tanks, and other military vehicles built in Detroit, to Cleveland, Ohio, for transshipment overseas. As a consequence, her main cargo deck became badly scored. Those who rode her after the war said she looked and sounded very tired, and speculated that her useful days were numbered.

After almost 50 years of service, the D & C vessels were all laid up. The EASTERN STATES, which had last run between Detroit, Michigan and Put-In-Bay, Ohio on excursion runs, was laid up on the Detroit waterfront awaiting her fate. On December 12, 1956, the once proud vessel was taken out onto Lake St. Clair where she was set afire. All her superstructure was burned off and the hull was taken to Hamilton, Ontario, where she was scrapped in 1957.

BUILT:	1902 Detroit Shipbuilding Co. Wyandotte, Michigan
HULL NUMBER:	144
LENGTH:	350.0
BREADTH:	44.0
DEPTH:	19.9
GRT:	3077
REGISTRY NUMBER:	US. 136981
ENGINES:	52", 72", 72" Diameter x 84" Stroke Inclined Compound
ENGINE BUILDER:	Shipyard, 1902

EASTERN STATES downbound Detroit River in her early days

EASTERN STATES leaving Toledo Harbor

EASTERN STATES approaching her Detroit docks

EASTERN STATES leaving her Detroit docks bound upriver

ISAAC L. ELLWOOD

This steel bulk freighter was built in 1900 for the newly-formed American Steel and Wire Company (A.S. & W.). The vessel was named after Mr. Ellwood of De Kalb, Illinois, who had been one of the main organizers of the American Steel and Wire Company in 1899.

One of four sister ships (the others were WILLIAM EDENBORN, JOHN W. GATES and JAMES J. HILL), the ISAAC L. ELLWOOD was the first on the Great Lakes to reach nearly 500 feet in overall length. The shipyard of F.W. Wheeler & Company in Bay City, Michigan built the vessel and launched her on May 5, 1900.

In the late 1800's, Mr. Ellwood was very active in promoting a merger of several mid-west iron and light steel companies. The collaborative efforts of Mr. Ellwood and Mr. Elbert H. Gary, an attorney from Naperville, Illinois, brought about the organization of the American Steel & Wire in 1898.

In 1901, American Steel & Wire became part of the United States Steel Corporation and the ISAAC L. ELLWOOD and her sister ships joined the Pittsburgh Steamship Company. The ship would remain in this fleet until scrapped in 1961.

BUILT:	1900 F.W. Wheeler & Co. West Bay City, Michigan
HULL NUMBER:	39
LENGTH:	478.0
BREADTH:	52.0
DEPTH:	25.2
GRT:	5085
REGISTRYNUMBER:	US. 100707
ENGINES:	16", 25", 38" 60" Diameter x 40" Stroke Quadruple Expansion
ENGINE BUILDER:	American Ship Building Co., 1900

ISAAC L. ELLWOOD leaving the Soo Locks downbound in 1900

ISAAC L. ELLWOOD entering Cleveland Harbor

ISAAC L. ELLWOOD leaving the Davis Lock at Sault Ste. Marie April 18, 1949

ISAAC L. ELLWOOD upbound light after leaving the Locks at the Soo

ISAAC L. ELLWOOD downbound in the St. Clair River in 1952

C. W. ELPHICKE

C.W. ELPHICKE upbound light leaving the Soo Locks in 1913

Built in 1889 for Charles W. Elphicke of Chicago, Illinois, by the Craig Ship Building Company at Trenton, Michigan, and launched on July 3, 1889, the C.W. ELPHICKE was a typical wooden bulk freighter for her time. She remained under the ownership of C.W. Elphicke until sold to G.W. Close of Berlin Heights, Ohio, around 1891. Her ownership was changed again when she was listed as being owned by James B. Wood of Belleview, Ohio, in 1896. In 1897, the vessel was purchased by J.C. Gilchrist of Cleveland, Ohio, and remained in the Gilchrist fleet until 1913 when her owners became the Kinney Transportation Company of Cleveland.

On October 21, 1913, the C.W. ELPHICKE became a victim of the fall season's first major storm, which would be a precursor to what would later be known as the Great Storm of 1913 a month later.

The steamer had loaded 106,000 bushels of Canadian grain at Fort William, Ontario and left on the long trip to Buffalo on Tuesday, October 14th, under the command of Captain Alonzo B. Comins and a crew of eighteen. The ELPHICKE had an uneventful journey proceeding down through Lakes Superior, Huron and St. Clair. However, while navigating the Detroit River on Sunday, October 19th, the steamer struck a submerged object. After the captain had made a quick inspection, he felt there was no need for concern as there appeared to be little damage done.

Continuing down the river, the ELPHICKE reached Lake Erie early Monday morning. Leaving the shelter of the Detroit River behind, the vessel found the waves to be moderate and the winds freshening. As she proceeded further east, the winds reached gale force and the waves increased in magnitude. Soon it was found that water was entering her hold. Captain Comins was not overly concerned about this problem, as he felt the bilge pumps could handle it. However, the water continued to gain, and upon closer inspection, a large hole was found on the starboard side, caused when the steamer hit the obstruction in the river. Again the captain decided that with vigorous working of the pumps, his ship could reach Long Point where he could make temporary repairs.

As the ELPHICKE continued east, she was punished severely by the angry waters. The entire crew working constantly could not keep up with the inrushing water. Unknown to all aboard, the seams from the hole to nearly 200 feet back, had opened several inches, allowing great quantities of water to enter the hull, thus sealing the fate of the freighter. Slowly the vessel began settling lower into the lake. The captain and his crew worked throughout Monday night in an effort to reach safety behind Long Point, however, the steamer continued filling. At daybreak, when the ship was within a mile of the Point and safety, it became obvious that the ELPHICKE would sink soon. The captain, rather than allowing the vessel to sink in deep water, gave orders to beach her. She was turned to port and proceeded only a short distance before standing 2,000 feet from shore.

The C.W. ELPHICKE lay in the surf on the southern shore, a mile west of the Long Point Lighthouse. A yawl waslowered and had just cleared the freighter when it was capsized by a large wave. All of the men that were thrown into the turbulent water were pulled safely back on board the vessel. By this time the Long Point lifesaving crew had reached the stranded freighter. With their assistance, a second yawl was launched. Seven of the crew reached shore safely after battling the breakers for nearly an hour. The captain and the remaining eleven were taken aboard the surfboat and also reached shore safely.

The C.W. ELPHICKE was officially abandoned on October 23rd, 1913; she had been found to have broken up and was not salvageable. The loss of both vessel and cargo amounted to $125,000. After an official investigation by the U.S. Steamboat Inspection Service, the captain and officers of the freighter were found to be blameless for the vessel's loss.

The gale season of 1913 had begun, claiming the ELPHICKE as its first victim. She would be the first of many that year.

BUILT:	1889 Craig Ship Building Co. Trenton, Michigan
HULL NUMBER:	39
LENGTH:	273.0
BREADTH:	42.0
DEPTH:	20.4
GRT:	2058.55
REGISTRYNUMBER:	US. 126568
ENGINES:	19", 30", 50" Diameter x 40" Stroke Triple Expansion
ENGINE BUILDER:	S.F. Hodge & Co., Detroit, Michigan 1889

ERIE ISLE

FREDERICA on the east coast in her early years

a) Frederica, b) ERIE ISLE

BUILT:	1894 Neafie & Levy Shipbuilding Co. Philadelphia, Pennsylvania
HULL NUMBER:	unknown
LENGTH:	117.8
BREADTH:	26.0
DEPTH:	6.8
GRT:	293.88
REGISTRY NUMBER:	US. 120979
ENGINES:	9", 18" Diameter x 14" Stroke Fore & Aft Compound
ENGINE BUILDER:	Shipyard, 1894

The twin-screw, steel-hulled, freight and passenger steamer, built in 1894 by the Neafie & Levy Shipbuilding Company in Philadelphia, Pennsylvania, for the Philadelphia Steam Navigation Company, was named a) FREDERICA. When built, she was supposedly 99 feet in length. After a year of service on the route from Philadelphia to Frederica, Delaware, on the Murderkill River, the owners found the vessel to be somewhat undersized for the business and she was returned to the builders and lengthened 18 feet; 293 GRT.

The FREDERICA ran on this route until 1926 when she was sent to the Vineyard Shipyard at Milford, Delaware, where her saloon deck and overnight cabins were removed and the pilot house lowered to better suit the vessel for her new trade of carrying fruit and produce. FREDERICA continued as a freight boat in the Chesapeake Bay area until 1930 when she was sold to the Erie Isles Ferry Company of Sandusky, Ohio for service as a passenger and auto ferry from Catawba to Put-In-Bay, with occasional trips to Sandusky.

FREDERICA arrived at Sandusky in early October, 1930, via the St. Lawrence River. She was inspected, renamed b) ERIE ISLE, (315 GRT) and licensed to carry 300 passengers and a dozen or so automobiles. The ferry service to Put-In-Bay usually consisted of five round trips per day from Catawba and occasional trips to Sandusky.

In 1942, the ERIE ISLE was replaced on the route by the motor vessel MYSTIC ISLE, and was retired. The steamer was dismantled in 1946 and the hull was used as a barge with the unofficial name of FUBAR. As a barge, she was used by the Neuman Boat Company to carry coal and other bulk freight to the islands until the late 1950's, when she was abandoned and sunk on the east side of Middle Bass Island.

ERIE ISLE at her dock in the 1930's

ERIE ISLE ready for her trip to the islands in Lake Erie

ERIE ISLE laid up for lack of service

FUBAR (unofficially renamed) as a tow barge

FUBAR at the dock on Lake Erie

ERINDALE

ERINDALE spent less than a decade in Great Lakes trading and proved to be the last of the old Westdale fleet to operate. She was under the banner of Dale Transports when she tied up for the winter of 1983-84 at the stone dock below Lock 8 of the Welland Canal at Port Colborne.

When spring came, the Dale fleet was out of business and the vessel was moved to a section of the old canal, north of Humberstone. On November 2, 1984, the tugs ATOMIC and ELMORE M. MISNER towed ERINDALE to the scrap dock of International Marine Salvage in Port Colborne harbor. Over the following winter, the veteran self-unloader was dismantled.

This ship was one of the earliest vessels on the Great Lakes built with self-unloading capability. Indeed, she was the largest such vessel when she was launched by the American Ship Building Company at Lorain, Ohio on July 24, 1915.

Christened a) W.F. WHITE, this ship went to work for the Bradley Transportation Company, which later became the Bradley Limestone Division of the United States Steel Corporation. She loaded coal as her first cargo and departed Erie, Pennsylvania for Menominee, Michigan on her maiden voyage on September 1, 1915. Coal and limestone were this ship's main cargoes and she hauled millions of tons in the years that followed.

For a period from 1962 to 1965, W.F. WHITE left the Great Lakes for Chesapeake Bay. There she carried coal to steel plants on the Delaware River until she cleared Baltimore April 18, 1965, for the return to the Great lakes.

W.F. WHITE spent ten more years in lakes trading and often carried more than 100 cargoes a season. Stone remained her number one commodity and in 1968, for example, the ship hauled 85 loads of stone with over half of the shipments taken on at Calcite, Michigan.

Coal accounted for fourteen shipments that year while only limited amounts of slag and cement clinker were carried. Detroit and Port Huron were her main discharge ports among the nineteen visited in 1968.

Even in her last year, W.F. WHITE carried 90 cargoes (86 stone, 4 coal) before heading to lay-up at Duluth on December 17, 1974.

She resumed trading in 1976 for Westdale Shipping Ltd., who bought the steamer and placed her in Canadian registry under the number C. 370934. She was towed down the Great Lakes in May and refitted at Toronto. She was also converted to burn oil instead of coal and re-entered service as b) ERINDALE.

Stone continued to dominate this vessel's trading in her early Westdale years as she carried it on the short haul up Lake Ontario between Colborne and Clarkson.

This ship made news on several occasions. In November 1954, she crushed the tug OHIO (1) against the pier at Buffalo. Then, on July 5, 1969, her crew rescued eight people from a foundering cruiser off Southeast Shoal on Lake Erie. Finally, on October 6, 1981, ERINDALE lost power in the Welland Canal and hit the east abutment of the Allanburg Bridge while bound for Cornwall with corn. She suffered bow damage and tied up at Toronto.

ERINDALE sat out the 1982 season but returned to service in 1983 after repairs, as a replacement for the damaged LEADALE (2), and sailed one last year before her retirement and subsequent sale for scrapping in 1984 at Port Colborne.

W.F. WHITE downbound in the Detroit River August 26, 1965

a) W.F. White, b) ERINDALE

BUILT:	1915 American Ship Building Co. Lorain, Ohio
HULL NUMBER:	712
LENGTH:	530.0
BREADTH:	60.0
DEPTH:	32.0
GRT:	7180
REGISTRY NUMBER:	US. 213555
ENGINES:	25 1/2", 39 1/4", 67" Diameter x 42" Stroke Triple Expansion
ENGINE BUILDER:	American Shipbuilding Co., 1915

W.F. WHITE on the ways July 28, 1915 at Lorain, Ohio

W.F. WHITE above Lock 3 Welland Canal May 10, 1976 in tow of the tug OKLAHOMA

W.F. WHITE stern shot April 13, 1965 at a dock on the east coast just before leaving for the Lakes.

ERINDALE above Lock 1 Welland Canal September 10, 1977

ERINDALE laid up awaiting scrap above Ramey's Bend in the Welland Canal April 10, 1984

ESCANABA

On the 30th of October, 1931, bids were opened by the United States Coast Guard for construction of cutter #55 which was to have a steel hull and was to be suitable for rescue and assistance work on Lake Michigan; it was also to be designed for ice breaking, having a cut-away forefoot. Defoe Boat and Motor Works, of Bay City, Michigan was awarded the contract for Cutter 55 (to be known as the ESCANABA) for the low bid of $408,800.00. Completion was not to be later than the 3rd of October, 1932.

She was launched on September 17, 1932, and arrived at her home port of Grand Haven, Michigan on the 9th of December, 1932.

On December 1, 1934, ESCANABA was involved in the rescue of the crew of the whaleback HENRY CORT off the piers at Muskegon, Michigan; also that winter, she delivered food to the residents of Beaver Island, who were isolated due to the bad weather.

With war raging in the Atlantic, the ESCANABA left Grand Haven and went to Manitowoc, Wisconsin where she was made ready for war service on salt water. At Manitowoc, she had her heavy mast removed and her forward bulwarks cut down to improve the field of fire for her three inch gun. Upon leaving Manitowoc, ESCANABA departed the Great Lakes and was assigned to the commander-in-chief, Atlantic Fleet, at Boston for duty on the Greenland Patrol. On the 15th of June, 1942, while running from Cape Cod to Halifax, she rescued 20 crewmen from the fleet tug USS CHEROKEE. On the 3rd of February, 1943, in convoy SG 19, bound from St. Johns, Newfoundland, to Skovfjord, Greenland, the transport SS DORCHESTER was torpedoed and sunk. The ESCANABA rescued 132 men, however, the famous Four Chaplains went down with the vessel.

ESCANABA's end came very suddenly when she was in convoy GS 24, Narsarssuak, Greenland, to St. Johns, on the 13th of June, 1943. At 0510 on that cold, misty morning, there was a violent explosion and the ESCANABA was gone. Of the 103 men aboard, only two survived and were picked up by the tug RARITAN. To this day, it has never been determined exactly what caused the loss of the ESCANABA. Enemy action is suspected but never proved, and at no time did the German authorities ever claim to have sunk ESCANABA.

BUILT:	1932 Defoe Boat and Motor Works Bay City, Michigan
HULL NUMBER:	149
LENGTH:	165.0
BREADTH:	36.0
DEPTH:	13.7
DISPLACEMENT TONNAGE:	715
REGISTRY NUMBER:	US Coast Guard
ENGINES:	Electric Double Reduction Turbine
ENGINE BUILDER:	DeLaval, 1932

USCG ESCANABA (1) in the ice on Whitefish Bay, Lake Superior

USCG ESCANABA (1) at her dock at Grand Haven, Michigan

USCG ESCANABA (1) in war colors

PARKER EVANS

A steel bulk carrier was launched on Saturday, the 21st of March, 1908, at the Great Lakes Engineering Works in Ecorse, Michigan for the Mutual Steamship Company, of Duluth. Christened by Miss Ruth Hartwell, of Chicago, she was given the name a) HARRY A. BERWIND. Within thirty minutes of her launching, the steamer was at the shear dock for the installation of her boilers.

For the next eight years, she sailed for Mutual Steamship under Tomlinson Management. In 1916, she was renamed b) HARVEY H. BROWN (2), operating for the Headwater Steamship Company. She sailed for Headwater for the next thirteen years, usually hauling coal or iron ore. She sailed for the Youngstown Steamship Company for one year in 1929, with Pickands Mather & Company as managers.

In 1930, the BROWN came under the ownership of the Interlake Steamship Company with Pickands Mather & Company, the managers. The BROWN was involved in a serious collision in the St. Clair River off Port Huron in November of 1951 with the steamer GEORGE F. RAND (1). While both ships were severely damaged, the RAND sank.

Her gross tonnage was altered to 6841 in 1955 when new after cabins were added.

During the fall of 1963, HARVEY H. BROWN was laid up at Erie, Pennsylvania, having outlived her usefulness. That winter, she was sold to Marine Salvage Ltd., of Port Colborne and then, in turn, on January 22, 1964, she was sold to the Hindman Transportation Company Ltd., of Owen Sound, Ontario. She was given the name of c) PARKER EVANS (C. 306052). Under the Hindman flag, the steamer usually was in the grain trade hauling out of the Lakehead to Georgian Bay or St. Lawrence River ports. Her Canadian dimensions were: 541.5 x 58.3 x 26.6; 7815 gross tons.

On June 5, 1972, PARKER EVANS made the news when, at 2:00 a.m., downbound under the Blue Water Bridge at Port Huron, she collided with the upbound steamer SYDNEY E. SMITH JR. (2). The SMITH was holed in the forward end and sank within fifteen minutes, fortunately with no loss of life. This collision rendered the SMITH a total loss.

On the 25th of June, when PARKER EVANS was upbound in Lake Huron after leaving the ship yard where her collision damage had been repaired, she and the German vessel ANNA KATRIN FRITZEN scraped together during reduced visibility causing only minor damage.

In 1979, Hindman Transportation sold its entire fleet to the Quebec & Ontario Transportation Company Ltd. PARKER EVANS then became d) MARLHILL. During the 1980 spring fit out at Toronto, it was found that the steamer's starboard boiler was cracked and not worth repairing. The MARLHILL was then put up for sale and she was sold in the early spring of 1981 for use as a grain storage barge at Tampico, Mexico.

In May of 1981, after her engine and cabins had been removed at Toronto, she departed the Great Lakes. While in heavy seas under tow of the IRVING BIRCH, on the 30th of May, 1981, along with her former fleetmate, LAC DES ISLES, the MARLHILL sank 150 miles east of Norfolk, Virginia. On the following morning, the LAC DES ISLES sank 61 miles off Cape Henry Light.

HARRY A. BERWIND downbound loaded at Mission Point, St. Marys River in 1916

HARVEY H. BROWN downbound out of the Locks at Sault Ste. Marie

a) Harry A. Berwind, b) Harvey H. Brown (2), c) PARKER EVANS, d) Marlhill

BUILT:	1908 Great Lakes Engineering Works Ecorse, Michigan
HULL NUMBER:	40
LENGTH:	532.0
BREADTH:	58.3
DEPTH:	32.0
GRT:	6634
REGISTRY NUMBER:	US. 205072
ENGINES:	24 3/8", 38 1/4", 65 1/4" Diameter x 42" Stroke Triple Expansion
ENGINE BUILDER:	Great Lakes Engineering Works, Ecorse, 1908

HARVEY H. BROWN downbound in the Detroit River July 4, 1953

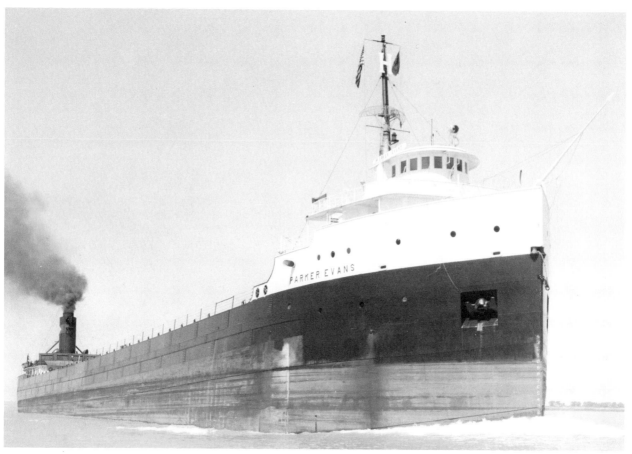

PARKER EVANS upbound light in the St. Clair River June 11, 1964

MARLHILL upbound with cargo in the St. Clair River September 16, 1979

PARKER EVANS after sinking the
SYDNEY E. SMITH JR. June 5, 1972

MARLHILL leaving Toronto in tow of the tug DANIEL McALLISTER on her way overseas

LEON FALK JR.

WINTER HILL after her service at the end of the war

WINTER HILL was built in 1945 at the Sun Shipbuilding & Dry Dock Company in Chester, Pennsylvania for the U.S. Maritime Commission. In 1949, she was sold to Ships, Inc. of New York City. In 1960, WINTER HILL was purchased by Skar-Ore Steamship Corporation, a subsidiary of M.A. Hanna, for conversion to Great Lakes operation.

WINTER HILL was converted at Bethlehem Shipbuilding Company's Key Highway Yard in Baltimore, Maryland. A former T-2 tanker, she was stretched with the insertion of a new mid body, increasing her length by 206 1/2 feet. The mid body was built as Hull Number 556 at Schlieker-Werft of Hamburg, Germany. Her engine room and power systems remained unchanged, including the 5,400 kw turbo-electric engine. The pilot house, originally situated amidships, was moved to the forward end.

While at the shipyard in Baltimore, WINTER HILL was renamed b)LEON FALK JR., in honor of Mr. Leon Falk, Jr., chairman of the board of Falk and Company and a director of the National Steel Corporation. Following trials held on Chesapeake Bay on June 26 and 27, 1961, LEON FALK JR. departed Baltimore on June 28, bound for Cleveland, on her first voyage after conversion. Her new dimensions were: 707.6 x 75.1 x 39.8; 10537 gross tons. Enroute, she stopped at Seven Islands, Quebec to load 20,748 tons of Labrador ore, arriving in Cleveland on July 8, 1961.

On April 8, 1969, LEON FALK JR. entered Duluth harbor to become the first vessel to arrive from the lower lake region opening the 1969 shipping season at the head of the lakes. She loaded almost 20,700 tons of iron ore bound for Great Lakes Steel in Detroit.

During the winter of 1971-72, LEON FALK JR. received new stern quarters and automated boilers at the American Ship Building's South Chicago yards.

On April 17, 1974, LEON FALK JR. arrived at the Burlington Northern docks in Superior, Wisconsin, opening the 1974 season there. She loaded 22,778 tons of iron ore bound for Huron, Ohio. On January 27, 1975, the FALK closed the 1974 season at Superior by loading 17,542 tons of ore bound for Detroit.

LEON FALK JR. laid up for the final time at the Nicholson slip in Ecorse, Michigan on August 19, 1981. In 1985, the FALK was sold by Skar-Ore Steamship Corporation to Desguaces Heme for overseas scrapping. LEON FALK JR. departed the Nicholson slip on August 15, 1985, under her own power, bound for Quebec City. Ironically, just two hours prior to her departure, her near-sister PAUL H. CARNAHAN arrived at Nicholson's and laid up for her final time.

LEON FALK JR. arrived at Quebec City on August 19, 1985. On August 30, 1985, the FALK along with MENIHEK LAKE, departed Quebec City under tow of the tug CAPT. IOANNIS S. The tow arrived safely in Gijon, Spain on September 28, 1985. Scrapping of LEON FALK JR. began at Gijon on November 6, 1985.

LEON FALK JR. downbound below the Blue Water Bridge, St. Clair River July 17, 1961

LEON FALK JR. August 29, 1976

LEON FALK JR. on her last trip at Port Weller August 17, 1985

a) Winter Hill, b) LEON FALK JR.

BUILT:	1945 Sun Shipbuilding & Dry Dock Co. Chester, Pennsylvania
HULL NUMBER:	477
LENGTH:	504.0
BREADTH:	68.2
DEPTH:	39.2
GRT:	10537
REGISTRY NUMBER:	US. 247576
ENGINES:	Steam Turbine/Generator and Electric Drive Motor
ENGINE BUILDER:	Westinghouse 1945

LEON FALK JR. with MENIHEK LAKE at Quebec City August 22, 1985

FAVORITE (2)

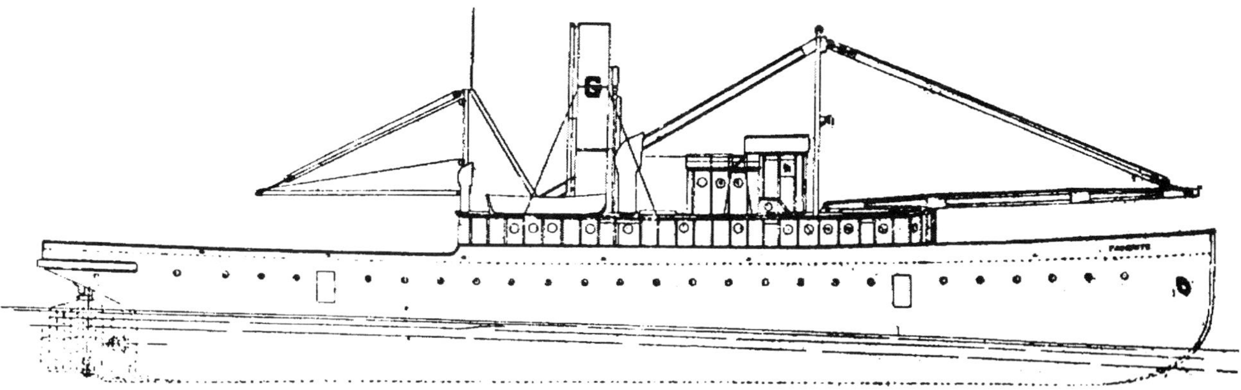

FAVORITE - outline view

Designed by Mr. W.I. Babcock, of New York, the wrecking tug FAVORITE (2) was built by the Buffalo Dry Dock Company in 1907, and was launched on the 2nd of February, 1907, for the Great Lakes Towing Company of Cleveland. When she was launched, the FAVORITE was the largest self-propelled vessel built for salvage and rescue work on the Great Lakes.

After her launching, and under the command of Captain Alex Cunning, she proceeded to St. Ignace to take up station. On her way, she stopped at both Cleveland and Detroit in order to be viewed by the public and the shipping industry.

During the next ten years, FAVORITE was involved in many notable salvages. One such event was on the 29th of May, 1909, at Manistique, Michigan, when the car ferry ANN ARBOR NO. 4 capsized at her dock. It took the FAVORITE until the 25th of June to raise and right the car ferry. In July of 1915, FAVORITE was involved in the grim task of raising the passenger steamer EASTLAND after she rolled over and sank in the Chicago River taking 835 lives with her.

On November 23, 1917, FAVORITE was taken over by the Navy Department. She was commissioned on the 23rd of January, 1918, as USS FAVORITE (#1385) under the command of Ensign W.F. Lakeman. On her way out of the lakes, FAVORITE assisted in freeing the vessels CODORUS and GEORGE N. ORR, which were ashore on Prince Edward Island. Until March of 1918, she broke ice off the coast of Maine.

During the summer of 1918, FAVORITE was made ready to go overseas. On the 5th of August, 1918, she arrived at Brest, France, to begin salvaging sunken vessels. She stayed in Europe until the 21st of June, 1919, when she sailed for New York. Arriving back in the United States, she was decommissioned and turned over to the Department of the Interior.

In October of 1940, the Navy again acquired FAVORITE for the 5th Naval District and reclassified her as IX-45. In 1943, FAVORITE was assigned to the Panama Canal District. She was returned by the Navy in 1948 and decommissioned.

She was then sold to the Peruvian Navy, her home port Lima, Peru. In the Peruvian Navy, she was converted to a submarine rescue vessel and renamed b) GUARDIAN RIOS. Her name was again changed in 1954 to c) RIOS. In 1958, after 51 years of operation, the RIOS was stricken from the Navy lists and apparently was scrapped.

FAVORITE in her white livery

FAVORITE upbound in the St. Clair River opposite Marine City

a) FAVORITE (2), b) Guardian Rios, c) Rios

BUILT:	1907 Buffalo Dry Dock Co. Buffalo, New York
HULL NUMBER:	209
LENGTH:	180.7
BREADTH:	43.0
DEPTH:	20.6
GRT:	1223
REGISTRY NUMBER:	US. 203983
ENGINES:	22", 36", 60" Diameter x 30" Stroke Triple Expansion
ENGINE BUILDER:	American Ship Building Co., Cleveland, 1907

FAVORITE on Portage Lake, Lake Superior January 30, 1914

FEDERAL PALM

The smart looking passenger-cargo ship FEDERAL PALM was built on the Great Lakes, but never served their ports. She was built in 1961, by Port Weller Dry Docks, Limited, for the newly-founded Federation of the West Indies. FEDERAL PALM, and her sister FEDERAL MAPLE, which was turned out at Montreal by Canadian Vickers, Limited, were gifts of the Canadian people to the infant Federation.

FEDERAL PALM was floated from the dry dock on June 21, but her planned late July christening had to be delayed at least twice. Finally, on August 26, then Immigration Minister, Helen Fairclough, christened the $3,600,000 ship. Two ships were but a part of Canada's aid package to the new nation.

Able to accommodate 50 passengers in berths, FEDERAL PALM could also carry some 200 deck passengers. Two, thirty foot landing barges were carried, in addition to the normal complement of life boats. Her schedule took her to all corners of the Federation, with stops at St. Kitts, Jamaica, Antigua, Monserrat, Dominica, St. Lucia, Barbados, St. Vincent, Grenada and Trinidad.

In the decade and more FEDERAL PALM trekked among the islands of the Caribbean, she was operated for the West Indian Federation by West Indies Shipping Corporation (Furness, Withy & Company Ltd., managers). When sold in 1972, FEDERAL PALM went to the Nauru Local Government Council, which gave her the name b) CENPAC ROUNDER. These owners placed her on an even more demanding island-hopping schedule. Her routes now took her from Nauru to New Zealand, Fiji, Singapore and Indonesia.

CENPAC ROUNDER's career came to an abrupt end in 1979. On the night of March 27-28, the unfortunate ship went hard aground near Suva in the Fijis. Refloated on March 29, she was found to have suffered very heavy hull damage and was, subsequently, declared a constructive total loss. Abandoned to the underwriters, she was sold and broken up at Pusan, South Korea.

FEDERAL PALM at Port Weller Dry Docks July 3, 1961

CENPAC ROUNDER

a) FEDERAL PALM, b) Cenpac Rounder

BUILT:	1961 Port Weller Dry Docks Limited Port Weller, Ontario
HULL NUMBER:	29
LENGTH:	274.5
BREADTH:	51.5
DEPTH:	26.5
GRT:	3171
REGISTRY NUMBER:	Br. 315791
ENGINES:	Diesel, 10 Cylinder, 1700 bhp, 750 rpm
ENGINE BUILDER:	Fairbanks Morse by Canadian Locomotive Ltd., Kingston, 1961

A.H. FERBERT (2)

A.H. FERBERT (2) downbound at Port Huron August 31, 1942 following grounding in the St. Marys River on her maiden voyage

In 1942, the United States Steel Corporation ordered five Great Lakes bulk freighters to help supply the ore to make steel to support the war effort. Three of these vessels were built at the Great Lakes Engineering Works at River Rouge, Michigan. The A.H. FERBERT, the third of the three, was launched on May 22, 1942. That day was designated as National Maritime Day, when 21 ships were launched in shipyards all over America.

The steamer was christened by Mrs. A.H. Ferbert, wife of the then president of the Pittsburgh Steamship Division. U.S. Steel classed her "AA-super class". When built, she and her sisters were 28 feet longer, 7 feet wider and 2 1/2 feet deeper than their most modern predecessors in the Pittsburgh fleet. Their 27% larger displacement and additional 3,400-ton capacity allowed the "supers" to add another 2,800,000 tons to the Pittsburgh fleet capacity.

She had the misfortune to run aground in the St. Marys River on her maiden voyage and had to return to her builder's yard for repairs before loading her first cargo.

In 1952, the ownership of the FERBERT was transferred to the United States Steel Corporation of Cleveland, Ohio. Defoe Ship Building converted her from coal to oil-fired boilers during the winter of 1971-72. During the winter of 1972-73, the FERBERT was the last ore carrier to pass through the Soo Locks for the 1972 season when she locked down on February 8, 1973. In the 1973 season, she made 54 trips and sailed 309 days. On June 5, 1981, her ownership was changed to USS Great Lakes Fleet, Inc.

She laid up for the final time on November 30, 1981. After being sold for scrap, she departed Duluth under tow of the tug GLENADA on September 15, 1987. The tow ran into difficulty on Lake Superior in heavy weather. The tug W.J. IVAN PURVIS, based at the Ontario Soo, was dispatched to her rescue. The FERBERT made it to the Soo on September 19, and departed on September 20. She broke her tow line in the St. Marys River near De Tour Village, Michigan on September 25, and, as a consequence, scraped her bottom and went to anchor for Coast Guard inspection. Four days later, FERBERT ran hard aground in the St. Clair Cutoff Channel and required six tugs to pull her off.

She passed downbound through Detroit for the final time on September 26, 1987. The vessel cleared the St. Lambert Lock in the Seaway October 6, and arrived at Lauzon, Quebec, October 7. She departed Quebec City December 3, along with SAMUEL MATHER (6) under tow of the tug CAPT. IOANNIS S. and arrived at Sydney, Nova Scotia on December 9, 1987. The A.H. FERBERT finally arrived at her final port, Aliaga, Turkey, along with SAMUEL MATHER on June 20, 1988 where they were broken up.

A.H. FERBERT (2) upbound at Mission Point, St. Marys River August 22, 1951

A.H. FERBERT (2) upbound, St. Marys River September 4, 1953

A.H. FERBERT (2) downbound Lake Huron under the Blue Water Bridge June 9, 1960

BUILT:	1942 Great Lakes Engineering Works River Rouge, Michigan	*DEPTH:*	30.3
HULL NUMBER:	289	*GRT:*	10294
LENGTH:	622.6	*REGISTRY NUMBER:*	US. 242024
BREADTH:	67.0	*ENGINES:*	DeLaval Cross Compound Steam Turbine
		ENGINE BUILDER:	DeLaval, 1942

A.H. FERBERT (2) in tow of the tugs GLENADA and W.J. IVAN PURVIS on her way to scrap, September 1987

FERNGLEN

The steamer WILLIAM A. AMBERG, launched September 15, 1917, at Lorain, Ohio, by the American Ship Building Company, was built for the Producers Steamship Company (M.A. Hanna Company, managers). In 1932, she was renamed b) ALBERT E. HEEKIN and in 1936 her ownership was transferred to the National Steel Corporation.

In 1955, she was renamed c) SILVER BAY after being traded, along with her sistership the LOUIS W. HILL, to the Wilson Transit Company for the steamer BEN MOREELL(1). In 1957, SILVER BAY was painted in the colors of the Republic Steel Corporation but still was managed by Wilson Marine. In 1961, her boilers were converted to burn oil.

On November 8, 1970, the SILVER BAY went out of control at about 1:30 a.m. when her propeller snagged the cable of red nun buoy number 34 above the Neebish Rock Cut in the St. Marys River. The cable wrapped around the vessel's shaft causing her to lose power and steerageway. The Captain dropped both anchors, bringing the ship to a halt at the entrance to the Rock Cut. Two divers from Sault Ste. Marie, Michigan, cut the cable and, with the assistance of tugs MISEFORD and JOHN McLEAN, SILVER BAY was underway by 10:30 a.m. The mishap caused the delay of 15 downbound vessels above and below the Soo Locks.

In 1971, the steamer was sold to Kinsman Marine Transit Company of Cleveland. In July 1973, she was laid up at Toledo, Ohio, immediately after the entry into service of the new motorship WILLIAM R. ROESCH.

In the spring of 1975, she was sold into Canadian registry to Robert Pierson Holdings Ltd. and was renamed d)JUDITH M. PIERSON C. 369249), during the course of her first trip which took her to Toronto with a cargo of soya beans. Westdale Shipping Ltd. acted as managers for the Pierson fleet, of which JUDITH M. PIERSON was the first ship. Her ownership was transferred to Pierson Steamships Ltd. in 1977.

Pierson's operating firm, the Soo River Company, went into receivership on August 6, 1982. About a month later, P & H Shipping Division, Parrish and Heimbecker, Limited, bought the entire Soo River fleet and at that time JUDITH M. PIERSON was renamed e) FERNGLEN. She operated only briefly however, and laid up in Toronto for the final time on November 10, 1982.

Sold for scrap in 1984, FERNGLEN was towed out of Toronto on April 30, 1985 by the tugs STORMONT and GLENSIDE arriving at Port Maitland, Ontario, May 1, 1985. Her scrapping began on June 20th by Port Maitland Shipbreaking Ltd. Her pilot house is still in use as a construction company office in Port Maitland.

a) William A. Amberg, b) Albert E. Heekin, c) Silver Bay, d) Judith M. Pierson, d) FERNGLEN

BUILT:	1917 American Ship Building Co. Lorain, Ohio
HULL NUMBER:	723
LENGTH:	525.0
BREADTH:	58.0
DEPTH:	31.0
GRT:	7031
REGISTRY NUMBER:	US. 215708
ENGINES:	23 1/2", 38", 63 1/2" Diameter x 42" Stroke Triple Expansion
ENGINE BUILDER:	Shipyard, 1917

WILLIAM A. AMBERG downbound at Mission Point, St. Marys River in 1918

ALBERT E. HEEKIN upbound light in the St. Marys River in 1950

SILVER BAY assisted by the tug TEXAS, entering Cleveland Harbor April 14, 1956

SILVER BAY downbound in the St. Clair River October 1, 1958

SILVER BAY upbound in the St. Marys River August 9, 1972

JUDITH M. PIERSON upbound in the St. Clair River in 1978

FERNGLEN at Huron, Ohio on her last trip in 1984

BENSON FORD (1)

In 1915, Henry Ford purchased property in Dearborn, Michigan where he built his Rouge automobile manufacturing complex. He specifically located this complex on the meandering Rouge River so water transportation could be used to supply raw materials. The Rouge River was straightened by creating the Short Cut Canal and, on July 2, 1923, the ONEIDA steamed into the new canal with Ford dignitaries aboard to celebrate the event. Nine days later, the CLETUS SCHNEIDER tied up at the Ford dock to unload the first cargo of iron ore.

Henry Ford contracted with the American Ship Building Company and Great Lakes Engineering Works for two "state of the art" bulk carriers. They were delivered and put into service in August of 1924. At that time, these were two of the largest, finest ships on the Great Lakes. Both had Sun-Doxford diesel engines of 3,000 horsepower. These two vessels were the first all-electric ships, equipped with electric winches, steering gears, heaters, stoves, etc.

The Ford Motor Company vessel BENSON FORD (1), built at the Great Lakes Engineering Works in River Rouge, was launched on April 26, 1924 by the ship's namesake, young Benson Ford, a grandson of Henry Ford.

Henry Ford requested that a system be set up so his grandson could throw a switch to launch the boat. The shipyard's electrical department designed guillotines which replaced the axe men at the ten triggers. All were now cut by throwing a switch on the launching platform. According to the accounts of the day, six-year-old Benson Ford stood next to his grandfather on the launch platform. Mr. Ford said, "All right, Benson, go ahead"; young Benson threw the switch and the ship was launched. Great Lakes Engineering Works used this method on all subsequent launchings. The BENSON FORD sailed on her maiden voyage on August 2, 1924, beautifully outfitted with inlaid mahogany in her staterooms and dining rooms.

She was equipped with a bow thruster in 1964.

After many years of faithful service, she laid up for the final time in the fall of 1981. Her name was changed to b) JOHN DYKSTRA (2) in the fall of 1982 so the Benson Ford name could be used for another vessel. In July, 1983, the DYKSTRA was sold to Lake Transportation, Inc. of Milwaukee, Wisconsin for use as a barge. She was towed out of the Rouge slip on June 23, 1983, and tied up at the old Solvay plant, where her engine was removed. She was towed from Detroit on December 21, 1984 enroute to Cleveland, Ohio. She was repainted and opened for tours and dinners during Cleveland's *River-Fest* for a brief period during the summer of 1985.

The plan was to convert the DYKSTRA to a self-unloading barge. But, the estimated $7 million cost to convert her was deemed too high, it was decided to scrap her. Before she was scrapped, however, her forward cabins were removed early in July, 1986 and taken to South Bass Island on the barge/tug combination THOR 101 and GREGORY J. BUSCH. The hull of the JOHN DYKSTRA was towed from Cleveland on July 10, 1986, to Marine Salvage Ltd's. scrapyard at Ramey's Bend in the Welland Canal by the McKeil tug GLENBROOK. The forward cabins of the JOHN DYKSTRA arrived at South Bass Island on July 18, where they serve as a cottage and are there to this very day.

BENSON FORD downbound in Lake St. Clair

BENSON FORD downbound in lower Lake Huron August 8, 1960

BENSON FORD downbound in the Detroit River June 13, 1969

JOHN DYKSTRA (2) being moved by the tugs

a) BENSON FORD (1), b) John Dykstra (2)

BUILT:	1924 Great Lakes Engineering Works River Rouge, Michigan
HULL NUMBER:	245
LENGTH:	596.7
BREADTH:	62.0
DEPTH:	27.7
GRT:	8170
REGISTRY NUMBER:	US. 223909
ENGINES:	23" Diameter x 45" Stroke Four Cylinder, Opposed Piston, Sun-Doxford Diesel
ENGINE BUILDER:	Sun Shipbuilding Co., 1924

BENSON FORD (2)

In April of 1951, officials of the Great Lakes Steamship Company of Cleveland, Ohio, deemed it necessary to increase the capacity of their fleet. This decision was made as a result of the constantly increasing demand for more tonnage. The company retained H.C. Downer & Associates, Cleveland, as its design agent and commissioned the firm to develop a specific hull form.

In consequence, the steamer RICHARD M. MARSHALL, built for the Great Lakes Steamship Company at Bay City, Michigan by the Defoe Shipbuilding Company, was launched January 29, 1953, and began service the following August, as the fleet flagship. At that time, the MARSHALL was the most completely welded large carrier designed and built on the Great Lakes. The completed vessel contained approximately 44,000 rivets; these being used primarily in one bilge-strake seam, the sheer strake, one seam on the strake below sheer, the gunwale bar, the spar-deck stringer and the corners of the hatch coamings.

In 1957, when the Great Lakes Steamship Company went out of business, the Northwestern Mutual Life Insurance Company of Milwaukee, bought the RICHARD M. MARSHALL and chartered her to the Wilson Marine Transit Company, Cleveland. Wilson renamed her b)JOSEPH S. WOOD and she became the flagship of the Wilson fleet. She was rechristened at Cleveland on May 7, 1957.

In 1966, Ford Motor Company Marine Operations, in the market for more tonnage for its fleet, found that the JOSEPH S. WOOD was available, because Wilson was having difficulties keeping the vessel busy. The Wilson fleet had long-term chartered the WOOD from Northwestern Mutual Life for $500,000 a year and, due to the business conditions at that time, the charter fees were causing a severe financial strain on Wilson's operations. Ford bought the WOOD from Northwestern Mutual Life for $4.3 million on February 14, 1966, while the ship was wintering in Ashtabula, Ohio.

On March 31, 1966, the WOOD was towed to American Ship Building's Toledo yard for a five-year inspection and to have a bow thruster installed. She departed the shipyard on April 23, 1966, and was towed to the Rouge complex at Dearborn, Michigan. Rechristening ceremonies were held at the Rouge on May 11, 1966, with Mrs. John Dykstra christening the ship, renaming her in honor of her husband.

The first trip of the steamer c) JOHN DYKSTRA (1) in Ford colors was to Marquette, Michigan, to load iron ore for the Rouge.

In 1982, after the retirement of the original BENSON FORD, the vessels' names were switched. The Ford fleet would always have a vessel name d) BENSON FORD. Thus she became d) BENSON FORD (2). Her ownership was changed to the Rouge Steel Company in 1984.

She laid up for the final time at the Rouge on December 18, 1984.

In 1985, Rouge Steel purchased the two remaining steamers of the Cleveland-Cliffs fleet. The EDWARD B. GREENE was renamed b) BENSON FORD (3) and the BENSON FORD (2), a) RICHARD M. MARSHALL, was renamed with her U.S. official number e) US. 265808. On August 18, 1986, US. 265808 was towed by Gaelic's tugs SUSAN HOEY, BANTRY BAY and SHANNON from the Rouge to Nicholson's slip at River Rouge. She departed Nicholson's on November 28, under tow of tugs TUSKER and GLENADA for Ramey's Bend. Ironically, upon US. 265808's arrival at Marine Salvage in Ramey's Bend, she was placed along side b) JOHN DYKSTRA (2), BENSON FORD (1), with whom she had switched names in 1982.

Late in December, 1986, US. 265808 was towed by the tugs THUNDER CAPE and GLENBROOK to Thorold and over the winter was loaded with a storage cargo of saltcake. In April, 1987, the saltcake was reloaded into the saltwater vessel ORESTIA and, on June 12, US. 265808 departed for Sorel under tow of the Sandrin tugs TUSKER and GLENADA.

On August 3, she departed Sorel for Quebec City arriving the next day. On August 11, the tug JANTAR cleared Quebec City with US. 265808 and T.W. ROBINSON in tow; their destination was Recife, Brazil where they arrived on September 22, 1987 for scrapping.

a) Richard M. Marshall, b) Joseph S. Wood, c) John Dykstra (1), d) BENSON FORD (2), e) U.S. 265808

BUILT:	1953 Defoe Shipbuilding Co. Bay City, Michigan
HULL NUMBER:	424
LENGTH:	629.6
BREADTH:	67.0
DEPTH:	30.3
GRT:	10606
REGISTRY NUMBER:	US. 265808
ENGINES:	Cross Compound Steam Turbine
ENGINE BUILDER:	DeLaval, 1943

RICHARD M. MARSHALL downbound in the Detroit River June 24, 1954

JOSEPH S. WOOD downbound St. Marys River August 12, 1960

JOHN DYKSTRA (1) upbound in the St. Marys River June 28, 1966

BENSON FORD (2) downbound in the St. Marys River July 18, 1983

BENSON FORD (2) upbound in the St. Marys River July 23, 1984

U.S. 265808, ex BENSON FORD (2), in the Detroit River being towed away for scrap in 1987

WILLIAM CLAY FORD (1)

WILLIAM CLAY FORD (1) launching at River Rouge May 5, 1953

This steel bulk freighter was the last of the eight "Pittsburgh" or "AAA-class" (if one uses U.S. Steel's designations) to be built on the Great Lakes. She was launched on May 5, 1953, at River Rouge, Michigan, by the Great Lakes Engineering Works, at a cost of $5.3 million to build.

When she sailed on her maiden voyage August 4, 1953, her first mate was Don Erickson. She served her whole career with the Ford Motor Company as flagship, and, unhappily, was the first of her class to be scrapped. When she was laid up for the last time at the Ford Rouge Plant on December 14, 1984, her Captain was Don Erickson, who had been Captain of the WILLIAM CLAY FORD since 1965 and was only the third Captain of the vessel.

The WILLIAM CLAY FORD carried a plaque, presented by the Great Lakes Maritime Institute, recognizing her participation in the search for the EDMUND FITZGERALD. It read "On the night of Nov. 10-11, 1975, these men voluntarily left a safe harbor to face the dangers of gale-force winds and vicious seas, in the blackness of a storm which had already claimed as a victim the steamer EDMUND FITZGERALD, to search for possible survivors of that disaster, exemplifying the finest traditions of the Maritime Profession." Captain Don Erickson said, "When we got to where the FITZGERALD went down, all we saw were (sic.) two ducks."

WILLIAM CLAY FORD arrived at Superior, Wisconsin, January 9, 1979, for lengthening by Fraser Shipyards. Her length was increased by 120 feet and a stern thruster was installed. Her new dimensions were: 749.4 x 70.3 x 31.3; 14,630 gross tons. She was the ninth vessel to be lengthened at Fraser. Her capacity was increased from 21,500 to 26,000 tons per trip with the same number of crew and only a small increase in fuel consumption. She departed Fraser on June 2, 1979.

Her ownership was transferred in 1984, to the Rouge Steel Company. In 1985, the "Ford Fleet" purchased two Cleveland-Cliffs steamers. The WALTER A. STERLING was renamed WILLIAM CLAY FORD (2) and the original WILLIAM CLAY FORD was renamed using her U.S. official number; she became b) U.S. 266029.

She departed, for the last time, from the Rouge slip on August 20, 1986, under tow of Gaelic tugs, and, she was taken to Detroit Marine Terminals in the Rouge River, where her pilot house was removed for an exhibit at Dossin Great Lakes Museum on Belle Isle. On August 27, she was towed to Nicholson's at River Rouge, looking much as she had when she was launched 33 1/4 years before. She arrived at Port Maitland, Ontario on December 8, 1986, after a stormy and difficult passage, towed by tugs TUSKER and GLENADA, and was scrapped during 1987.

WILLIAM CLAY FORD (1) downbound in the St. Clair River

WILLIAM CLAY FORD (1) upbound in lower Lake Huron August 17, 1970

WILLIAM CLAY FORD (1) being lengthened at Fraser Shipyards. Superior, Wisconsin in 1979

a) WILLIAM CLAY FORD (1), b) U.S. 266029

BUILT:	1953 Great Lakes Engineering Works River Rouge, Michigan
HULL NUMBER:	300
LENGTH:	629.4
BREADTH:	70.3
DEPTH:	31.3
GRT:	11590
REGISTRY NUMBER:	US. 266029
ENGINES:	Cross Compound Steam Turbine
ENGINE BUILDER:	Westinghouse 1953

WILLIAM CLAY FORD (1) upbound in the St. Marys River July 25, 1984

U.S. 266029 ex WILLIAM CLAY FORD (1) being towed out of the Rouge River by the tug SUSAN HOEY in 1986

G1 - CARPORT

The tug CARPORT and barge G1 were highly unorthodox craft by Great Lakes standards when they operated here in the 1950's and early 1960s. Built by the Christy Corporation shipyard at Sturgeon Bay, Wisconsin, for Cargo Carriers, Inc. (Cargill) in 1950, the G1 - CARPORT were designed for specialized service with Cargill grain interests that included being able to negotiate the New York State Barge Canal between the Great Lakes and the Atlantic Seaboard.

The barge G1 featured a notched stern that formed a saddle into which the towboat CARPORT would fit. The two units were held together in a tongue and groove arrangement and secured by three heavy turnbuckles at the bow of the tug. It was the plan, originally, to have six barges and three tugs in operation, but G1 - CARPORT were the only ones completed.

Tug CARPORT was powered by a 1,280 H.P. Fairbanks Morse diesel engine with diesel auxiliary engines for electric power, etc. Normally, the tug supplied power for the barge's pumps, lights, etc., but G1 did have a diesel electric generator set for stand-by use. A feature of the tug was a retractable pilot house that could be lowered nine feet on a hydraulic ram to give a minimum height of 15 feet 2 inches, for passages under bridges along the barge canal. All living spaces for crew were located in the tug.

Barge G1 had eight compartments for dry cargo and eight side tanks and an after tank fitted for liquid cargo, giving it a carrying capacity of about 120,000 bushels of grain and 300,000 gallons of liquid cargo. The main cargo holds were also fitted with six inch suction lines so liquids could be carried in them as well.

The most unique feature of the barge was a 48 inch propeller mounted athwartships in a tunnel in the bow that was probably the first bow-thruster employed on the Great Lakes. The thruster was powered by a GM 6-71 diesel engine remotely controlled from the tug pilot house.

A typical run for G1 - CARPORT would be to carry grain from the Canadian Lakehead to Chicago, then load a combination cargo of grain and soybean, or linseed oil, to her maximum draft of 15 feet 2 inches at Chicago and proceed down the lakes to Oswego, New York, on Lake Ontario. At this point, the grain cargo was off-loaded and the ship would continue on down the New York State Barge Canal and Hudson River at canal draft of 10 feet 8 inches, to off-load the oil cargo at Edgewater, New Jersey. The return load was usually made light. During the winter months, the ship would be employed in the coastwise trades on the Eastern Seaboard and Gulf of Mexico between various Cargill installations.

The ship carried a minimal towboat crew and eventually disagreements surfaced among the owners, maritime unions and U.S. Coast Guard as to manning the vessel, and, as a result, the operation, as far as the Great Lakes were concerned, concluded in 1963.

G1 - CARPORT was sold in 1963 to Aztec Trading Co., S.A., and placed under Panamanian flag. Aztec renamed her b) AZTEC CHIEF and continued operating the vessel on salt water.

The ultimate disposition of the ship is unknown to us. It last appeared in Lloyd's Registry of Ships 1981-82.

G1 - CARPORT and at Mission Point, St. Marys River

G1 - CARPORT moving outbound Duluth Harbor in July, 1955

a) G1 - CARPORT, b) Aztec Chief

BUILT:	1950 Christy Corporation Sturgeon Bay, Wisconsin
HULL NUMBER:	367 Barge / 368 Tug
LENGTH:	287.9 / 63.7
BREADTH:	43.6 / 27.6
DEPTH:	18.7 / 7.6
GRT:	1,892 / 99
REGISTRY NUMBER:	US. 261191 / US. 260922
ENGINES:	8 1/4" Diameter x 10" Stroke 8 Cylinder Diesel
ENGINE BUILDER:	Fairbanks Morse, Beloit, Wisconsin, 1950

G1 - CARPORT at Occident Elevator, Duluth in October, 1955

G1 - CARPORT at Occident Elevator, Duluth in October, 1955

W.H. GILCHER

On December 18, 1890, the Cleveland Shipbuilding Company launched the steel bulk freighter W.H. GILCHER for the Gilchrist Transportation Company. She was almost an exact duplicate of the steamer WESTERN RESERVE. Both vessels, launched only four months apart, competed for top cargo carrying records during the seasons of 1891 and 1892.

On August 30, 1892, the WESTERN RESERVE broke in two 60 miles above Whitefish Point on Lake Superior, only one of the crew surviving. Just a few months later her near-sister would suffer a similar, but more mysterious fate.

In the fall of 1892, the GILCHER departed Buffalo, New York, with a 3,000 ton coal cargo, bound for Milwaukee, Wisconsin. A severe gale lashed Lake Michigan on the 28th of October as the GILCHER left the Straits of Mackinac and headed into the fury of the storm. The GILCHER vanished, with all 18 hands, from the face of the angry lake. The storm continued for several days and, on November 4th, wreckage from two vessels washed ashore on High Island. Pieces of wreckage were found bearing the names of W.H. GILCHER and of the wooden schooner OSTRICH. The latter had sailed with a load of hemlock timber and carried a crew of 7; she was under the command of her owner John McKay. No bodies were ever recovered.

The post-mortems about the fate of the W.H. GILCHER and WESTERN RESERVE were begun by masters, crewmen, shipbuilding firms, owners, insurance underwriters and historians. To this day, the reason the GILCHER disappeared is unknown. The exact cause, be it collision, structural steel failure, ship design, safety or navigational hazards, will probably never be known. Both ships, the GILCHER and the OSTRICH, simply vanished with all hands during severe weather conditions.

Artists' conceptions of the GILCHER are shown, since no photographs of it exist.

W.H. GILCHER drawing by Samuel Ward Stanton

BUILT:	1891 Cleveland Shipbuilding Co. Cleveland, Ohio
HULL NUMBER:	15
LENGTH:	301.5
BREADTH:	41.2
DEPTH:	21.1
GRT:	2414
REGISTRY NUMBER:	US. 81326
ENGINES:	20", 33", 54" Diameter x 40" Stroke Triple Expansion
ENGINE BUILDER:	Shipyard 1891

W.H. GILCHER painting by Seth Arca Whipple

MARY S. GORDON

In 1882, shipbuilder William Watts launched into the Penetangore River, the two-masted schooner MARY S. GORDON. After being fitted out in Kincardine harbour, she was presented to the owner, Alex Gordon, of Kincardine.

The little schooner was engaged in servicing the small ports along the eastern Lake Huron shoreline and also Georgian Bay. On a typical trip, she carried salt from Kincardine to Owen Sound, discharging there to run light to the north shore of Georgian Bay for a load of lumber, which was to be shipped out on the railroad at Kincardine after being unloaded from the schooner.

MARY S. GORDON was in serious trouble during the first week in December, 1885. She had gone on the rocks near Chantry Island, off Southampton, Ontario, and was in danger of breaking up. The crew had been rescued and part of her cargo of fish had been unloaded on the island. The Port Elgin tug ALICE BROOKS was attempting to pull the schooner off the shoal when she too was driven ashore and totally wrecked.

The Goderich tugs JAMES CLARK and EVENING STAR took off the remaining cargo and delivered it to Goderich. They later returned and retrieved the fish from the island. About 130 packages of fish were lost out of a cargo of 1,000 packages. The GORDON was eventually salvaged and repaired.

In May of 1890, she battled against the elements for two weeks on a trip from Goderich to Owen Sound. Enduring huge seas driven by high winds, she lost a major portion of her salt cargo and narrowly escaped foundering. She discharged the remaining cargo at Owen Sound on May 13, then sailed light for the North Shore.

In 1892, Alex Gordon accepted Malcom McDonald of Goderich as a partner in the ownership of the schooner. McDonald was sole owner by 1894 and he sold her to Colin Graham, of Kincardine, in 1895. She continued to sail in the area of the Bruce Peninsula, often carrying lumber cargoes southbound.

By 1899, Graham had sold the GORDON to T. Strong, of Port Elgin, because Graham needed money to buy the larger schooner SARAH. Strong may have towed the GORDON with his tug C.M. BOWMAN, rather than sail the schooner. John Corstan, of Owen Sound, owned the MARY S. GORDON from 1902 until she was dropped from the register many years later, sometime after 1917. Her final disposition is not known.

MARY S. GORDON with barreled salt leaving harbor outbound on Lake Huron

BUILT:	1882 William Watts Kincardine, Ontario
HULL NUMBER:	None
LENGTH:	56.0
BREADTH:	17.0
DEPTH:	4.9
GRT:	28
REGISTRY NUMBER:	C. 77780

E.G. GRACE

E.G. GRACE was the first of the "Maritime Class" vessels to go for scrap. She had tied up at Ashtabula, Ohio on December 25, 1976, and remained idle for eight years.

The vessel was a product of the American Ship Building Company's Lorain, Ohio shipyard. Her keel was laid December 5, 1942 and she slid into the water the following July 5th. This was the last of the six ships built by Amship in the L6-S-A1 class for the United States Maritime Commission which had intended to name this bulk carrier "LINCOLNSHIRE". She was traded to the Interlake Steamship Company in exchange for older tonnage, and actually entered service as E.G. GRACE in honor of the then-president of Bethlehem Steel. She began service on October 2, 1943, clearing Lorain to load iron ore at Superior, Wisconsin.

E.G. GRACE operated mainly in the iron ore trade, also carrying stone and coal and, occasionally, grain. During her final twenty years, from 1957 through 1976, E.G. GRACE carried over 770 cargoes. Taconite Harbor, Minnesota was the most frequent of her iron ore loading ports in later years. Most of her coal came aboard at Toledo, Ohio, while the majority of stone came out of Stoneport, Michigan. The twin ports of Duluth/Superior accounted for virtually all of the grain. South Chicago and Cleveland were the most common destinations for ore while Taconite Harbor and Milwaukee led the coal receiving ports. Indiana Harbor easily led the ports receiving most all of the stone while all of the grain went to Buffalo, New York in this twenty year period.

On June 4, 1959, E.G. GRACE made the first of eleven trips down the seaway for Labrador ore. She loaded at Sept Isles, Quebec, and delivered the cargoes to Cleveland, Toledo and Ashtabula.

On July 11, 1969, E.G. GRACE ran aground in Lake Nicolet in the St. Marys River and had to be lightered before tugs could pull her free.

The last cargo for E.G. GRACE was 14,797 tons of taconite pellets delivered from Taconite Harbor to South Chicago. Like many of the Amship "Maritimers", the vessel had engine problems late in her career, and these contributed to her retirement.

The tugs GLENSIDE and GLENEVIS towed E.G. GRACE to Port Colborne, Ontario on May 17, 1984, and the men of Marine Salvage Ltd. began to scrap the hull almost immediately. The work continued through 1985 and the last remnants were broken up early in 1986.

E.G. GRACE upbound in the St. Clair River at Port Huron

E.G. GRACE upbound in the Detroit River May 30, 1969

E.G. GRACE arriving at Port Colborne in tow of the tugs GLENEVIS and GLENSIDE May 17, 1984

E.G. GRACE scrapping under way July 28, 1984 at Ramey's Bend, Welland Canal

BUILT:	1943 American Ship Building Co. Lorain, Ohio
HULL NUMBER:	829
LENGTH:	604.8
BREADTH:	60.2
DEPTH:	30.2
GRT:	8758
REGISTRY NUMBER:	US. 243830
ENGINES:	50", 22 5/8", 22 5/8", 50" Diameter x 48" Stroke Lentz-Poppet Double Compound
ENGINE BUILDER:	American Shipbuilding Company, 1943

GEORGE A. GRAHAM

The steel-hulled bulk carrier MARINA was constructed as Hull No.1 by the Chicago Shipbuilding Company, built to the order of the Minnesota Steamship Company, of which Pickands Mather & Company were managers. The keel of the was laid on July 1st, 1890, and launched on March 14, 1891. She was christened by Mrs. L.I. Babcock.

The steamer's big triple expansion engine produced 1,200 i.h.p. on steam supplied by two cylindrical, single-ended, coal-fired boilers, which measured 14 feet by 12.6 feet.

The Minnesota Steamship Company was absorbed into the Federal Steel Company in 1900, and the following year Federal Steel itself was swallowed up by the newly formed United States Steel Corporation, whose lake shipping affiliate was the Pittsburgh Steamship Company, of Cleveland.

MARINA, which was far surpassed in both size and cargo capacity by the newer vessels in the "*Tinstack fleet*", was sold on August 10, 1910 to the Lakewood Steamship Company, Cleveland, which was managed by Captain Charles L. Hutchinson. In 1912, her ownership was transferred to another Hutchinson affiliate, the Mesaba Steamship Company, of Charleston, West Virginia.

On June 12, 1912, MARINA was sold to O'Brien and O'Gorman, of Toronto, and she was transferred to the Canadian Northwest Steamship Company Ltd., of Port Arthur, Ontario. At this time, she was renamed b) GEORGE A. GRAHAM and was registered in Canada under Registry Number C. 131051. The Canadian register showed her dimensions as 310.5 x 39.1 x 21.3; 2410 GRT.

GEORGE A. GRAHAM operated successfully for her Canadian owners for half a decade. In 1917, the Canadian Northwest Steamship Company Ltd. was taken over by the Montreal Transportation Company Ltd., Montreal, and the GRAHAM joined the famous M.T.Co. fleet.

Early in October 1917, GEORGE A. GRAHAM loaded grain at the Canadian Lakehead for delivery at Midland. In the early morning hours of October 7th, she cleared DeTour Passage and headed into a heavy gale on northern Lake Huron. She was headed for shelter at South Bay on Manitoulin Island, but became particularly unmanageable in the heavy seas and eventually became stranded on Fitzwilliam Island where she soon broke in two.

The crew members were rescued by local fishermen from South Baymouth. The steamer, however, was abandoned as a total loss, and she was in such a position, close inshore, that she could not be refloated. The hull was finally cut up by salvagers in 1937.

MARINA and MARIPOSA in the Poe Lock at Sault Ste. Marie in 1896

MARINA upbound in the St. Clair River

GEORGE A. GRAHAM upbound at Mission Point, St. Marys River in 1915

a) Marina, b) GEORGE A. GRAHAM

BUILT:	1891 Chicago Shipbuilding Co. Chicago, Illinois
HULL NUMBER:	1
LENGTH:	292.0
BREADTH:	40.2
DEPTH:	20.8
GRT:	2431
REGISTRY NUMBER:	US. 92282
ENGINES:	24", 38", 61" Diameter x 42" Stroke Triple Expansion
ENGINE BUILDER:	Globe Iron Works, Cleveland, Ohio 1891

GEORGE A. GRAHAM aground

GRAINMOTOR

The GRAINMOTOR was expected to be the first of a new class of diesel-powered bulk carriers designed for trading through the St. Lawrence River canals. Unfortunately, as a result of the effects of the Great Depression, she also proved to be the only vessel of her class ever built.

GRAINMOTOR was contracted by Davie Shipbuilding Company and launched at Lauzon, Quebec in August of 1929. She began service that year for Canada Steamship Lines Ltd. and was employed mainly in the grain trade from the Great Lakes to the ports of the St. Lawrence River.

Navigation through the confined locks and channels of the Welland Canal and the old St. Lawrence River canals was difficult; accidents occurred and GRAINMOTOR was involved in several. The vessel made an unintentional 180 degree turn between Bridges 12 and 11 of the Welland Canal on July 30, 1948, when her engine failed and she went out of control. A year later, on April 25, 1949, GRAINMOTOR collided with the abutment of the railroad bridge above Lock 2 of the Lachine Canal. Then, on November 9, 1952, GRAINMOTOR hit the bank near Cornwall and began to take water in her number 2 bilge. Fortunately, none of these incidents resulted in major damage.

Even after the 1959 opening of the new St. Lawrence Seaway (which rendered most canal-sized ships obsolete), GRAINMOTOR remained a profitable carrier for CSL. She was deepened to 23.4 feet at Kingston early in 1961 and this increased her GRT to 2252 and carrying capacity from 3,200 to 3,800 tons. The ship continued to operate through the 1964 season and then was laid up at Kingston.

Although she had been facing a bleak future, the vessel got a reprieve in June 1966 when she was sold to Bahamas Shipowners Ltd. After loading grain at Port Colborne, GRAINMOTOR left the Seaway and was soon in service under the new name b) BULK GOLD. The ship was later transferred to Bahamas Package Freighters Ltd., and operated by the Gold Line in the cement and general cargo trades between Miami and Nassau.

BULK GOLD went to anchor at Montagu Bay, Bahamas, January 10, 1968 and remained there until her sale in January 1971 to Michael Zapatos. She was towed to Charleston, South Carolina for a refit at the Detyens Shipyards but remained either docked or anchored at that port for most of the year. By December 1971, BULK GOLD was at Miami, Florida and she resumed trading on the Gulf of Mexico the next year for the Antilles Lines.

BULK GOLD was plagued with engine problems, no doubt caused by age and a lack of maintenance during her periods of idleness. Then, in July 1972, Hurricane Agnes wrecked havoc on the Florida Peninsula. BULK GOLD, having suffered damage in the hurricane, was brought to Tampa. Plans to operate the vessel to Colombia and Ecuador, hauling phosphate and potash, did not materialize immediately, for legal problems apparently developed. It was reported that the ship was repowered early in 1973. She finally departed Tampa on May 4, 1973, for Guayaquil, Ecuador, with a phosphate cargo which she had stored for almost a year. Finally, in 1974, the vessel was reported resold to Carlos Vandano, of Bluefields, Nicaragua. The veteran motor vessel was renamed c) ANDY but sank July 24, 1974, off Isla de Providentia while on a voyage between Pensacola, Florida and Guayaquil.

GRAINMOTOR in the old St. Lawrence River Canals

GRAINMOTOR upbound in the St. Marys River August 3, 1962

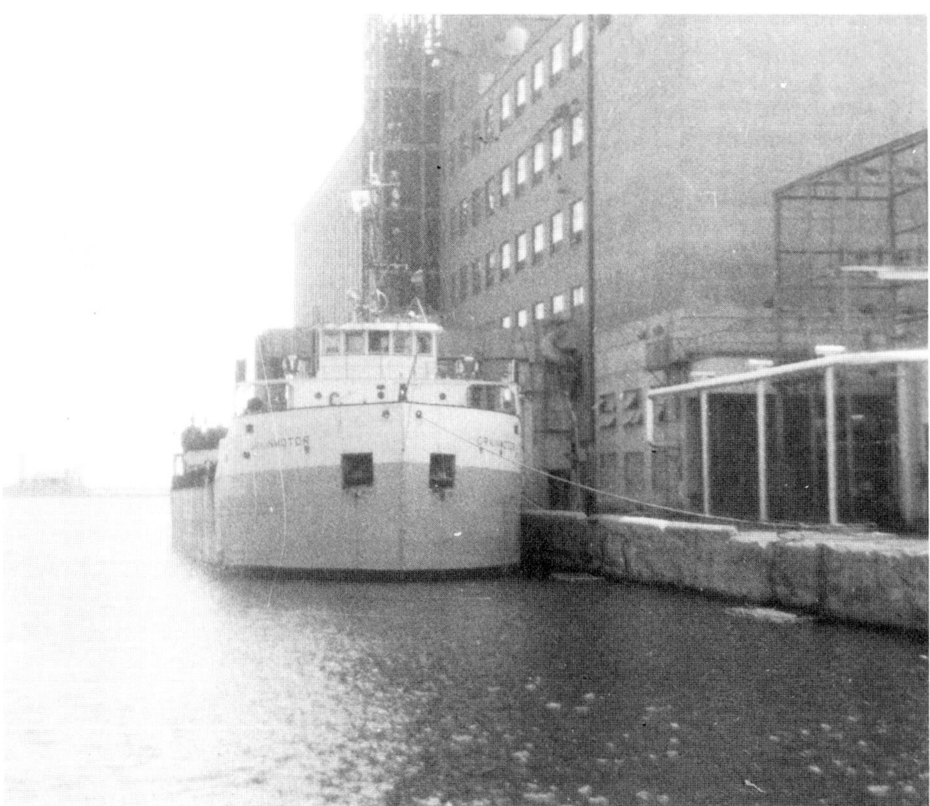

GRAINMOTOR with a gray hull, loading at Port Colborne with her last lakes cargo June 28, 1966

BULK GOLD anchored in the Bahamas

BULK GOLD at Charleston, South Carolina

ANDY with her cabins aft

a) GRAINMOTOR, b) Bulk Gold, c) Andy

BUILT:	1929 Davie Shipbuilding Co. Lauzon, Quebec
HULL NUMBER:	503
LENGTH:	251.9
BREADTH:	43.1
DEPTH:	18.3
GRT:	1829
REGISTRY NUMBER:	C. 154473
	ENGINES: 8 Cylinder, 16" Diameter x 20" Stroke Diesel
ENGINE BUILDER:	Bessemer Gas Engine Co., Grove City 1929

FRED W. GREEN

The canal-sized steamer CRAYCROFT was built by the Great Lakes Engineering Works at Ecorse, Michigan, and was launched on September 26th, 1918 for the U.S. Shipping Board. She was taken to salt water and, after some use, was laid up in the reserve fleet at Norfolk, Virginia. In 1927, she was acquired by Captain John Roen and Ira J. Lyons for the purchase price of $42,150. After fitting out the ship, the owners obtained a cargo of sugar from Baltimore, Maryland for Milwaukee and Green Bay, Wisconsin. Captain Roen was master for the delivery trip to the lakes.

After the cargo was discharged the ship was taken to Muskegon, Michigan where two thirty-ton cranes with clam buckets were installed. At this time, the name of the steamer was changed to b) FRED W. GREEN in honor of the then-governor of Michigan. In 1932, the Northwestern Transportation Company was formed by the two partners to operate the ship.

Because of her inability to discharge cargo further back from the dock face it was decided to install an unloading conveyor and boom. This was done during the winter of 1928-29 at a cost of $58,000. The unloading conveyor enabled the GREEN to discharge cargo back nearly 100 feet on the dock, which made her a little bit more competitive over conventional self-unloading vessels. This conveyor, however, could only discharge straight ahead or off the port bow.

The FRED W. GREEN was used mostly in the crushed stone, gravel and sand trades. She also was used to carry rip-rap stone for breakwater jobs contracted by the owners, with occasional rip-rap, stone and coal carried for others. The GREEN was employed in these trades until 1941.

The company had received several inquiries regarding the purchase of the ship for use on the high seas in the war effort. She eventually was sold in late October, 1941 through Mr. H. Harris Robson, a ship broker, to the U.S. Maritime Commission for a little over $200,000. The FRED W. GREEN departed Sturgeon Bay, Wisconsin, on November 12, 1941, for New York, where the unloading gear was removed. Shortly after, the ownership was again changed, this time to the British Ministry of War Transport.

On May 24, 1942, the GREEN departed New York for Freetown, Africa, with a cargo of miscellaneous freight, which included nitric acid and ammonia, and a deck load of army trucks. She was making the trip independently, without benefit of convoy or escort. After running the U-boat gauntlet along the east coast, and even though she was unescorted and trailing a long plume of coal smoke, the crew had begun to relax after passing Bermuda. The quietness of the evening of May 30th was shattered by gunfire as the FRED W. GREEN was attacked by the German submarine U-506. The gunfire set the ship afire and in the smoke and fumes from the acid and ammonia, the crew lowered the boats and abandoned the ship. At 11:45 p.m., she went down in position 30.20N/62.00W. The thirty-two survivors were picked up 36 hours later by the destroyer U.S.S. LUDLOW. Five of the crew were lost, including the master.

CRAYCROFT in dry dock prior to leaving the lakes in 1919

a) Craycroft, b) FRED W. GREEN

BUILT:	1918 Great Lakes Engineering Works Ecorse, Michigan
HULL NUMBER:	205
LENGTH:	253.5
BREADTH:	43.8
DEPTH:	20.4
GRT:	2308
REGISTRY NUMBER:	US. 217055
ENGINES:	19", 32", 54" Diameter x 40" Stroke Triple Expansion
ENGINE BUILDER:	Shipyard 1918

FRED W. GREEN being used to dredge the bottom

FRED W. GREEN unloading stone

FRED W. GREEN underway

FRED W. GREEN in the Chicago River

HAMILTON

HAMILTON at the shipyard in Buffalo October 9, 1918

The composite-hulled barge HAMILTON was built at Hamilton, Ontario, as Hull 4 of the Hamilton Bridge and Iron Works and launched on September 21, 1901. She was built to the order of the Montreal Transportation Company Ltd., Montreal.

There is some question concerning her original statistics. The Canadian Register of Shipping gave her depth as 11.5 feet and her gross tonnage as 970 while the Great Lakes Register indicated that her depth was 13.1 feet and her GRT 996. Hull modifications were carried out on HAMILTON by the Bertram Iron Works at Toronto in 1905.

The fleet of the Montreal Transportation Company Ltd. was officially taken over by Canada Steamship Lines Ltd., Montreal in 1920, but an operating agreement had existed between the M.T.Co. and C.S.L. as early as 1916. During that period there was a certain overlapping of fleet management between the two concerns.

In 1921, HAMILTON was converted to a twin-screw bulk carrier and, according to Lloyd's Register, the work was carried out by the Davie Shipbuilding and Repair Company, at Lauzon, Quebec. The hull was lengthened to 249.6 feet, 1,614 GRT, and into the vessel were fitted two triple expansion steam engines which had been built in 1898 by the National Shipbuilding Company, of Goderich, Ontario. They had cylinders of 12 3/4 inches, 21 1/2 inches and 35 inches and a stroke of 24 inches.

HAMILTON operated for Canada Steamship Lines in the lower lakes bulk trades until she was forced into lay-up at Kingston about 1930 as a result of the effects of the Great Depression. She lay at Kingston in deteriorating condition. In 1937 she was sold to Les Chantiers Manseau, Ltee., of Montreal and Sorel and then towed to Sorel where eventually she was dismantled.

BUILT:	1901 Hamilton Bridge and Iron Works Hamilton, Ontario	*BREADTH:*	40.0
HULL NUMBER:	4	*DEPTH:*	11.5
LENGTH:	202.2	*GRT:*	970
		REGISTRY NUMBER:	C. 111661

HAMILTON at an elevator at Montreal

NED HANLAN

The steel harbor tug NED HANLAN was built in 1932 by the Toronto Dry Dock Company Ltd. for the Corporation of the City of Toronto. Launched in September of 1932, she was fitted with a powerful fore-and-aft compound engine. Steam was supplied by one scotch boiler, which measured 10 feet by 10.9 feet.

NED HANLAN was used for general harbor duties at Toronto. In addition, the city operated a large water pumping and filtration station at Gibraltar Point on the Toronto Islands. And the HANLAN, being fitted for passenger service, carried the shift crews to and from the city and the Island Waterworks. She also towed maintenance vessels for the purpose of inspecting and servicing the several municipal water intake pipes located in Lake Ontario.

NED HANLAN is remembered for the winter ferry service which she operated for the residents of the Toronto Islands, and also for her icebreaking work in the harbor to facilitate the movement of winter storage vessels to and from the various grain elevators.

When the Municipality of Metropolitan Toronto was formed in 1953 as a regional government to provide services for the whole Toronto area, it assumed ownership of the two City of Toronto tugs, namely NED HANLAN and the older G. R. GEARY. The HANLAN continued to operate until, a victim of high operating expenses, she was retired late in 1965, and was laid up in the Rees Street slip.

In 1967, NED HANLAN was turned over to the Marine Museum of Upper Canada for preservation purposes. After much difficulty, the necessary financing was finally arranged. On October 29, 1971, the tug was hauled out of the water at the Metro Marine Yard, placed on a large, flat-bed trailer, and was hauled overland to a permanent display site beside the Marine Museum of Upper Canada in Exhibition Park, Toronto. The tug's preservation was largely spearheaded by Toronto Marine Historian Allan Howard.

Her name, commemorating the famous Toronto oarsman, has been carried on by the small diesel tug NED HANLAN II, which was built for the Municipality of Metropolitan Toronto in 1966.

BUILT:	1932 Toronto Dry Dock Co. Toronto, Ontario
HULL NUMBER:	none
LENGTH:	74.8
BREADTH:	19.1
DEPTH:	9.0
GRT:	105
REGISTRY NUMBER:	C. 157362
ENGINES:	13", 26" Diameter x 18" Stroke Fore and Aft Compound
ENGINE BUILDER:	John Inglis Co. Ltd., Toronto1932

NED HANLAN at work during the winter in Toronto Harbour

NED HANLAN at her dock in Toronto with many guests. (Alan Howard is pictured in the right background)

NED HANLAN being moved to her new site in Exhibition Park, Toronto, October 29, 1971

L. EDWARD HINES

This wooden freighter was built at Marine City, Michigan by John J. Hill in 1893. Since 1893 was the year of the World's Columbian Exposition in Chicago, the ship was named in honor of Christopher Columbus' flagship. SANTA MARIA was built for M. Sicken of Marine City and was a typical steam barge of the era. She was launched on November 15, 1893.

In 1899, the ship was purchased by the Edward Hines Lumber Company, of Chicago. She was renamed b) L. EDWARD HINES in 1903, in honor of the son of the company's founder and owner. Lumber, destined for the Hines yards on the Chicago River, was the principal cargo carried by the steam barge and often by one or two barges which she towed.

With the decline of the lumber trade on the Great Lakes, the vessels of the Hines fleet, including the L. EDWARD HINES, were sold or junked. The L. EDWARD HINES was sold in 1916 to owners in Nicaragua and traded in the Caribbean very briefly. The steamer was reported to have foundered in heavy weather at a point some five miles off Belize, British Honduras, on October 1, 1916.

SANTA MARIA downbound in the St. Marys River after leaving the Soo Locks in 1900

L. EDWARD HINES in the locks at Sault Ste. Marie

a) Santa Maria, b) L. EDWARD HINES

BUILT:	1893 John J. Hill Marine City, Michigan
HULL NUMBER:	none
LENGTH:	203.0
BREADTH:	37.3
DEPTH:	14.1
GRT:	982
REGISTRY NUMBER:	US. 116606
ENGINES:	24", 48" Diameter x 40" Stroke Fore and Aft Compound
ENGINE BUILDER:	S.F. Hodge & Co., Detroit 1893

W.W. HOLLOWAY

On Saturday, September 8, 1906 at the Cleveland yard of the American Ship Building Company, Miss Helen A. Hawgood christened the HENRY A. HAWGOOD in honor of her father who had died the previous April. The steamer was the last of three that Henry Hawgood had ordered before his death. This vessel, built for the Minerva Steamship Company of Cleveland, was to be managed by William A. Hawgood. The other two vessels ordered at the same time were the HARVEY D. GOULDER and the J.Q. RIDDLE. All three served long and useful lives on the lakes. The HENRY A. HAWGOOD outlasted the other two.

Henry A. Hawgood was born in Wales in 1846, emigrated to Wisconsin at the age of five, started sailing the Lakes at the age of sixteen and became a chief engineer at age eighteen. In due course, he bought the schooner-barge CHICAGO BOARD OF TRADE, then other vessels and, at the time of his death in 1906, the Hawgood fleets which he and other members of his family managed were a major force on the Lakes. But the Hawgood fleets came apart in 1911 with a series of law suits among the Hawgoods, Acme Transit Company, Commonwealth Steamship Company, American Ship Building Company and stockholders of the various companies. In the suits it was alleged that the Hawgoods had received "commissions" or kickbacks from the shipbuilder. One of the suits claimed that Henry A. Hawgood had received a $35,000 commission on his namesake vessel and that the building price of $420,000 that Minerva Steamship Company had paid for the HAWGOOD was $60,000 over what then was the fair market price of a similar vessel. As a result of the a number of the Hawgood vessels reverted to the American Ship Building Company but, before the judgment was rendered, HENRY A. HAWGOOD was quickly sold to the Hubbard Steamship Company, W.C. Richardson, manager.

In late 1912, or early 1913, Richardson renamed the vessel b) C. RUSSELL HUBBARD. In 1921, she was transferred to the Columbia Steamship Company (later Columbia Transportation Company) which would operate her into the 1980's. In 1937, she was renamed c) W.W. HOLLOWAY in honor of William W. Holloway, the president of Wheeling Steel Corporation, one of Columbia's customers.

In 1957, the HOLLOWAY was given a new lease on life when she was converted to a self-unloader by the Christy Corporation of Sturgeon Bay. This increased her gross registered tonnage to 7213. To complete her modernization, during the winter of 1962-63, the American Ship Building Company's Lorain yard replaced the HOLLOWAY's original triple-expansion steam engine with a new eight cylinder, 2,250 horsepower diesel engine constructed by the Nordberg Manufacturing Company at Milwaukee. This reduced the vessel's tonnage to 7166 gross tons.

As a self-unloader, the HOLLOWAY was involved in a number of mishaps, mostly minor. On April 15, 1963, while on dry dock at Lorain following her repowering, she sufffered a $15,000 fire in her fantail. In late May of 1967, while in the Trenton Channel of the Detroit River, she dropped her KaMeWa propeller and part of her shaft. The year 1974 was not a good year for the HOLLOWAY either. On July 10, she grounded in the Detroit River's Fighting Island Channel as a result of steering gear problems. She was released by two tugs later in the day. Later in the same month, on July 29, steering gear failure was again blamed when the HOLLOWAY, downbound with stone, grounded in Lake St. Clair near the Grosse Pointe Yacht Club. This time part of her cargo had to be transferred to the J.F. SCHOELLKOPF, JR. Four tugs finally pulled her free on July 31. Then on November 15 she struck the bank at Burns Harbor causing extensive damage to herself.

The HOLLOWAY's next reported mishap occurred on February 16, 1977 at American Ship Building's Chicago yard when a four-hour fire burned her forward crew's quarters. On June 4 of the following year, the HOLLOWAY struck an abutment at South Chicago inflicting $224,000 damage to herself.

All of these mishaps, plus the passing years, took their toll on the W.W. HOLLOWAY. She laid up for the last time at Toledo on December 7, 1981. In 1985, she was sold for scrap to Marine Salvage Ltd. which, the following year, sold her to Siderurgica Aco Norte, S.A. of Brazil. On August 20, 1986, the HOLLOWAY departed Toledo for Quebec City in tow of the tug SALVAGE MONARCH. The Polish tug JANTAR cleared Quebec City in mid September with W.W. HOLLOWAY and PHILIP D. BLOCK in tow, arriving at Recife, Brazil on October 24, 1986. Almost immediately cutting began on W.W. HOLLOWAY, one of the last remnants of the old Hawgood fleets.

a) Henry A. Hawgood, b) C. Russell Hubbard, c) W.W. HOLLOWAY

BUILT:	1906 American Ship Building Co. Cleveland, Ohio
HULL NUMBER:	435
LENGTH:	532.0
BREADTH:	56.0
DEPTH:	31.0
GRT:	6839
REGISTRY NUMBER:	US. 203582
ENGINES:	23 1/2", 38", 63" Diameter x 42" Stroke Triple Expansion
ENGINE BUILDER:	American Ship Building Company 1906

HENRY A. HAWGOOD approaching the locks at Sault Ste. Marie in 1909

C. RUSSELL HUBBARD upbound at Mission Point, St. Marys River in 1912

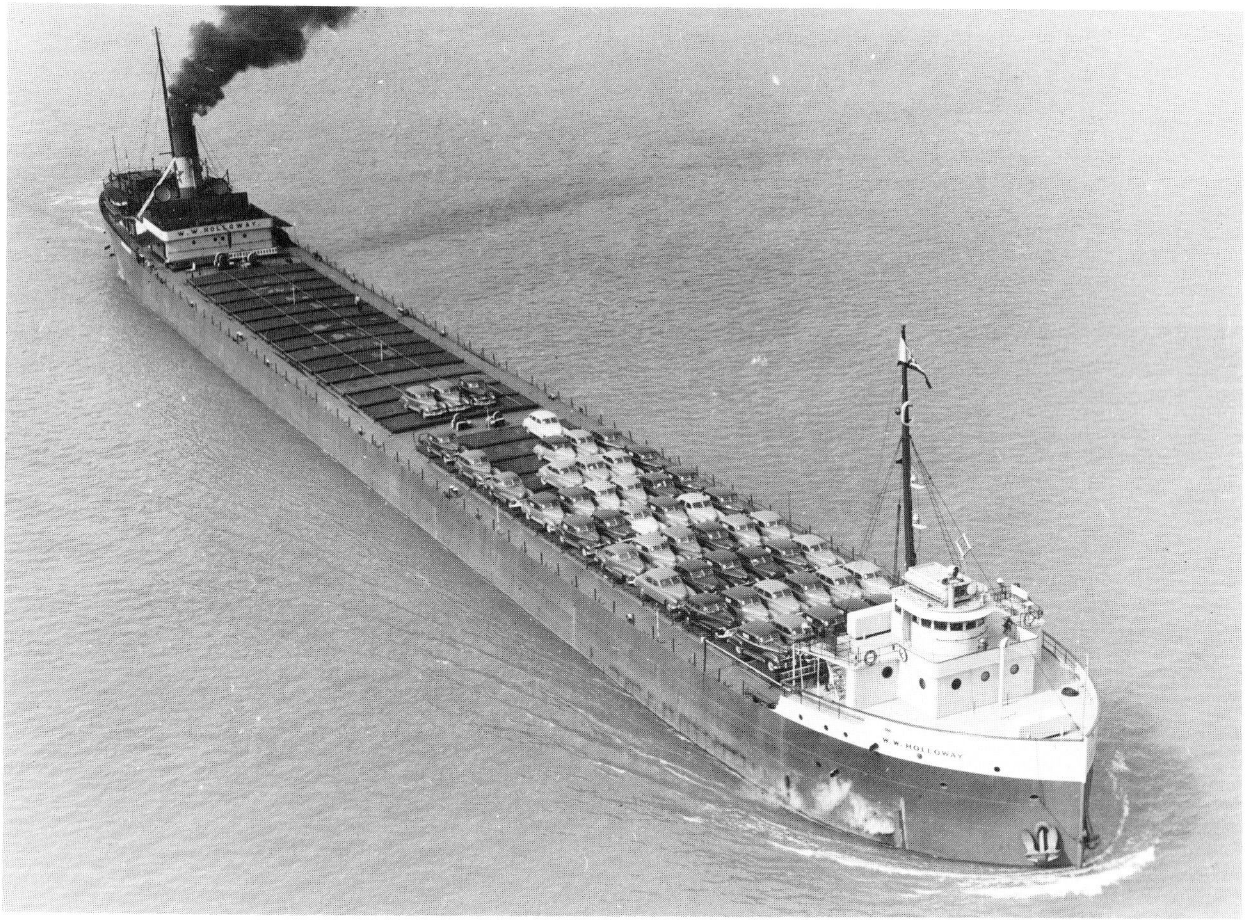

W.W. HOLLOWAY upbound in the Detroit River under the Ambassador Bridge

W.W. HOLLOWAY downbound in lower Lake Huron, June 9, 1960

W.W. HOLLOWAY upbound in the Detroit River, June 28, 1963

W.W. HOLLOWAY on her way to the scrapyard in tow of the tug SALVAGE MONARCH in the Welland Canal August,1986

WILLIAM HOOPES

The depression year of 1934 saw the launch of the small but sturdy steam tug WILLIAM HOOPES, by the American Ship Building Company's Lorain yard.

Designed by the noted Montreal naval architects Milne, Gilmore and German, HOOPES was intended for the St. Lawrence River Power Company, a wholly-owned subsidiary of the Aluminum Company of America.

Alcoa's "fleet", used to maintain its hydraulic canal at Massena, New York, had been in existence since about 1906. It was in that year that the power canal, low head power house, and appurtenances were transferred from Lord Kelvin and others of the original British investors, to Alcoa's immediate forerunner, the Pittsburgh Reduction Company. The company shipyard both built and repaired their wooden tugs, dredges and scows. Last of the yard's products was the tug DE GRASSE of 1914, finally broken up some 30 years later.

WILLIAM HOOPES had been designed as an icebreaker. This feature enabled her to service the ice scows anchored in line above the canal entrance during the severest of winter weather.

The HOOPES delivery trip, Lorain to Massena, proved to be an arduous extension of her trails. Beset by late Fall conditions even more foul than normal, it took the little tug from November 9, at 0715 until November 28, at 1130, to make her way to her home port. The tug had traveled Lake Erie to Buffalo, the New York State Barge Canal to Oswego, then Lake Ontario and the St. Lawrence to Massena.

Placed in service immediately, the HOOPES performed each task assigned to her for the next 23 years. By 1957, with the completion of the Seaway and power projects in the offing, it was apparent to Alcoa that her floating plant would be redundant. They, therefore, made plans to dispose of the ice scows, their remaining dredge, A.K. LAWRIE, the smaller tug JAMES W. RICKEY, and, finally, the HOOPES.

The WILLIAM HOOPES was sold off to the A.S. Wikstrom Construction Company of Skaneateles, New York. On September 12, 1957, she was towed from Massena by the Wikstrom tug ST. REGIS bound for Weedsport. By 1960, the HOOPES had been laid up and was out of documentation. In 1970, Wikstrom re-engined her with a new 12 cylinder Cummins diesel. She was redocumented and reentered the company's service in May, 1971.

A.S. Wikstrom finally disposed of WILLIAM HOOPES in 1976 to the Environmental Dredging Company of Wenonah, New Jersey.

WILLIAM HOOPES at Dodge's Bay September 9, 1953

WILLIAM HOOPES in the Cornwall Dry Dock July 10, 1956

BUILT:	1934 American Ship Building Co. Lorain, Ohio
HULL NUMBER:	809
LENGTH:	50.0
BREADTH:	14.1
DEPTH:	7.5
GRT:	30
REGISTRY NUMBER:	US. 233545
ENGINES:	11", 22" Diameter x 12" Stroke Two Cylinder Compound
ENGINE BUILDER:	Marion Machine Works, Marion, Ohio 1934

H. HOUGHTEN

The lumber hooker H. HOUGHTEN was an 1889 product of the Wheeler yard in West Bay City, Michigan, but one of their smaller hulls. She was built in the old style, with her houses all aft, and referred to by the old sailors as a "rabbit". Like her larger counterparts, she carried immense loads of lumber above and below decks and towed barges as well. She was built for Henry Houghten and others of Detroit, Michigan who were in the building materials business. Towing various schooners and barges, she hauled lumber, coal, sand and gravel for her owners from the time of her construction until she changed hands in 1919. After the turn of the century, Mr. Houghten also operated the small sand dredge MARY. It is assumed that the HOUGHTEN was relegated to the sand trade more and more as he grew older.

At some time, around 1920, the HOUGHTEN was given a clamshell dredging rig to make her exclusively a sand boat. She was operated as such by W.L. Emery of Detroit from 1920 to 1925. Emery also ran the sand dredges HARLOW and JOHN R. EMERY. The HOUGHTEN's pilot house was moved to her forecastle in a 1921 refurbishing.

In 1926, the ship was bought by the Service Gravel Company of Marysville, Michigan. She was reported burned near Harper's Point in the Sny Bora Channel at the Flats on November 20th of the same year. Although her documents were surrendered a month later, she was listed for several years afterward in the Great Lakes Red Book with the notation that she was "not in commission". While she was never restored to documentation, it is suspected that she was removed from the Sny Bora Channel for repairs which never materialized.

The HOUGHTEN is known to have suffered a number of accidents and two sinkings during her career. She sank at a dock in Detroit on September 9, 1902, and capsized and filled at the Mullen Coal Dock in Sandwich on September 6, 1916, both without loss of life.

H. HOUGHTEN at the Soo in 1900

H. HOUGHTEN and others at Marine City

BUILT:	1889 F.W. Wheeler & Co. West Bay City, Michigan
HULL NUMBER:	59
LENGTH:	126.0
BREADTH:	27.0
DEPTH:	8.2
GRT:	210
REGISTRY NUMBER:	US. 96006
ENGINES:	15", 27" Diameter x 22" Stroke Fore and Aft Compound
ENGINE BUILDER:	J.B. Wilson Detroit, Michigan 1889

JOHN C. HOWARD (1)

The steel canaller JOHN C. HOWARD (1) was launched on June 20, 1903 at St. Clair, Michigan by the newly-formed, but ill-fated, Columbia Iron Works for the George Hall Coal Company of Ogdensburg, New York. This was the second and last of the vessels built by this firm. The Columbia Iron Works was declared bankrupt in 1904 and was taken over by the Great Lakes Engineering Works of Ecorse, Michigan. They built various vessels at the yard until the machinery was transferred to Ashtabula, Ohio in 1912.

In 1906, the HOWARD was purchased by the Dollar Steamship Company and taken to the Pacific to run in the lumber trade in Washington and Oregon. She was renamed b) MELVILLE DOLLAR (2) at this time. In 1916, the Iwaki Company of Japan bought the vessel and renamed her c) JINYO MARU. From this time she operated in the Western Pacific between Japan, China, the Philippines and South-east Asia ports. In 1919, she was bought by Chinese parties and renamed d) SHIN PING. In 1930, she was owned by the San Peh Steam Navigation Company of Shanghai. In 1932, the little canaller was scrapped in Shanghai. China.

a) JOHN C. HOWARD (1), b) Melville Dollar (2), c) Jinyo Maru, d) Shin Ping

BUILT:	1903 Columbia Iron Works St. Clair, Michigan
HULL NUMBER:	P295
LENGTH:	220.0
BREADTH:	39.3
DEPTH:	13.7
GRT:	1244
REGISTRY NUMBER:	US. 200151
ENGINES:	16", 26", 44" Diameter x 36" Stroke Triple Expansion
ENGINE BUILDER:	Shipyard 1903

JOHN C. HOWARD (1) unloading coal

BRUCE HUDSON

The steel-hulled tanker barge BRUCE HUDSON, built by the Horton Steel Works Ltd. at Fort Erie, Ontario, entered service early in 1935 for Lloyd Tankers Ltd., Toronto, Ontario. Her first year of operation was anything but auspicious. On July 16, 1935, she capsized off Cobourg, on Lake Ontario, while in tow of the big, wooden-hulled tug MUSCALLONGE. The barge was towed, upside-down, to Toronto where her cargo was unloaded. The HUDSON was then towed to Port Weller where she was righted by GATE LIFTER NO. 1 after which the necessary repairs were made.

On November 15, 1935, the HUDSON was on Lake Ontario in tow of the tug ETHEL. The tug ran out of fuel and left the barge adrift on the lake while she went off to seek bunkers. After wallowing helplessly in heavy weather, the barge and her crew were rescued by the passing freighter BRULIN. BRUCE HUDSON was adrift again in 1937 when she broke away from the tug RIVAL.

In 1939, BRUCE HUDSON was converted to a steamer at the Muir Bros. drydock at Port Dalhousie. She was given twin triple expansion steam engines, 10 1/8 inches, 16 1/2 inches, 27 inches diameter by 15 inches stroke, which were built in 1909 by the Collingwood Shipbuilding Company Ltd., and which had come from the passenger steamer WAUBIC. Her boiler came from the scrapped CSL freighter MARTIAN (1). As rebuilt, the HUDSON's hull was 172.0 feet by 30.0 feet by 15.2 feet; 753 GRT.

BRUCE HUDSON was involved in an unfortunate incident which occurred at East Chicago on July 26, 1943. While loading cargo for Toronto she caught fire and lives were lost in the conflagration. The steamer was taken to Port Dalhousie for the necessary repairs. The BRUCE HUDSON was returned to service in 1944.

In 1946, the HUDSON was sent to Port Weller Dry Docks where she was lengthened, her new dimensions being, 212.7 feet by 30.1 feet by 15.3 feet; 1,071 GRT. When she returned to service in 1947, she was sold to Transit Tankers & Terminals Ltd., Montreal, which was an enterprise of Gaston Elie. In 1952, she was renamed b) COASTAL CLIFF and transferred to the ownership of the Affiliated CoastalakeTankers Ltd., of Ottawa, Ontario.

During 1957, COASTAL CLIFF was taken to the St. Lawrence Drydocks, Montreal where she was lengthened to 249.3 feet. The reconstruction increased her GRT to 1,319 and, at the same time, the vessel was converted to a motorship with the fitting of two new 12 cylinder diesel engines manufactured by the Cummins Engine Company Ltd.

In 1964, she was taken over by another affiliate, Canadian Sealakers Ltd., of Edmundston, New Brunswick. In 1968, she was transferred back to Transit Tankers & Terminals Ltd.

In 1969, COASTAL CLIFF was sold to Challenger Ltd. and was renamed c) WITCROIX. She was taken to the Virgin Islands in the Caribbean for use as a water carrier, and her ownership was later transferred to the Witcroix Corp. of Panama, R.P. The last report received had the ship laid up at St. Thomas, U.S. Virgin Islands. Her final disposition is unknown, although she still was listed in the 1982-1983 issue of Lloyds Register.

BRUCE HUDSON turning over on Lake Ontario in July 1935

BRUCE HUDSON upside down with barge ROY K. RUSSELL and tug RIVAL assisting

BRUCE HUDSON after righting at Port Weller July 1935 with tug RIVAL

BRUCE HUDSON in the old St. Lawrence Canals

BRUCE HUDSON upbound in the Detroit River

COASTAL CLIFF in the Cornwall Canal in 1958

a) BRUCE HUDSON, b) Coastal Cliff, c) Witcroix

BUILT: 1935 Horton Steel Works
Fort Erie, Ontario
HULL NUMBER: none
LENGTH: 164.0
BREADTH: 30.0
DEPTH: 10.2
GRT: 452
REGISTRYNUMBER: C. 158658

GEORGE M. HUMPHREY (2)

This vessel was never launched! She was built by the American Ship Building Company at Lorain, Ohio in a dry dock. On June 19, 1954 without ceremonies, she was floated. The festivities took place the following October 5th when she was christened GEORGE M. HUMPHREY in honor of the man, who at that time was Secretary of the Treasury in the Eisenhower Administration. Prior to his service in Washington, and following it, Mr. Humphrey was Chairman of the Board of the Hanna Mining Company, the firm which managed the steamer HUMPHREY for National Steel Corporation.

The HUMPHREY was the first vessel built on the Lakes with a 75 foot beam and this soon paid off. On October 21, 1954, she broke the lakes' ore record when she loaded 22,605 gross tons at Allouez, Wisconsin—a record that stood until 1960. Besides being a good carrier, she handled well and, by and large, was a dependable performer. Her usual run was from Superior, Wisconsin to the Great Lakes Steel works at Detroit's Zug Island, but over her years, she wandered all over the lakes and also operated down the St. Lawrence Seaway during several seasons. She was the first laker on which the hatch covers were not placed between hatches when loading or unloading. Instead, the HUMPHREY's hatch covers were stacked 6 and 7 high. Thus, she was fitted with an unusually high deck crane.

But she did have her share of mishaps, the most serious of which occurred in shifting ice on April 13, 1956, when she was pushed on a shoal near Gros Cap in Lake Superior's Whitefish Bay. For a time, it appeared that she would sink but was finally saved and taken to Lorain for repairs. By comparison, her other scrapes were less serious. On July 11, 1965, she and ALEXANDER LESLIE brushed on Lake St. Clair. A fender boom fell on her pilot house in the Poe Lock at the Soo on April 29, 1971. On June 11, 1976, she suffered $107,500 damages when she struck an obstruction in the St. Marys River. And, finally, she sustained an 8-foot gash in her hull when she struck part of the structure of the Soo's MacArthur Lock on August 30, 1978.

Fortunately, what could have been the HUMPHREY's biggest mishap never happened. On November 10, 1975, she battled her way down a stormy Lake Superior about 10 hours ahead of EDMUND FITZGERALD. When word came of the tragic loss of the FITZGERALD, the HUMPHREY was safely anchored in the lower St. Marys River.

The HUMPHREY was part of the first wave of 24 new Lakers and 11 saltwater conversions that, following World War II, rebuilt the U.S. Lakes' fleets in the years 1949 through 1961. In hindsight, it is unfortunate that all of these vessels were steamers and only six of them self-unloaders. In the second wave of shipbuilding for the U.S. Lakes' fleets, from 1972 through 1981, a total of 27 larger new boats were built—all self-unloaders and all powered by diesel engines. When the steel industry fell on hard times in the early 1980's, these new boats made those of the "first wave" economically vulnerable. Fifteen of the "first wave" steamers were converted to self-unloaders and, with a few exceptions, these were the boats that survived into the better days of the late 1980's. Unfortunately, GEORGE M. HUMPHREY was one that did not.

The HUMPHREY laid up at Ecorse on December 31, 1983. In August of 1986, a crew, made up mostly of retired Hanna sailors, fitted her out for a one-way trip to Quebec City. On August 13, under the command of Captain G. Victor Chamberlain, she cleared Ecorse and tied up at Lauzon a few days later. For Captain Chamberlain it was an especially nostalgic voyage. While serving his initial year as first mate aboard the HUMPHREY in 1962, the captain was called ashore and Chamberlain sailed the HUMPHREY for one trip—his first command. He remained as first mate aboard the HUMPHREY through the 1965 season and in 1975 returned to her for three seasons as captain, leaving her in 1978 to bring out the new Hanna flagship, GEORGE A. STINSON. In 1986, he came out of retirement to sail GEORGE M. HUMPHREY one more time.

The HUMPHREY did not remain long at Lauzon. The crew that delivered her returned to Ecorse and, on August 21, departed with another "first wave" vessel, PAUL H. CARNAHAN. Then on September 3, 1986, the Dutch tug SMIT LLOYD 109 departed Lauzon with both HUMPHREY and CARNAHAN in tow. In late September the tow locked through the Panama Canal and arrived on December 10 at Kaohsiung, Taiwan where the steamers were soon cut up by their new owners, Shiong Yek Steel Corporation.

BUILT:	1954 American Ship Building Co. Lorain, Ohio
HULL NUMBER:	871
LENGTH:	690.4
BREADTH:	75.9
DEPTH:	32.9
GRT:	14034
REGISTRY NUMBER:	US. 268564
ENGINES:	Cross Compound Steam Turbine
ENGINE BUILDER:	General Electric Co. 1954

GEORGE M. HUMPHREY (2) downbound in lower Lake Huron August 16, 1971

GEORGE M. HUMPHREY (2) downbound in the St. Clair River June 5, 1978

IMPERIAL CORNWALL

The IMPERIAL CORNWALL was a member of the Imperial Oil fleet for forty-one years. She was built as ACADIALITE and was launched at the Furness Shipbuilding Company Ltd. yard at Haverton Hill-on-Tees, England, in 1930.

The vessel had ten tanks for transporting various grades of petroleum and had a 21,500 barrel capacity. She was designed for trading through the locks of the Welland and the old St. Lawrence Canals and she operated out of Imperial Oil docks at Sarnia or Montreal most of the time.

Imperial Oil renamed their vessels in 1947 and this ship became b) IMPERIAL CORNWALL. She was later fitted with special, high-priced valves for carrying benzene, varsol, marvelube and jet fuel.

IMPERIAL CORNWALL was a busy ship. She opened the navigation season on the Welland Canal both in 1951 and again in 1955. She also won "Top Hat" honors as first arrived of the season at various ports.

When another of the fleet's tankers, IMPERIAL KINGSTON, was sold and cut down to a barge in 1960, IMPERIAL CORNWALL received the other steamer's more modern bridge structure to replace her own.

In 1969, IMPERIAL CORNWALL headed east. There she was based at Halifax to carry bunkers. She also supplied plants of the Nova Scotia Power & Light Company. Then, in February of 1970, she was called to lighter the grounded tanker ARROW on Chedebucto Bay to help to reduce the effect of one of Canada's worst environmental disasters.

IMPERIAL CORNWALL was retired on February 11, 1971, and she was replaced at Halifax by IMPERIAL DARTMOUTH. She was sold to Penn Shipping Ltd. and reportedly made only two trips before laying up. She was renamed c) GOLDEN SABLE while idle at Montreal and was seized by the crew for back wages of over $15,000.

GOLDEN SABLE resumed trading in July, 1971 for Neal Petroleum and made one trip to the Great Lakes to deliver a cargo to Buffalo. She then had to tie up again as her boiler and tanks were condemned.

The ship was sold to Steel Factors Ltd. and resold to Louiseville General Enterprises. The tug R.F. GRANT towed the hull to Louiseville, Quebec, on August 12, 1972. She served there as a floating dock. GOLDEN SABLE was gone from the port by March, 1981 and is believed to have been broken up on the St. Lawrence. Her Canadian registry was closed in October, 1981.

ACADIALITE upbound in Lake St. Clair

IMPERIAL CORNWALL downbound under the Blue Water Bridge

IMPERIAL CORNWALL downbound in lower Lake Huron June 8, 1960

GOLDEN SABLE above Lock 1 in the Welland Canal August 25, 1971

a) Acadialite, b) IMPERIAL CORNWALL, c) Golden Sable

BUILT:	1930 Furness Shipbuilding Co. Haverton Hill-on-Tees, U.K.
HULL NUMBER:	170
LENGTH:	250.0
BREADTH:	43.1
DEPTH:	17.7
GRT:	1991
REGISTRY NUMBER:	C. 154480
ENGINES:	17", 28", 46" Diameter x 36" Stroke Triple Expansion
ENGINE BUILDER:	North Eastern Marine Engineering Co. Ltd. 1930

GOLDEN SABLE idle on the St. Lawrence River July 14, 1976

IMPERIAL REDWATER

The post World War II shipbuilding boom that saw some 40 large new vessels added to the Great Lakes bulk fleet in the early 1950s, included introduction of the largest freshwater tankers in the world. For a brief time, crude oil from Canada's new oil fields in Alberta was moved by tanker from a pipeline terminus at Superior, Wisconsin, to refineries at Sarnia, Ontario, and the Toronto area. Four of these 120,000 barrel capacity tankers were built in 1951 and 1952 at a cost of about $4.5 million each; they were IMPERIAL LEDUC, IMPERIAL REDWATER and IMPERIAL WOODBEND, operated by Imperial Oil Ltd. and B A PEERLESS for British American Oil Company Ltd. (A fifth tanker for Canadian Oil Company Ltd., was started at Collingwood, but was completed as a dry bulk freighter - GEORGIAN BAY of Canada Steamship Lines Ltd.)

The lives of these tankers were short because extension of the Interprovincial/Lakehead pipe line across Wisconsin and Michigan to Sarnia in 1953 (and to the Toronto area in 1957) brought a virtual close to this unique chapter in Great Lakes shipping.

The Imperial tankers (named for oil fields near Edmonton) had the classic hull design of ocean-going tankers, and presented a trim appearance with black hull, burgundy red deck houses, yellow kingposts, masts and booms, and white catwalks, railings and other topside rigging. Safety was a paramount concern in the operation of these tankers as the crude, with all the highly volatile light ends present, had a wide flash-point range, so the 36-man ship crews and terminal personnel were highly trained and followed strict safety procedures. Timber rubbing strakes protected the ship's sides from creating sparks as they warped along lock walls and docks.

The Superior/Sarnia round trip was made every four days with the run across Lake Superior taking 23 hours light (25 hours loaded) and the run from the Soo to Sarnia taking 19 hours. At Superior, the average time in port was 10 hours with ballast pumping (into separator tanks on the dock) taking from two to four hours, and six and a half hours for actual loading with Lakehead Pipe Line Company's terminal pumps delivering the oil. At the other end of the trip, 10 hours was the average time in Sarnia with ship's pumps discharging crude in around seven plus hours, and taking on some return trip ballast before leaving the dock. The tankers were especially good foul weather ships and their punctuality in scheduling was phenomenal.

When IMPERIAL REDWATER was launched at the Canadian Shipbuilding & Engineering Company Ltd.'s shipyard at Port Arthur, Ontario, on November 18, 1950, local newspapers proclaimed it the largest ship ever built on Lake Superior. It was the only one of the four tankers to be built there. The ship loaded its first cargo of crude at Lakehead Pipe Line Company's Superior, Wisconsin, terminal on May 15, 1951, and two and a half years later discharged her final cargo at Imperial Oil's Sarnia refinery on November 5, 1953. REDWATER carried the greatest amount of cargo of any of the big Imperial tankers in its three operating seasons.

In 1952, IMPERIAL REDWATER carried the greatest amount of cargo of any of the new Great Lakes ships in operation at that time, and its 106 passages through the Soo Locks exceeded that of any other major cargo vessel. The largest single cargo loaded by the ship was 126,618 barrels.

In November, 1953, after "Butterworthing" and gas-freeing her tanks at Sarnia, IMPERIAL REDWATER moved to the Collingwood shipyard where she was rebuilt as a dry bulk freighter for Upper Lakes & St. Lawrence Transportation Company Ltd., of Toronto. The ship received conventional bottom and side tanks in place of its 27 liquid cargo tanks, and was fitted with a six-compartment hold and a regular freighter spar deck with one-piece hatch covers handled by an electric deck gantry. The midship house, with some modifications, was repositioned atop the forecastle in the normal position of a lake bulk carrier, the move being made on rollers and with the ship's own anchor windlass providing the pulling power. The lower block coefficient of her tanker hull form gave a respectable operating speed of around 17 mph.

The ship was rechristened b) R. BRUCE ANGUS in honor of an Upper Lakes' fleet captain, who was one of the original officers of the UL&StL fleet. Captain Angus brought a unique background to the lakes, for his sailing career began at age 14 in the British square-rigger PRIDE OF SCOTLAND, where he rose from apprentice to mate, sailing in the "around the Horn" Australian grain trade. Captain Angus was named Great Lakes "Man of the Year" in 1958, the year of his retirement.

The R. BRUCE ANGUS loaded her first dry bulk cargo (503,000 bushels of wheat) on June 23, 1954, at the Canadian Lakehead, and took on its first iron ore cargo at the D.M. & I.R. ore docks at Two Harbors, Minnesota, on July 3, 1954.

After almost 20 years in the ore, coal and grain trades on the lakes, the ship lay idle for a few years at Toronto, and finally was sold for scrapping. The R. BRUCE ANGUS departed Toronto on July 15, 1985, for Quebec and subsequent overseas towing. She arrived at her final berth at Setubal, Portugal, on August 20, 1985, and there she was dismantled.

a) IMPERIAL REDWATER, b) R. Bruce Angus

BUILT:	1951 Canadian Shipbuilding & Engineering Co. Port Arthur, Ontario
HULL NUMBER:	106
LENGTH:	601.5
BREADTH:	68.3
DEPTH:	31.0
GRT:	11816
REGISTRY NUMBER:	C. 192769
ENGINES:	Steam Turbine
ENGINE BUILDER:	John Inglis Co. 1950

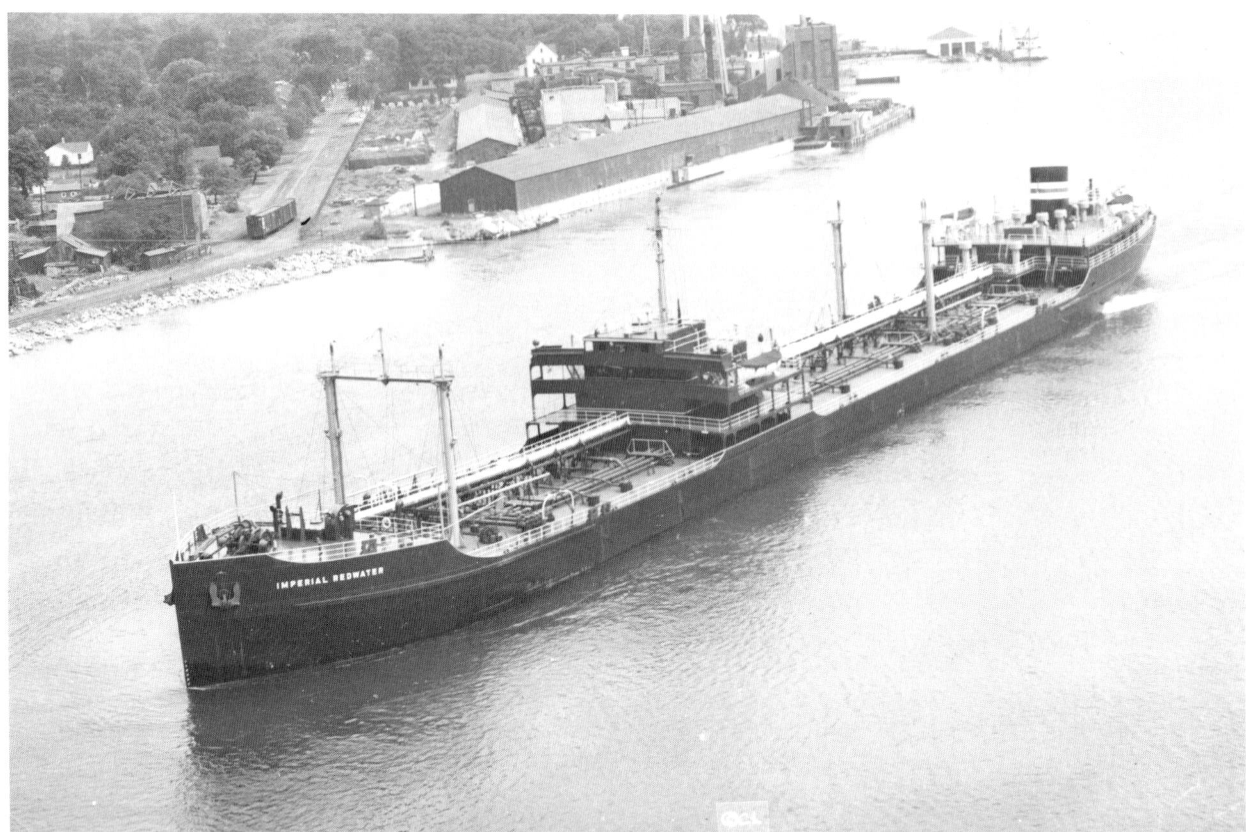

IMPERIAL REDWATER downbound under the Blue Water Bridge

Lakehead Pipe Line Co. crude oil loading dock at Superior, Wisconsin with B A PEERLESS and IMPERIAL LEDUC tied up

R. BRUCE ANGUS downbound in lower Lake Huron September 24, 1960

R. BRUCE ANGUS upbound in the St. Clair River July 20, 1977

IMPERIAL SIMCOE

Imperial Oil Limited, of Toronto, Ontario started shipping its products by water in 1902, using chartered vessels, and in 1910 started to operate its own tank ships. In 1930, the Furness Shipbuilding Company at Haverton Hill-on-Tees, Great Britain, built two sister tankers for Imperial Oil, the ACADIALITE (C. 154480) and SIMCOLITE.

After arriving in Canadian waters, the SIMCOLITE hauled petroleum products for Imperial Oil around the Great Lakes and St. Lawrence River often loading at the Sarnia refinery. In 1947, SIMCOLITE had her name changed to b) IMPERIAL SIMCOE. In 1962, her ownership changed to Chargord Investments Ltd., of Toronto, with Imperial Oil being her manager.

In 1965, after 35 years of service, IMPERIAL SIMCOE was laid up at Lauzon, Quebec, along with her older fleetmate, IMPERIAL WELLAND, a) ROYALITE. They were sold to Steel Factors Ltd., Montreal, and were then resold to German and then Spanish breakers. They cleared Lauzon on September 9, 1965, in tow of the Dutch tug LOIRE, but on two occasions the tankers broke the tow in the North Atlantic during heavy weather, and it was only with extreme difficulty that the tug got them back in tow again. IMPERIAL SIMCOE and IMPERIAL WELLAND finally arrived safely at Santander, Spain on October 13, 1965 where they were cut up for scrap.

a) Simcolite, b) IMPERIAL SIMCOE

BUILT:	1930 Furness Shipbuilding Co. Haverton Hill-on-Tees, U.K.
HULL NUMBER:	171
LENGTH:	250.0
BREADTH:	43.2
DEPTH:	17.9
GRT:	1919
REGISTRY NUMBER:	C. 155282
ENGINES:	17", 28", 46" Diameter x 36" Stroke Triple Expansion
ENGINE BUILDER:	North Eastern Marine Engineering Co. Ltd. 1930

SIMCOLITE upbound at Mission Point, St. Marys River

SIMCOLITE in heavy seas

IMPERIAL SIMCOE upbound in the St. Clair River opposite St. Clair June 28, 1963

IMPERIAL WOODBEND

The IMPERIAL WOODBEND was the newest, and had the shortest career, of the trio of 120,000 barrel tankers operated by Imperial Oil Ltd., in the crude oil trade from Superior, Wisconsin, to Sarnia, Ontario, in the early 1950s. She was built by the Canadian Shipbuilding & Engineering Company Ltd. shipyard at Collingwood, Ontario, and was launched on December 6, 1951.

The big tanker loaded its initial cargo of crude at Lakehead Pipe Line Company's Superior terminal on April 20, 1952. Her final (99th) cargo was discharged at Imperial Oil's Sarnia refinery on November 7, 1953. In her brief, two-year, stint as one of the largest freshwater tankers in the world, IMPERIAL WOODBEND had the distinction of loading the largest single cargo of any of the big crude tankers (126,876 barrels), and due to a modification of her pumping system (as compared to IMPERIAL LEDUC and IMPERIAL REDWATER) held the record for the fastest off-loading of cargo at Sarnia (six hours, 50 minutes).

IMPERIAL WOODBEND's cargo tanks were formed by two longitudinal bulkheads that divided the cargo space fore and aft, while ten oil-tight bulkheads segregated the nine tanks transversely, giving a total of 27 oil compartments. The center tanks had a capacity of 9,000 barrels and the wing tanks 4,000 barrels each. In normal practice midship tanks No. 4 and No. 6 were used as trim tanks and were usually lightly loaded to meet the 24 and 25 foot St. Marys River draft conditions of the early 1950s. No. 5 was a buoyancy tank and not used for cargo.

Loading at Superior, after ballast water had been pumped into special separation tanks on the dock, was done through 14 inch shore connection hoses to the ship's three deck lines, with terminal pumps (and gravity) delivering oil. Two deck crews, supervised by the ship's Chief Mate and a Terminal "Gauger", loaded the ship, with one crew starting forward, the other aft, and working toward midships manipulating valves to provide an even and maximum flow of crude to the ship's tanks. Off-loading at Sarnia was accomplished by the ship's three 4,100 gpm turbo-driven centrifugal pumps, augmented by two reciprocating "stripper" pumps for final cargo clean-out. The ship's Pumpman and First Officer set up and monitored the unloading.

The big tankers were powered by 4,500 shaft horsepower Parsons-Inglis steam turbines driving double reduction gearing delivering 90 output shaft rpm for a ship speed of about 17 mph. Two oil-fired Foster-Wheeler "D" type boilers supplied 55,000 pounds of steam per hour normally and 68,000 pounds per hour maximum at 500 psi and 750 degrees F.

These large tankers with their highly flammable cargoes, having operated in the congested waters of the Great Lakes system without a major mishap, reflects considerable credit on the companies and the crews involved. Stringent safety rules, and training of ship and terminal personnel, resulted in an enviable safety record for the ships. Only one incident, an explosion and fire in a tank aboard IMPERIAL LEDUC, while docked at Sarnia at the close of the 1951 season, marred a perfect no-accident performance.

After discharging her final crude cargo and "Butterworthing" and gas-freeing her tanks at Sarnia, IMPERIAL WOODBEND sailed to Port Colborne, Ontario, where E.B. Magee Ltd., converted the ship to a dry bulk freighter for Mohawk Navigation Company Ltd., of Montreal, over the 1953-54 winter.

The ship's 27 liquid cargo tanks were replaced by a four-compartment cargo hold with standard laker tank top and side tanks, and the pilot house was moved forward to the forecastle head. The spar deck was fitted with a four-foot-high trunk to increase cubic capacity for dry cargo. The trunk deck had 16 hatches with patented MacGregor fore-and-aft-moveable type covers that were removed by winches and stowed between hatches during loading and unloading.

Conversion of the ship was completed in the early summer of 1954 and she was rechristened b) GOLDEN HIND, honoring Sir Francis Drake's historic flagship in which he circumnavigated the globe in 1577-80. GOLDEN HIND then sailed for the Canadian Lakehead where she loaded her first dry bulk cargo of 641,000 bushels of oats and barley, and departed on July 17, 1954 for Buffalo, New York. GOLDEN HIND was the largest and fastest ship in the Mohawk fleet and continued to operate with its unusual blue and green hull colors until 1969. At that time, it was announced that the Scott Misener Steamship Company would operate the Mohawk boats, and GOLDEN HIND remained under charter to Misener until the end of the 1972 season.

In 1973, the ship was sold to the Quebec & Ontario Transportation Company Ltd., of Thorold, Ontario, and became a part of Groupe Desgagnes, Inc., of Quebec, when the Q & O fleet was purchased by that concern in 1984. The ship operated infrequently during her period of Desgagnes ownership and in the Autumn of 1986, (35 years after her launching) she was sold for scrap and towed overseas. GOLDEN HIND arrived at her final berth at Mamonal, Colombia, on October 28, 1986, and soon was dismantled.

a) IMPERIAL WOODBEND, b) Golden Hind

BUILT:	1952 Canadian Shipbuilding & Engineering Co. Collingwood, Ontario
HULL NUMBER:	147
LENGTH:	601.6
BREADTH:	68.2
DEPTH:	34.6
GRT:	12639
REGISTRY NUMBER:	C. 193679
ENGINES:	Steam Turbine
ENGINE BUILDER:	John Inglis Co. 1952

View looking forward from the after deckhouse showing the piping arrangement and catwalk to the mid-ship castle

Picturesque photo of tanker IMPERIAL WOODBEND

IMPERIAL WOODBEND upbound at Mission Point, St. Marys River, August 31, 1953

GOLDEN HIND upbound in the Welland Canal

GOLDEN HIND upbound in the St. Marys River, July 19, 1976

GOLDEN HIND upbound in Welland Canal in 1984

ITORORO

The steel-hulled, twin-screw, refrigerated meat carrier ITORORO was built in 1920 by the Moore Plant of the Bethlehem Shipbuilding Corporation at Elizabethport, New Jersey. Steam for her twin triple expansion engines was produced by two oil-fired, watertube boilers. Her original owner was the International Products Steamship Company, of New York and Asuncion, Paraguay.

Although Lloyds Register classed ITORORO and her almost exact sistership, AQUIDIBAN "For River Purposes Only", both steamers came into the Great Lakes during 1923. Press reports indicate that ITORORO arrived at Port Arthur, Ontario, on her first lake trip on October 13, 1923, to load grain. At the time, ITORORO apparently was managed by the Southgate Marine Corporation, of Norfolk, Virginia.

In 1926, ITORORO was acquired by the Brown Navigation Company Ltd., Quebec, and she was brought into the Canadian register (C.153066) for the pulpwood trade between Bersimis and Quebec City. She was adapted for this trade by the Morton Engineering and Drydock Company Ltd., Quebec. The shipyard fitted a raised forecastle on the steamer, and placed the texas and pilothouse (which originally were located amidships) on it. A trunk, running the full length of the cargo deck, was built to increase her carrying capacity.

In 1939, after a considerable period in lay-up, ITORORO was purchased by Gaston Elie, manager of Transit Tankers & Terminals Ltd., Montreal, and was converted into a tanker at the Davie Shipbuilding and Repairing Company Ltd., Lauzon, Quebec. She emerged from the reconstruction with 1,755 GRT.

Transit Tankers & Terminals operated ITORORO in the St. Lawrence River and lower lakes trades until 1944, when she was sold to Cia. Petrolero de Chile, Valparaiso, and renamed b) DON PANCHO for South American coastal service. In 1949, she was transferred to Navegacion Petrolero Goytizolo Cia., of Callao, Peru, which renamed her c) DON JOSE.

The steamer was destroyed in a fire and explosion which occurred at Talara, Peru, on March 3rd, 1958.

a) ITORORO, b) Don Pancho, c) Don Jose

BUILT:	1920 Bethlehem Shipbuilding Corp. Elizabethport, New Jersey
HULL NUMBER:	2153
LENGTH:	245.0
BREADTH:	40.1
DEPTH:	17.7
GRT:	1625
REGISTRY NUMBER:	US. 223067
2 ENGINES:	11", 18", 29" Diameter x 20" Stroke Triple Expansion
ENGINE BUILDER:	H.G. Trout & Co., Buffalo, New York 1920

ITORORO in winter quarters at Toronto

ITORORO upbound

ITORORO laid up before being sold for service in South America

JOHNSTOWN (2)

Although a few saltwater ships have been converted for use on the Great Lakes, the JOHNSTOWN (2) and her sistership, SPARROWS POINT, were built on saltwater for exclusive use on the Lakes. Built by the Sparrows Point Yard of Bethlehem Shipbuilding Company in Baltimore, Maryland, the JOHNSTOWN was christened on the 23rd of January, 1952, by Mrs. Robert E. McMath, the wife of the vice-president of Bethlehem Steel Corporation. Due to high winds and low tide, the JOHNSTOWN was not end-launched into the Patapsco River until high tide on the 24th.

On May 5, 1952, JOHNSTOWN departed Baltimore under tow for New Orleans, arriving on May 21st. She departed New Orleans that same day and headed up the Mississippi River, being pushed by the tug TENARU RIVER. JOHNSTOWN arrived at Lockport, Illinois on June 4th and then it took two days to transit the Chicago Sanitary and Ship Canal. She finally arrived at the American Ship Building yard at South Chicago on the 6th of June after spending 32 days, 10½ hours in transit from Baltimore. To this date, at 621 feet 1 inch (overall), she still holds the record as the longest vessel ever to make this river passage. At American Ship Building, the vessel's stack and parts of her superstructure were installed and upon leaving South Chicago, she proceeded to Cleveland where she laid up due to a steel strike. In late August of 1952, JOHNSTOWN was able to sail on her maiden voyage after the strike had been settled.

In 1958, she went to the American Ship Building yard at South Chicago where a new mid-section was installed. When she sailed from there, she left with a new 72 foot mid-section now making her 683 feet long with a gross tonnage of 10,317.

In 1981, she laid up at Erie, Pennsylvania, staying there until 1985. On the 28th of May, 1985, JOHNSTOWN cleared Quebec City along with the PONTIAC (2), formerly of the Cleveland Cliffs Steamship Company behind the tug KORAL. On the 24th of June, JOHNSTOWN arrived at San Estaban de Pravia, Spain for dismantling. She was the first of the post-war built United States lakers to be scrapped.

JOHNSTOWN (2) downbound at Mission Point, St. Marys River, August 26, 1952

JOHNSTOWN (2) upbound in the St. Marys River, July 27, 1974

BUILT:	1952 Bethlehem Shipbuilding Co. Sparrows Point, Maryland
HULL NUMBER:	4504
LENGTH:	611.0
BREADTH:	70.2
DEPTH:	33.7
GRT:	9164
REGISTRY NUMBER:	US. 263877
ENGINES:	Cross Compound Steam Turbine
ENGINE BUILDER:	Bethlehem Steel 1952

FRED KELLEY

The wooden-hulled barge FRED KELLEY was built at Toledo, Ohio by the Bailey Brothers shipyard. When she came out as a barge for her owners, Shepard, Henry & Company of Erie, Pennsylvania, she was towed by the steamer MARY JARECKI. A steeple compound steam engine was installed in Toledo after her first two seasons of operation and she sailed thereafter as a steam barge. In May of 1875, the FRED KELLEY was in a collision with the steam barge SWALLOW in Toledo harbor but neither vessel was severely damaged.

In 1879, H.J. Johnson of Cleveland, Ohio became her owner and sailed her for his iron ore and coal trades. M.A. Bradley of Cleveland purchased FRED KELLEY in 1889, and the vessel had no other owners for the rest of her life. In 1894, she was slightly altered topside and her tonnage was changed to 770 gross tons. The vessel sailed until the 1910 season when she was abandoned due to her condition and age.

BUILT:	1871 Bailey Brothers shipyard Toledo, Ohio
HULL NUMBER:	none
LENGTH:	212.2
BREADTH:	32.8
DEPTH:	14.2
GRT:	926.54
REGISTRY NUMBER:	US. 120074
ENGINES:	24", 44" Diameter x 38" Stroke Steeple Compound
ENGINE BUILDER:	Globe Iron Works 1871

FRED KELLEY downbound at Mission Point, St. Marys River in 1900

D.G. KERR (1)

The steel bulk freighter D.G. KERR was built at West Superior, Wisconsin by the Superior Shipbuilding Company and launched on May 20, 1903 for Wolvin's Provident Steamship Company. She was similar to the D.M. CLEMSON (1) and the JAMES H. REED. She had a "sunken" dining room and six firemen shared one room below decks aft. She originally had no after cabins above her main deck and her tall natural-draft stack made her definitely an unusual looking vessel. D.G. KERR was one of the first vessels to have 12 foot center hatches along with the JAMES H. HOYT of 1902.

In 1915, she was remeasured to the following dimensions: 448.0 x 52.0 x 25.0; 5,315 gross tons. In 1916, D.G. KERR was sold to the Interlake Steamship Company and renamed b) HARRY R. JONES. After cabins were added to the vessel in 1937 and she was rebuilt considerably. Her new dimensions at this time were: 455.2 x 52.2 x 24.9; 5,265 gross tons. She was used mainly in the ore trade and carried an occasional cargo of grain.

In 1956, HARRY R. JONES was sold to Cargo Carriers, Inc. and operated until the 1960 season when she was sold for scrap. Many Great Lakes ships have been towed overseas for scrapping, but this is the only one which went to Scotland. However, her trip overseas was not smooth. Rather reluctantly did she go to the scrapyard. She went aground at Androsan, Scotland on January 6, 1961 and it wasn't until February 15, that she arrived at her final port of Troon, Scotland. She was cut up for scrap there in the same year.

D.G. KERR (1) leaving the locks at the Soo at the turn of the century

D.G. KERR (1) downbound in the St. Clair River opposite Marine City, Michigan

a) D.G. KERR (1), b) Harry R. Jones

BUILT:	1903 Superior Shipbuilding Co. West Superior, Wisconsin	*GRT:*	5531
HULL NUMBER:	509	*REGISTRY NUMBER:*	US. 157696
LENGTH:	468.0	*ENGINES:*	15", 23 3/4", 36 1/2", 56" Diameter x 40" Stroke Quadruple Expansion
BREADTH:	52.0		
DEPTH:	28.0	*ENGINE BUILDER:*	Superior Shipbuilding Co. 1903

HARRY R. JONES downbound in Lake St. Clair, June 19, 1949

HARRY R. JONES downbound in the Detroit River under the Ambassador Bridge

HARRY R. JONES at Dock 24 in Cleveland, Ohio during 1958

KINSMAN ENTERPRISE (1)

The steel bulk freighter NORMAN B. REAM was built by the Chicago Shipbuilding Company at Chicago, Illinois for the Pittsburgh Steamship Company and launched on August 18, 1906. One of a class of 580 footers, NORMAN B. REAM worked in the iron ore trade almost exclusively, carrying a variety of limestone and coal cargoes on occasion.

Various corporate changes occurred beginning in 1952, but she and her sister vessels remained in the Tin Stack fleet until they were declared surplus in the 1960's. NORMAN B. REAM was sold to the Kinsman Transit Company in 1965 and was renamed b) KINSMAN ENTERPRISE (1). In Steinbrenner's Kinsman fleet, she served mainly in the grain trade for the next thirteen years. Her career was rather uneventful and she was finally declared "outdated" and laid up at Toledo, Ohio in late 1978 after performing one unusual task. She arrived at Lorain, Ohio from South Chicago on August 8, 1978 with the cabins for Hull Number 908, EDGAR B. SPEER, one of the new 1,000 footers. After a few more trips, she laid up in the Frog Pond at Toledo at the end of the season.

On August 23, 1979, KINSMAN ENTERPRISE was towed out of the Frog Pond, having escaped the scrapper's torch, and sold to the Port Huron Seaway Terminal to be used as a storage barge. She was tied up at the Seaway Terminal and renamed c) HULL #1, to be used to store beans which were shipped later to overseas ports or to domestic ports from the fields of Michigan's Thumb district. A conveyor was built for the vessel to facilitate loading and unloading.

After ten more years of service, in July of 1989, she was again declared surplus, the conveyor removed, and she was welded shut for the trip overseas to the scrapper. She was purchased by Marine Salvage Company Ltd., of Port Colborne, Ontario, and began the tow on August 26, 1989, arriving at Aliaga, Turkey on October 10th.

a) Norman B. Ream, b) KINSMAN ENTERPRISE (1), c) Hull #1

BUILT:	1906 Chicago Shipbuilding Co. South Chicago, Illinois
HULL NUMBER:	70
LENGTH:	580.0
BREADTH:	58.0
DEPTH:	27.4
GRT:	7692
REGISTRY NUMBER:	US. 203543
ENGINES:	24", 39", 65" Diameter x 42" Stroke Triple Expansion
ENGINE BUILDER:	American Ship Building Co., Cleveland 1906

NORMAN B. REAM upbound at Mission Point, St. Marys River in 1928

NORMAN B. REAM upbound after leaving the Locks at the Soo

KINSMAN ENTERPRISE upbound in the St. Marys River, July 27, 1974

HULL no. 1, ex KINSMAN ENTERPRISE, at the Seaway Terminal dock at Port Huron, August 31, 1979

HULL No. 1 "Buttoning up" at Port Huron, August 17, 1989 in preparation for her trip overseas

JOHN A. KLING

JOHN A. KLING was one of the early self-unloaders on the Great Lakes, and was launched by the Manitowoc Shipbuilding Company at Manitowoc, Wisconsin on August 5, 1922. The freighter took on her first cargo, a load of stone, on October 2, 1922, at Rockport, Michigan.

JOHN A. KLING operated for the Reiss fleet under its subsidiary, the Rockport Steamship Company. Much of the vessel's work was concentrated on Lakes Erie, Huron and Michigan, but she made occasional trips to Lake Superior and, on April 18, 1932, came down the Welland Canal to Lake Ontario for the first time.

The vessel returned to Manitowoc in 1940 and was lengthened to 546.5 feet; 6,825 GRT. This increased her carrying capacity to almost 11,000 tons.

Her duties varied from year to year. In 1960, JOHN A. KLING hauled 76 cargoes. These included 400,642 tons of stone on 37 trips, 277,409 tons of coal on 31 voyages and 90,296 tons of sand on eight trips. Drummond Island, where she stopped to take on stone on 16 occasions, was the most frequent of the 30 different ports visited. Apart from one trip to Toronto with coal, the vessel remained on the middle three Great Lakes. However, JOHN A. KLING was idle at Manitowoc from July 1 to 25, 1960, for work on her boom which had collapsed on a dock.

In 1961, JOHN A. KLING hauled 86 loads. These included eight cargoes of ore out of Silver Bay, Minnesota. All but one load of ore went to Detroit, the one exception being consigned to Buffalo. Drummond Island was again the most frequent loading port and the steamer stopped there 21 times for stone.

In 1966, the vessel's original 1,600 horsepower triple expansion engine was replaced by the Christy Corporation at Sturgeon Bay, Wisconsin. A 3,400 horsepower Cooper-Bessemer diesel was installed, and a new pilothouse was constructed at the same time.

The Reiss fleet was sold to the American Steamship Company, of Buffalo, New York, in 1969 and JOHN A. KLING spent a decade in its colors.

Dale Transports Ltd. purchased the ship late in the 1980 season, wintered her at Toronto, and sent her back to work the next year as b) LEADALE (2). As such, she operated in the stone and salt trades much of the time and even traveled down the Seaway. She ran aground in the St. Lawrence River on August 4, 1981, off Caughnawaga and had to be lightered so that she could be refloated.

Another accident, which occurred on December 7, 1982, ended her career. LEADALE had just unloaded salt at Thorold, Ontario and, while departing her dock, backed into a concrete dolphin, punched a hole in her hull near the stern, and sank a few feet off the dock in 30 feet of water. All crew members were rescued.

LEADALE was refloated on December 19th and was towed to Ramey's Bend at Port Colborne three days later. She was sold to Marine Salvage in April 1983, and scrapping began almost immediately.

JOHN A. KLING downbound in the Detroit River under the Ambassador Bridge

JOHN A. KLING downbound in Lake St. Clair, August 21, 1950

JOHN A. KLING downbound in the Detroit River, August 10, 1967

JOHN A. KLING downbound in the St. Clair River at Sarnia, June 11, 1971

LEADALE at the Homer Bridge, Welland Canal, September 12, 1981

LEADALE sunk at Thorold, December 11, 1982

LEADALE under tow to the scrapyard by the tug GLENEVIS December 22, 1982

a) JOHN A. KLING, B) Leadale (2)

BUILT:	1922 Manitowoc Shipbuilding Co. Manitowoc, Wisconsin
HULL NUMBER:	204
LENGTH:	438.0
BREADTH:	56.2
DEPTH:	28.4
GRT:	5412
REGISTRY NUMBER:	US. 222512
ENGINES:	21", 35", 59" Diameter x 42" Stroke Triple Expansion
ENGINE BUILDER:	Shipyard 1922

LAKE WINNIPEG

LAKE WINNIPEG was one of a number of straight deck bulk carriers that were constructed using the stern, including the engineroom and after-end accommodations, of a deep sea T-2 tanker. These tankers were a part of the emergency shipbuilding program of World War II. They were constructed by the United States Maritime Commission to serve as fleet oilers.

Kaiser Incorporated, of Portland, Oregon, was heavily engaged in the construction of the T-2 class tankers. She was launched November 9, 1943, as a) TABLE ROCK. After the war, the tanker was sold to the French government (Cie Nationale de Nav.) and renamed b) NIVOSE. The vessel likely was engaged in trade between North Africa and France.

The size of ocean-going tankers grew rapidly in the post-war years and soon the T-2's were no longer competitive. Some were converted to dry bulk carriers but most went for scrap. A few, such as NIVOSE, survived through reconstruction.

The Seaway ore and grain trade was expanding rapidly in the early sixties. Great Lakes shipyards could not produce the needed vessels quickly enough. Overseas reconstruction projects were not only cheaper, but also the work was completed faster than building an entirely new ship.

Nipigon Transports Ltd. purchased NIVOSE and sent her to Glasgow, Scotland for conversion. The cargo section was removed and scrapped, while a new bow and mid-body were built and connected to the old stern section. The bow of the vessel was launched May 7, 1962, and the two sections were soon joined at the Barclay, Curle & Company shipyard. The result was c) LAKE WINNIPEG, a 702 x 75 x 42.6 foot Great Lakes bulk carrier of 18,660 gross tons. She was enrolled in the Canadian Registry (C. 304310) and on August 21, 1962, cleared for Canada. Her hatches had not yet been cut out which provided extra strength for the transatlantic voyage. The hatch cutting was done at Lauzon, Quebec, and by September 23, 1962, LAKE WINNIPEG was upbound in the Seaway, with 22,584 tons of iron ore from Sept Isles, Quebec.

During 1963, her first full year on the Great Lakes, LAKE WINNIPEG carried 27 cargoes, including 14 shipments of ore and 13 of grain. All of the grain was loaded at the Canadian Lakehead and was destined for Baie Comeau, Quebec. The ore moved west from Sept Isles to Cleveland, Toledo, Ashtabula and Detroit. Two loads of ore from Taconite Harbor came down the lakes in October for Stelco at Hamilton, Ontario.

LAKE WINNIPEG was first of the season down the St. Lawrence Seaway in 1975 and the last ship down in 1979. She received heavy bow damage after striking a dock in Montreal late in 1976 and was reported aground near DeTour Passage on May 25, 1980 as a result of gear failure.

LAKE WINNIPEG saw only limited service in 1983 and was idle at Montreal in 1984. She was sold in 1985 via Gibson Shipbrokers to Batista E. Iramos Ltd. for scrap. The tug IRVING CEDAR pulled her out of Montreal on May 2, 1985, and they arrived at Lisbon, Portugal, May 19th. LAKE WINNIPEG thus became the first 730 foot laker to go for scrap but others would soon follow.

NIVOSE underway on the east coast

Bow section of LAKE WINNIPEG at Blythswood Shipyard in 1962

LAKE WINNIPEG upbound at Port Huron, October 18, 1962

LAKE WINNIPEG above Lock 3 in the Welland Canal, November 12, 1983

a) Table Rock, b) Nivose, c) LAKE WINNIPEG

BUILT:	1943 Kaiser Incorporated Portland, Oregon
HULL NUMBER:	41
LENGTH:	504.0
BREADTH:	68.2
DEPTH:	39.2
GRT:	10448
REGISTRY NUMBER:	US. 244865
ENGINES:	Steam Turbine/Generator and Electric Motor Drive
ENGINE BUILDER:	General Electric 1943

LAKESIDE

The wooden-hulled, propeller passenger steamer LAKESIDE was built in 1888 at Windsor, Ontario, by Lane from a design by Captain A.M. Kirby. She was constructed to the order of the Lakeside Navigation Company, of Walkerville, Ontario, and was launched on April 10, 1888. She entered service on a route from Windsor and Detroit to Leamington and Pelee Island, under the command of Captain N.J. Wigle.

Later in 1888, Captain Wigle brought LAKESIDE down the Welland Canal to Toronto, for the Lakeside Navigation Company had decided to enter into direct competition with A.W. Hepburn's Niagara Falls Line by operating between Toronto and Port Dalhousie in opposition to the wooden-hulled side-wheeler EMPRESS OF INDIA. The competition became even more fierce in 1892 when the newly-formed St. Catharines, Grimsby and Toronto Navigation Company placed its new, steel-hulled side-wheeler GARDEN CITY on the route.

During 1892, the S.G. & T. chartered LAKESIDE to run with GARDEN CITY, and peace came to the route when the company merged its operations with those of Captain Hepburn in 1893. Hepburn and Wigle shared the management of the pooled service, and in due course the ownership of LAKESIDE passed to the Niagara, St. Catharines & Toronto Navigation Company Ltd., which was a subsidiary of McKenzie and Mann's Niagara, St. Catharines & Toronto Railway Company.

Hepburn withdrew EMPRESS OF INDIA from the pooled service in 1898, after which LAKESIDE and GARDEN CITY carried on together for many years. LAKESIDE proved to be very popular on the Toronto - Port Dalhousie run, and also carried excursions direct from Port Dalhousie to Toronto's Island Park.

LAKESIDE was withdrawn from the route when the new DALHOUSIE CITY was commissioned in 1911, and in July of that year, she was sold to M.J. Hogan, a Port Colborne contractor, who used her to carry supplies to various construction sites.

In July of 1920, LAKESIDE was acquired by John E. Russell, of Toronto, and he had the Toronto Dry Dock Company (in which he had an interest) convert her to a double-decked tug, 118.4 x 25.9 x 9.0; 200 GRT. She was renamed b) JOSEPH L. RUSSELL, in honor of the owner's eldest son, and not only towed Russell's various barges but also served as a wrecking tug.

In May of 1929, the John E. Russell Towing Company, of Toronto, was one of the companies merged to form Sinmac Lines Ltd., Montreal, and JOSEPH L. RUSSELL joined the new firm. She did not last long, however, for she foundered on Lake Ontario on November 15, 1929. Bound from Montreal for Toronto with the barge AUGUSTUS in tow, she began to take in water while off Point Petre, and her pumps could not stem the flow. Her crew left the sinking tug in the lifeboat and landed ashore safely at Cobourg, Ontario.

LAKESIDE at her dock at Port Dalhousie Harbour

LAKESIDE laid up in Muir's Pond above Lock 1 at Port Dalhousie in 1911

a) LAKESIDE, b) Joseph L. Russell

BUILT:	1888 Lane Windsor, Ontario
HULL NUMBER:	none
LENGTH:	121.0
BREADTH:	26.0
DEPTH:	9.3
GRT:	348
REGISTRY NUMBER:	C. 90778
ENGINES:	19", 32" Diameter x 26" Stroke Fore and Aft Compound
ENGINE BUILDER:	Kerr Brothers, Windsor 1888

C.G.S. LAMBTON

The LAMBTON was built at the Canadian Government shipyards at Sorel, Quebec, during the winter of 1909. She was a twin-engine, twin-screw lighthouse supply and service ship equipped with passenger cabins on the main deck for the conveyance of lightkeepers and their families.

LAMBTON was based at the Parry Sound Agency of the Department of Marine and Fisheries. She and her sistership, SIMCOE, provided service to the navigation aids in harbors and channels of Georgian Bay, Lake Huron, Lake Superior and, occasionally, Lake Erie.

On April 18, 1922, LAMBTON departed Sault Ste. Marie, Ontario with lightkeepers and supplies for Isle Parisienne, Caribou Island and Michipicoten Island. She had to buck heavy ice to clear Whitefish Bay, and, in the process, broke her steering gear. LAMBTON had a Drake steering engine located in her pilothouse and the damage was corrected by a temporary jury rig of one inch cables connecting the steering engine to the steering quadrant shaft. In this condition, she sailed into Lake Superior in a severe northeast gale.

On April 19, she was sighted by the steamers GLENLIVET, OSLER and WESTMOUNT (2) when they were approximately 40 miles north of Whitefish Point. About noon that day, she was last seen by the steamer MIDLAND PRINCE, and soon afterwards the storm reached its peak with winds up to 60 mph.

When the lighthouse remained darkened for days afterward, the alarm was raised that LAMBTON was missing. The tug G.R. GRAY was chartered for the search and the U.S. Coast Guard cutter COOK also was requested to search eastern Lake Superior. Wreckage, which was identified as coming from LAMBTON, was located east of Caribou Island on April 30, by the COOK. The LAMBTON, her entire crew and the lightkeepers had been swallowed up by the cold waters of Lake Superior.

BUILT:	1909 Canadian Government shipyards Sorel, Quebec	*GRT:*	323
HULL NUMBER:	unknown	*REGISTRY NUMBER:*	C. 126409
LENGTH:	108.0	*Twin ENGINES:*	11", 18", 30" Diameter x 22" Stroke Triple Expansion
BREADTH:	25.1	*ENGINE BUILDER:*	Fleming & Ferguson, Paisley, Scotland 1908
DEPTH:	12.7		

LAMBTON on the stocks

LAMBTON in winter lay-up at Parry Sound

LAMBTON under way

THOMAS W. LAMONT

THOMAS W. LAMONT was built by the Toledo Shipbuilding Company in Toledo, Ohio for the Pittsburgh Steamship Company and was launched on March 22, 1930. Shortly thereafter, she departed on her maiden voyage, bound for Duluth, Minnesota, to load her first cargo of iron ore, on May 28. The THOMAS W. LAMONT was named after a long-standing director of the United States Steel Corporation who also served as vice-chairman of the board and director of J.P. Morgan and Company.

After almost twenty-five years of uneventful service for Pittsburgh, THOMAS W. LAMONT entered Fraser-Nelson Shipbuilding and Dry Dock Company in Superior, Wisconsin, in December, 1964, where during the winter of 1964-65, she received a 3,200 bhp Nordberg diesel engine with reverse reduction gear and water-cooled clutches, two 150 kw diesel generators, one 30 kw emergency diesel generator, two package steam generators, fuel oil bunker tanks, and a new streamlined stack. Also added was a 635 hp bow thruster, making the LAMONT the first vessel in the Pittsburgh fleet to be so equipped.

For her first cargo after repowering, THOMAS W. LAMONT loaded 14,049 gross tons of iron ore at the Missabe ore docks in Duluth on May 1, 1965. On December 18, 1970, she loaded the last cargo of the 1970 iron ore season at the D.M. & I.R. ore docks in Duluth, departing with 11,972 gross tons of Minntac pellets. On April 7, 1974, she loaded the initial shipment of ore for the 1974 season at those same docks, departing on April 8 with 12,511 gross tons bound for U.S. Steel's Lorain, Ohio plant. On July 30, 1977, the LAMONT made a rare trip into the Rouge River delivering a cargo of iron ore to the Ford Motor Company. Ford had been stockpiling iron ore in 1977 in anticipation of an iron miners' strike.

The THOMAS W. LAMONT was involved in a dramatic rescue during the 1979 season. On June 5, Hall Corporation's CARTIERCLIFFE HALL was upbound on Lake Superior when she caught fire. The first vessel on the scene was the LAMONT, alerted by smoke on the horizon. When she arrived, the LAMONT found the after end cabins of the CARTIERCLIFFE HALL enveloped in fire and smoke.

The crew of the LAMONT took seventeen survivors aboard and cared for them until they were evacuated by a Coast Guard helicopter later in the morning. Many of the seventeen were not properly clothed, a few were burned, and some were unconscious.

Rear Admiral A.F. Fugaro of the U.S. Coast Guard later said the efforts of the LAMONT were "exemplary" and that her initial report to the Coast Guard significantly aided in speeding the rescue.

On September 3, 1981, the THOMAS W. LAMONT laid up in Duluth for the final time. In 1987, the LAMONT was sold by the USS Great Lakes Fleet, through Aaron Ferer & Sons, to Sonmez Denizclilik Han of Istanbul, Turkey, for overseas scrapping. On August 22, 1987, THOMAS W. LAMONT departed Duluth under tow of Wellington Towing's CHIPPEWA, bound for Quebec City, where they arrived on September 3, 1987, six years to the date of her final lay-up. On September 15, 1987, the LAMONT and her former fleetmate, the ENDERS M. VOORHEES, left Quebec City with the British-flag tug IRVING CEDAR towing. On October 24, the tow arrived in Alegeciras, Spain. On December 15, 1987, the Greek tug EVEREST cleared Alegeciras with the LAMONT arriving in Aliaga, Turkey on December 27.

BUILT:	1930 Toledo Shipbuilding Co. Toledo, Ohio	*GRT:*	7790
HULL NUMBER:	184	*REGISTRY NUMBER:*	US. 229753
LENGTH:	587.9	*ENGINES:*	24", 41", 65" Diameter x 42" Stroke Triple Expansion
BREADTH:	60.2	*ENGINE BUILDER:*	Toledo Shipbuilding Co. 1930
DEPTH:	27.9		

THOMAS W. LAMONT upbound light in the Detroit River

THOMAS W. LAMONT downbound at Mission Point, St. Marys River

THOMAS W. LAMONT downbound at Mission Point, St. Marys River, August 29, 1953

THOMAS W. LAMONT downbound in the St. Clair River opposite Harsens Island, August 6, 1965

THOMAS W. LAMONT at Port Colborne, August 29, 1987, on her way to scrap. Tugs GLENEVIS and CHIPPEWA

ALEXANDER LESLIE

In 1837, in Oswego, New York, John T. Hutchinson was born. He was to become one of the most successful vessel owners on the Great Lakes. At 24 years of age, he purchased part interest in the scow MONITOR, which started his career in lake shipping.

In 1901, the J.T. HUTCHINSON was launched at Cleveland, Ohio by the American Ship Building Company for the Pioneer Steamship Company which was managed by Hutchinson. Launched on February 9, she was the first steel-hulled vessel built for the fleet for which she served until 1923.

During the time she sailed for Pioneer, she was involved in a few incidents. On November 29, 1903, J.T. HUTCHINSON ran aground on an uncharted reef off Five Mile Point, west of Eagle Harbor on Michigan's Keweenaw Peninsula in Lake Superior. At the time, she was hauling 187,000 bushels of flax, bound for Buffalo, New York. She was finally refloated on December 4th and was towed to Buffalo by the tugs M.F. MERICK and FAVORITE (1). On the 10th of November, 1913, she again stranded in Lake Superior, this time on Point Iroquois on Whitefish Bay; she suffered $20,000 damage. During the winter of 1919, she was rebuilt at Cleveland. Her new dimensions were: 346.0 x 48.0 x 24.3 feet; 3,690 GRT.

In 1923, J.T. HUTCHINSON was sold to the Forest City Steamship Company which renamed her b) H.A. ROCK. Due to a lack of cargoes, Forest City went into receivership in 1927 and the H.A. ROCK became the property of the Lake Erie Coal Company, of Walkerville, Ontario which renamed her c) ALEXANDER LESLIE (C. 154692). Her Canadian dimensions were: 353.6 x 48.2 x 23.7 feet; 3,509 gross tons. During her days with the Lake Erie Coal Company, she was a common sight in Erieau, Ontario, where she delivered coal from American Lake Erie ports. In November of 1957, she grounded on a sand bar off Erieau while loaded with 5,000 tons of coal from Toledo. After five days, with assistance from the tug PRUDENCE, she was finally pulled free and limped to her dock.

In 1964, the LESLIE came under the ownership of Norlake Steamships Ltd., Toronto, which operated her until 1969, hauling grain out of the Lakehead to Georgian Bay ports and down the Seaway.

In December of 1969, she was downbound in the system headed for Trois-Rivieres, Quebec, with a load of grain. After discharging, she proceeded back to Sorel for lay-up, having been sold to Steel Factors Ltd., of Montreal. On May 31, 1971, along with the STONEFAX, she departed Sorel behind the Polish tug JANTAR. She arrived at Santander, Spain on the 19th of June, and was dismantled there.

a) J.T. Hutchinson, b) H.A. Rock, c) ALEXANDER LESLIE

BUILT:	1901 American Ship Building Co. Cleveland, Ohio
HULL NUMBER:	405
LENGTH:	346.0
BREADTH:	48.0
DEPTH:	28.0
GRT:	3734
REGISTRY NUMBER:	US. 77457
ENGINES:	22", 35", 58" Diameter x 40" Stroke Triple Expansion
ENGINE BUILDER:	Shipyard 1901

J.T. HUTCHINSON downbound at Mission Point, St. Marys River in 1919

H.A. ROCK downbound at Mission Point, St. Marys River

ALEXANDER LESLIE upbound at Mission Point, St. Marys River in 1927

ALEXANDER LESLIE upbound in the St. Clair River opposite Sarnia, October 10, 1962

ALEXANDER LESLIE downbound at Mission Point, St. Marys River, August 15, 1969

LILLIAN

The pulpwood barge LILLIAN, of the Roen Steamship Company, at Sturgeon Bay, Wisconsin, had her beginnings as a Lake Erie railroad carferry. She was launched as MARQUETTE & BESSEMER NO. 2 (2) at the Cleveland yard of the American Ship Building Company on September 3, 1910. The ferry, with a capacity of 32 railroad cars on four tracks, was owned by the Marquette & Bessemer Dock & Navigation Company, and was built to replace a carferry of the same name that had foundered in Lake Erie en route from Conneaut, Ohio to Port Stanley, Ontario in early December, 1909.

Normally, these carferries were employed in carrying coal cars, destined for Steel Company of Canada's mills at Hamilton, Ontario, across Lake Erie from Conneaut and Ashtabula on the American side to Port Stanley and Erieau on the Canadian shore. The 60 mile run took about five hours and a ferry could move about 80 cars a day. As this coal traffic dwindled in the early and mid 1920's, it became difficult to keep the ferries fully occupied and MARQUETTE & BESSEMER NO. 2 made occasional trips elsewhere. She was reported in the St. Lawrence River in 1921 and 1922, and in 1926 was involved in a minor accident in Toledo, Ohio while outbound with coal for Erieau.

MARQUETTE & BESSEMER NO. 2 had a propensity for minor mishaps, in part because she was difficult to handle at slow speeds. In fact, she seemed to have more than her share of minor collisions and mishaps.

Carferry service to Erieau ended in November, 1927, when a storm damaged the landing facilities, and abandonment of the ferry service entirely was approved by the ICC in February, 1932.

MARQUETTE & BESSEMER NO. 2 lay idle until 1937, when she was taken to Cleveland to serve as a show boat at the Great Lakes Exposition at which time she was lettered MOSES CLEVELAND although she was never enrolled under that name. After the Exposition, she lay idle at Cleveland and Port Huron, Michigan until she was sold in 1942 to the Filer Fiber Company. This firm, which operated a paper mill at Manistee, Michigan, reduced the ferry to an open-decked barge and she served out the war years carrying pulpwood. In 1946, Filer decided to get out of the shipping business and sold the barge to Captain John Roen who had previously hauled for Filer.

"Cap" Roen renamed the barge LILLIAN, for his daughter-in-law (Marquis Roen's wife), and used it in his pulpwood fleet. Under the Roen gray hull and white cabin colors, the LILLIAN was fitted with a 50 ton rail-mounted crane, and her 3,200 ton capacity enabled her to carry 1,700 cords of pulpwood, or approximately 2,600,000 board feet of lumber.

In the early days of pulpwood hauling, Roen loaded frequently from North Channel points in Lake Huron, including Sheguindah Bay, Manitowaning, Hensley Bay, Murphy's Harbor, Campbell's Bay, Gore Bay, South Bay, McBean Harbor, Burnt Island, Rabbit Island, Spragge, Spanish, New Point, Thessalon, Blind River and others. Many of them were very difficult places to get in and out of, and some of Roen's less daring competitors claimed that there was "Roen Gray" on every rock in the North Channel.

In 1949, the Roen Salvage Company was formed and LILLIAN, in addition to hauling pulpwood, was used in a number of dock and harbor building projects, dredging jobs and marine salvages. Work was performed for the Corps of Engineers, Merritt, Chapman & Scott, Peter Kiewit Sons Company, Edward Gillen Company and other private interests. LILLIAN's jobs included dredging and breakwall work at Manitowoc, Milwaukee, Calumet Harbor, Illinois, Grand Marais, Minnesota, Leland and Harrisville, Michigan. In 1962, she was fitted with spuds and did extensive dredging on Lansing Shoal in Lake Michigan. LILLIAN was used to install the water intake pipe and cell for Port Huron.

An unusual assignment came in 1965 when a United Airlines passenger plane, bound for Chicago's O'Hare Field, plunged into Lake Michigan off Waukegan, Illinois. LILLIAN was employed by Merritt, Chapman & Scott under contract to the U.S. Navy in an attempt to salvage parts of the airplane. LILLIAN also worked on the construction of McCormick Place in downtown Chicago, and hauled mattress stone for breakwalls at Charlevoix and Harbor Beach, Michigan.

A picturesque cargo trip for LILLIAN was delivering crushed stone from Marblehead, Ohio, to Wallaceburg, Ontario, which is located 12 miles up the Sydenham River from the St. Clair River near Algonac, Michigan. Since there was no dock for unloading, the barge was brought close to the river bank and its crane cast the stone ashore to be repiled by the highway builder's bulldozers.

The death of Captain Roen on December 7, 1970, marked the beginning of the end of a unique era in Great Lakes maritime history. Cargoes for the company's vessels were dwindling and the stockholders, who were heirs of John Roen, decided in late 1971 to sell off major pieces of equipment as purchasers could be found. Thus, in June, 1972, LILLIAN was sold to The Manitowoc Company and, although the vessel no longer plies the open waters of the Great Lakes, she continues to serve as a crane lighter in the shipyard of Manitowoc's subsidiary, Bay Shipbuilding Company at Sturgeon Bay, Wisconsin.

In April, 1989, crane barge LILLIAN was towed to Green Bay where she took part in raising the sunken tug MINNIE SELVICK.

MARQUETTE & BESSEMER NO. 2 (2)

MARQUETTE & BESSEMER NO. 2 (2) entering the harbor in the ice

MOSES CLEVELAND as a "Showboat" at Cleveland, Ohio in the late thrities

LILLIAN upbound at Mission Point, St. Marys River, July 16, 1955

a) Marquette & Bessemer No. 2 (2), b) LILLIAN

BUILT:	1910 American Ship Building Co. Cleveland, Ohio
HULL NUMBER:	450
LENGTH:	338.0
BREADTH:	56.0
DEPTH:	19.5
GRT:	2583
REGISTRY NUMBER:	US. 208021
2 ENGINES:	19", 31", 52" Diameter x 36" Stroke Triple Expansion
ENGINE BUILDER:	Shipyard 1910

LILLIAN at Sturgeon Bay, Wisconsin, March, 1989

LILLIAN at Grand Marais, Minnesota, June 20, 1956

LIQUILASSIE

On April 3, 1943, the tanker TEMBLADOR was launched on the site of the old McDougall-Duluth yard by the Barnes-Duluth Shipbuilding Company, a firm started by Julius Barnes two years earlier. TEMBLADOR was built for the Creole Petroleum Company, a subsidiary of Standard Oil of New Jersey, along with six sister tankers, for service around the Lake Maracaibo area of northern Venezuela. The TEMBLADOR and her sisters were never given official U.S. registry numbers, as they were flagged in Panama.

When the TEMBLADOR was launched, she and her six sisters were, at 366 feet overall, the largest ships built on the Great Lakes for ocean service. Due to their size, they were unable to go through the old St. Lawrence canals, so they went to salt water via the Chicago Sanitary Canal and the Mississippi River.

During World War II, TEMBLADOR hauled petroleum products out of the oil fields of Lake Maracaibo to Aruba. Until 1960, she traded in the Gulf of Mexico and the Caribbean. In 1960, she was purchased by the Canada Import Company, of Montreal, to be managed by Porter Shipping for service on the Great Lakes and St. Lawrence River. Her Canadian registry was: C. 199395

In 1961, TEMBLADOR was renamed b) LIQUILASSIE and there followed a series of corporate changes; from 1965 to 1966, she was owned by Eagle Shipping and Investment, and from 1966 to 1971, Liquilassie Shipping, managed by Porter Shipping. In 1971, Porter Holdings became her owner, and with Liquilassie Shipping as her manager, she stayed this way until 1977.

In August of 1977, she was purchased by L.B. Tanker, Inc., owned by Raymond Bergeron. In the fall of 1977, she was towed to United Metals at Hamilton, Ontario, where her after cabins and machinery were removed. She was then towed by the tug SHANNON to Windsor, Ontario, where the remainder of her stern was removed and a towing notch partially built. Her forward cabins were taken off and placed ashore at Windsor. She was towed to Port Arthur Shipbuilding at Thunder Bay, Ontario, where the notch was completed.

In 1979, LIQUILASSIE was again in service, this time as a tank barge with a new length of 306 feet and a gross tonnage of 3,358. During the winter of 1980-81, LIQUILASSIE again departed the Great Lakes, this time under tow of the tug TUSKER, bound for the Gulf of Mexico. On the 6th of February, 1981, LIQUILASSIE hit the Gandy Bridge at Tampa, Florida, closing it for three months. After much litigation, on January 27, 1983, LIQUILASSIE was sold Panamanian and headed for the South Pacific. During the spring of 1987, the vessel's tanks were cleaned and she was sunk as an artificial reef at Tonga. Thus ended her 44 years of service, the longest of any of the seven sistership tankers.

a) Temblador, b) LIQUILASSIE

BUILT:	1943 Barnes-Duluth Shipbuilding Co. Duluth, Minnesota
HULL NUMBER:	15
LENGTH:	355.0
BREADTH:	60.0
DEPTH:	17.6
GRT:	3401
REGISTRY NUMBER:	Panamanian
2 ENGINES:	16", 26", 43" Diameter x 27" Stroke Triple Expansion
ENGINE BUILDER:	Vulcan Iron Works, Duluth 1943

TEMBLADOR at Iroquois August 21, 1960

LIQUILASSIE downbound in the St. Clair River at Port Huron August 30, 1961

LIQUILASSIE in the Toronto Ship Channel June 6, 1979

LUBROLAKE

MERCURY (1) was built by the Pennsylvania Shipyard of Beaumont, Texas, and was launched in June, 1937, for Tankers, Inc. She was later part of the fleet of Cleveland Tankers, Inc. before moving to Lakeland Tankers Ltd., its Canadian subsidiary, in 1947.

The Armistice Day storm of November, 1940 ranks among the most severe in Great Lakes history. Many believed that this ship had been a casualty, for MERCURY was severely mauled by the rough weather on Lake Michigan and had to seek shelter behind North Manitou Island. When she was late reporting, the worst was feared. Great relief was experienced when it was found that the tanker had survived.

After reconstruction at the Port Weller Drydock, in 1947, this vessel resumed trading as b) LUBROLAKE. Her Canadian registry number was C. 178932. Her new GRT was 1,645. Although LUBROLAKE traveled throughout the Great Lakes system, she spent most of her time on the Lake Ontario-St. Lawrence section in the petroleum trade. She usually loaded at Montreal, occasionally at Toronto, for ports such as Oshawa, Cobourg, Kingston, Prescott, Morrisburg, Trois-Rivieres, Quebec City and Chicoutimi. She operated to the end of the 1966 season and then was retired at Toronto.

LUBROLAKE was sold to United Metals Ltd. for scrap in 1967, but was resold to K.C. Irving Enterprises. She was towed through the Iroquois Lock en route east on September 18, 1967, by the tugs ARGUE MARTIN and STORMONT.

The ship's forward cabins were removed, likely at Montreal, and she was towed to Saint John, New Brunswick, for use as an auxiliary tanker for the fishing fleet. As she was being moved under tow for east coast service, she went aground. The tug IRVING BEECH lost her off Cape Breton Island and LUBROLAKE came ashore near New Waterford, Nova Scotia, on December 2, 1967. There she was abandoned.

a) Mercury (1), b) LUBROLAKE

BUILT:	1937 Pennsylvania Shipyard Beaumont, Texas
HULL NUMBER:	116
LENGTH:	250.8
BREADTH:	43.0
DEPTH:	16.3
GRT:	1518
REGISTRY NUMBER:	US. 236327
ENGINES:	14" Diameter x 16" Stroke 6 cylinder diesel
ENGINE BUILDER:	Winton Engine Co., Cleveland 1937

MERCURY downbound in the Detroit River under the Ambassador Bridge

MERCURY upbound in the Detroit River

LUBROLAKE downbound in the St. Clair River opposite Sarnia June 9, 1961

LUBROLAKE in tow of the tug ARGUE MARTIN at Iroquois September 17, 1967

LUBROLAKE aground at Cape Breton December, 1967

LYCOMING

On August 14th, 1880, the shipyard of F.W. Wheeler at West Bay City, Michigan, launched the wooden package freighter LYCOMING for the Erie & Western Transportation Company's Anchor Line. She was placed in the package freight trade, sailing between various Great Lakes ports. The steamer performed her duties for approximately twenty-five years, until her age and the advent of more modern package freighters rendered her obsolete in the package freight trade.

In 1906, LYCOMING was sold to James O'Connor of Tonawanda, New York, and was converted for use in the coarse freight trade by the Buffalo Dry Dock Company, of Buffalo, New York. Her upper works were cut down to the main deck, leaving her distinctive arches exposed, thus giving the vessel a new profile.

On October 22nd, 1910, the steamer met her end when she was caught in a storm on Lake Erie and, while trying to reach the safety of the harbor at Rondeau, Ontario, struck the west pier of the entrance, caught fire and burned. The steamer became a total loss in the accident.

BUILT:	1880 F.W. Wheeler & Co. West Bay City, Michigan
HULL NUMBER:	7
LENGTH:	251.0
BREADTH:	36.0
DEPTH:	15.3
GRT:	1609
REGISTRY NUMBER:	US. 140416
ENGINES:	26", 54" Diameter x 36" Stroke Steeple Compound
ENGINE BUILDER:	H.G. Trout, Buffalo, New York 1880

LYCOMING leaving the docks at the Soo

LYCOMING downbound at Mission Point, St. Marys River in 1909

MADEIRA

The steel barge MADEIRA was launched on January 24, 1900, by the Chicago Shipbuilding Company, of Chicago, Illinois, for the Minnesota Steamship Company for the iron ore trade. In 1901, she and the rest of the Minnesota fleet were absorbed by U.S. Steel's Pittsburgh Steamship Company.

In tow of the steamer WILLIAM EDENBORN, the MADEIRA suffered the fate of many other vessels in the November 28, 1905 storm that struck Lake Superior. Inbound to Duluth, Minnesota, the two vessels were weathering the blow when, at 3:00 am, the tow line broke. Both vessels were now on their own in the boiling seas and the blinding wind-driven snow. The EDENBORN was driven ashore at the mouth of the Split Rock River, 45 miles northeast of Duluth, and broke in two. The crew managed to get ashore.

The MADEIRA's fate was far more horrendous. About 5:30 a.m., she suddenly smashed broadside on a huge cliff that towered above her. The crewmen were horrified to discover that the ship was disintegrating before their very eyes. One crewman was able to reach the top of the cliff and drop a line to enable three others to scramble up the face of the cliff from the sinking bow. He tossed down the weighted line again and drew up a stronger hawser. Five more men climbed to safety. Unfortunately one man fell overboard and was drowned.

The remaining crewmen managed to find a logging camp. Through their tales of woe, the residents realized that the vessel had grounded and broken up at the base of Gold Rock, just northeast of Split Rock Lighthouse. Two days later, frostbitten and suffering severely from exposure, they were picked up at Split Rock, Minnesota.

Even though in 1974, wrecking crews removed most of the wreck because of high scrap prices, pieces of the badly battered barge still litter the bottom where she sank, and the site is now a favorite scuba divers' rendezvous.

MADEIRA being assisted by the tug M.F. MERICK in the St. Marys River

BUILT:	1900 Chicago Shipbuilding Co. Chicago, Illinois
HULL NUMBER:	38
LENGTH:	436.0
BREADTH:	50.2
DEPTH:	24.2
GRT:	5039
REGISTRY NUMBER:	US. 93020

MADEIRA at the ore dock at Lorain

MAITLAND NO. 1

The pulpwood barge MAITLAND NO. 1, of the Roen Steamship Company, Sturgeon Bay, Wisconsin, had its beginnings as a Lake Erie carferry. Built in 1916 by the Great Lakes Engineering Works, Ecorse, Michigan, at a cost of $350,000, she was owned by the newly formed Toronto, Hamilton & Buffalo Navigation Company, of Ashtabula, Ohio, an affiliate of New York Central and Canadian Pacific Railways. The ferry, with a four track 30 car capacity, operated on the 90 mile run from the NYC slip in Ashtabula to newly built landing facilities at Port Maitland, Ontario, with cargoes of Pennsylvania coal for the Steel Company of Canada's mills at Hamilton, Ontario. The ferry did not carry passengers.

MAITLAND NO. 1 had a relatively short career as a carferry, because by 1928, the source of much of the coal for Hamilton had become the Appalachian field, and that coal moved through Sodus Point, New York, on Lake Ontario. Further reduction in Lake Erie traffic occurred during the Depression, and the opening of the new Welland Ship Canal in 1932, resulted in larger freighters usurping the trade. Thus, TH&B had to suspend service in June, 1932, and laid MAITLAND NO. 1 up at Ashtabula after 16 years of work.

The ferry was kept in serviceable condition and, late in 1935, she was leased to the Nicholson Universal Steamship Company to carry new automobiles between Milwaukee and Muskegon on Lake Michigan. However, competitors brought to light the Canadian part-ownership of MAITLAND NO. 1 and, after 16 months, this U.S. port-to-U.S. port service was stopped and she was returned to lay-up at Ashtabula in 1937.

In 1942, the U.S. War Shipping Administration requisitioned the ship to recover her two triple expansion steam engines which were removed and placed in the newly rebuilt steamers LAKE PLEASANT and LAKE SAPOR. The hull was sold to the Roen Steamship Company in November, 1942.

Roen reduced the ferry to a flat-deck pulpwood barge at Sturgeon Bay and the next spring towed her to Copper Harbor, Michigan, at the tip of the Keweenaw Peninsula, where Roen's barge TRANSPORT had grounded as a total loss in a storm the previous fall. The TRANSPORT's 25 ton diesel, Monighan crane was skidded onto MAITLAND's deck and other equipment was transferred, including a large diesel engine and generator.

The next year 1944, MAITLAND played a key role in the greatest salvage achievement on the Great Lakes, the recovery of the 580 foot Kinsman steamer GEORGE M. HUMPHREY (1) from the Straits of Mackinac where she had sunk on June 15, 1943, in 80 feet of water after a collision with the D.M. CLEMSON (2). The HUMPHREY was carrying 13,992 tons of iron ore. The story of this salvage, which projected Cap Roen to international fame, is well known, and MAITLAND NO. 1's role was unique in salvage annals.

Much work was done to bring the ship to near floatable condition, including clamming out most of her ore cargo. Then 50 sheaves were affixed to the gunwale bar on each side of the HUMPHREY's deck, with a like number of sheaves placed on each side of the barge MAITLAND. Four cables were reeved through these blocks and attached to steam winches on the barge. MAITLAND, floated into position over the sunken ore carrier, was then ballasted to her usual load line, the cables were pulled tight and the water was then pumped out of the barge. The first lift in this operation, on August 1, 1944, was able to lift the HUMPHREY about six to eight feet and the two vessels were then towed by Roen tugs into shallower water.

This operation was repeated until it was impossible to ballast down MAITLAND without striking HUMPHREY's deck. Then two barges, MAITLAND and HILDA, straddled the sunken ship and in a like manner raised her until her decks were awash. In this way, HUMPHREY was moved a mile and a half into shallow water. Pumps were then placed on board, the hole in the ship patched with canvas, and, when she was dry, the salvage was completed by September 11, 1944.

Repair work on the HUMPHREY was done at Sturgeon Bay and Manitowoc and she was back in service as b) CAPTAIN JOHN ROEN in the spring of 1945. The ship was later sold to the American Steamship Company for whom she operated for years as ADAM E. CORNELIUS (2) and finally CONSUMERS POWER (2).

MAITLAND NO. 1 also carried sizable lumber cargoes loaded at Blind River, Ontario, on the North Channel of Lake Huron, for delivery to Tonawanda, New York. Her record lumber cargo was one of 2,223,000 board feet, stacked 35 feet high on deck, that took two days to load and 36 hours to unload.

The versatile barge was also involved in a number of salvage jobs for the Roen Salvage Company, where she was used as a lighter to off-load cargo from stranded ships so Roen tugs could free them. Included among MAITLAND's salvage jobs was the lightering of grain from the Midland Steamship Company's ANGELINE in the Soo River, and from ALEXANDER T. WOOD in the Detroit River, iron ore from Interlake's E.G. GRACE in the St. Marys River, and from the salty FREIDA aground on the Poe Reef in the Straits. When the ocean-going ship FRANCISCO MORAZAN stranded on South Manitou Island in Lake Michigan in 1960, it was MAITLAND NO. 1 that was called upon to remove her general cargo, although the ship could not be saved.

Following the death of Captain John Roen on December 7, 1970, the unique operations of the Roen Companies were pared down and, in late 1971, the stockholders, who were heirs of John Roen, decided to sell off the equipment as buyers could be found. MAITLAND NO. 1 was sold to Eder Barge & Towing, Inc., of Milwaukee, in November, 1973 for $155,000. In 1978, Eder sold her to Bultema Marine Transportation Company, which soon merged with Canonie companies of Muskegon, Michigan.

In December, 1980, MAITLAND NO. 1 was loaded with scrap iron at Holland, Michigan, for her farewell trip from the Lakes, and she departed in tow of the tug JOHN

ROEN V, bound for a Mexican port. At Quebec, she was given Honduran registry and a new name b) TRIO TRADO by her new owners Trio Shipping Group, but it is questionable whether that name was ever painted on the barge. Her crew was taken off at Quebec and she continued as a "dead ship" tow from Quebec to the Straits of Canso, but was icing up badly in the Gulf of St. Lawrence. The tug, which had been renamed c) TRIO BRAVO, was considered too light for the tow and was replaced by a heavier salt-water tug which continued the tow southward from the Gulf of Canso. Between Yarmouth, Nova Scotia, and Rockland, Maine, the barge, heavy with ice and listing badly, capsized on January 10, 1981. The big tug attempted to tow her upside down, but the barge ultimately sank in deep water. The tug, TRIO BRAVO, sailed on to Port Everglades, Florida, where she later sank at the dock. She was raised and then was sunk intentionally as a fishing reef off Fort Lauderdale in 1982.

a) MAITLAND NO. 1, b) Trio Trado

BUILT: 1916 Great Lakes Engineering Works Ecorse, Michigan
HULL NUMBER: 129
LENGTH: 338.0
BREADTH: 56.0
DEPTH: 18.3
GRT: 2757
REGISTRY NUMBER: US. 214213
2 ENGINES: 19 1/2", 31", 52" Diameter x 36" Stroke Triple Expansion
ENGINE BUILDER: Shipyard 1916

MAITLAND NO. 1 in dry dock at Buffalo, January 2, 1920

MAITLAND NO. 1 helping raise the GEORGE M. HUMPHREY in the Straits of Mackinac, 1944

MAITLAND NO. 1 loading pulpwood in Grand Marais, Minnesota harbor in 1953

MAITLAND NO. 1 downbound at Mission Point, St. Marys River, August 21, 1957

MAITLAND NO. 1 unloading a cargo of grinding balls at the Superior, Wisconsin Shipyard in 1956

JESSIE MARTIN

The trim, two-masted schooner JESSIE MARTIN was built in 1881 at Muskegon, Michigan, by Henry J. Footlander for the Muskegon businessman William Martin. The schooner was typical of the many small vessels that were built around the Great Lakes for carrying cargo between various ports and landings, especially those that the larger craft could not reach.

On November 23, 1882, the MARTIN came to grief when she was overtaken by a gale blowing out of the northwest. The schooner had taken onboard a cargo of flour and oats at Milwaukee, Wisconsin, and was bound for Muskegon under the command of the first mate William Welcher. When the vessel's course became impossible to hold, the mate had the sail shortened and ran for safety of the harbor at Grand Haven, Michigan.

As the schooner approached the pierheads, she was swept too far to leeward and struck the south pier. The keeper of the Grand Haven Life Saving Station saw what was about to happen. His crew launched their surfboat and raced for the pier entrance, arriving just in time to catch a line thrown to them from the stricken vessel. They were able to hold the schooner to the pier just long enough for the mate and his two crewmen to jump onto the pier. The line then parted and the vessel was driven ashore.

Several days later, the wreck was inspected and was found not to be severely damaged, however, the hull had been holed in two places when she struck the pier.

The owner contacted John Dibble, a salvager from Muskegon, to release the schooner off the beach and into the harbor where she could be repaired. Dibble plugged the holes with gunny sacks held in place with wooden braces fastened to the deck beams. He then salvaged as much of the cargo as possible and pumped the vessel free of water.

By November 30th, preparations had been completed to refloat the beached schooner. The tug WEBSTER BATCHELLER was made fast to the JESSIE MARTIN by a seven hundred foot towline. A southwest gale was blowing at thirty miles per hour and the lake was running in great waves, throwing showers of spray onto the schooner, coating her hull, spars and rigging with ice. At ten in the morning, the tug cast off her lines and steamed out into the stormy Lake Michigan. As the towline became taut, the schooner came off the beach with a plunge.

Because she lay in shallow waters, the breakers raked over the vessel constantly. Each time that she pitched, she would strike the bottom hard. The crew had to hold onto anything that was solid in order to keep from being thrown overboard or dashed against deck fittings and severely injured. Unknown to the crew, the gunny sack packing jarred loose, allowing the water to rush into the hull.

As the tug began to turn around and tow the MARTIN in between the piers, the schooner began to follow the same arc. However, without buoyancy, she simply dragged around and rolled over like a log, settling on her starboard side. The crew were able to reach the rigging, but Dibble, who had been walking on the starboard side of the cabin when she rolled over, became trapped and drowned.

The tug, meanwhile, was signaling for help with her whistle. The lifesaving crew, upon hearing the signal, immediately launched their surfboat and rowed towards the wreck. After a wild and terrifying trip though the raging waters, they arrived at the site with great difficulty and removed the survivors to safety. After the storm subsided, the lifesavers returned to the wreck and recovered Dibble's body.

The JESSIE MARTIN was then towed to the Mechanics Dry Dock at Grand Haven, where she was pumped out, repaired and returned to service. She lasted another 25 years, during which time she was a frequent recipient of aid from the U.S. Life Saving Service.

The schooner's ownership changed several times in her career. In 1886, she was shown as being owned by A. Cochrane, of Muskegon. Then, in 1889, Avery of Muskegon was listed as her owner. The vessel was sold to John Hausen, of Chicago, in 1891 and then was sold for the last time, around 1897, to C.D. Christenson, of Muskegon.

The JESSIE MARTIN's career came to an end on August 20th, 1908 off Big Point Sable. She was bound for Manitowoc from Ludington, Michigan, with a cargo of lumber when she was caught by a storm. A distress signal was spotted by the lookout at the Ludington Life Saving Station and the crew responded quickly. Soon after leaving, they met the MARTIN's crew coming ashore in the schooner's yawl. The next morning, the 21st, the schooner was discovered stranded and broken up on the beach off Big Point Sable. The vessel was a total loss and had a value of $1,500, while the cargo was valued at $800. Only the sails and spars were salvageable.

BUILT:	1881 Henry J. Footlander Muskegon, Michigan
HULL NUMBER:	none
LENGTH:	68.0
BREADTH:	17.0
DEPTH:	5.7
GRT:	42
REGISTRYNUMBER:	US. 76212

JESSIE MARTIN at a dock on Lake Michigan

JESSIE MARTIN leaving the harbor

MASSENA

In 1878, the Buffalo shipyard of G.H. Notter was the launch site of the small wooden-hulled combination steamer MASSENA. She had been built for a group of local men, Guy Bridges and Captain James Fox of Massena, and Omar Hines of Watertown, who operated the vessel through their Massena Steamboat Company.

MASSENA's white hull and white superstructure remained so during her early years, as her steam engine and four bladed propeller moved her easily though the St. Lawrence and its tributaries. By 1882, Captain Fox had become sole owner, and he sailed her on her local routes. Normally, MASSENA carried freight and passengers between Dundee, Quebec on the east, and Ogdensburg on the west, making at least two trips per week during the shipping season. Intermediate stops were made at Massena Point, International Park, Tracey's Landing, Cornwall, Dickinson Landing, Louisville Landing and Waddington. MASSENA was especially sought after in the fall, when area apple growers pushed her 40 ton capacity to its limit.

By 1888, Captain Fox found MASSENA's small size restricting. Therefore he disposed of her to Captain Frank Dana, who employed her on the Ogdensburg - Alexandria Bay run, where she again proved very popular. So much so, that he had her lengthened by almost twenty feet in 1894; 94.4 x 18.0 x 5.5 feet; 89 gross tons. Meanwhile, Captain Fox purchased the 95 foot ALGONA, to carry even more passengers between Ogdensburg and Massena's healing springs.

In April, 1897, the MASSENA's seams opened while she was buffeted by strong winds west of Ogdensburg. Upbound for Alexandria Bay at the time, Captain Dana steamed hard for Maitland, where the vessel sank in two fathoms off the dock. Raised, she was returned to service within a very few days.

On August 20, 1903, in the early morning hours, the end came. Her crew finished loading a cargo of 120 barrels of slaked lime for the Hackett Hardware Company that evening. A typical summer storm swept down the river and lightning struck the MASSENA starting a huge fire. Cut loose and allowed to drift to save the dock, the locals watched as she fetched up on a bar opposite the dock. There she burned to the waterline in an hour. Captain Dana and his crew had made it to shore safely, but lost their possessions. Only half of MASSENA's $12,000 value was covered by insurance. It is claimed that both engine and boiler were saved and later salvaged.

BUILT:	1878 G.H. Notter Shipyard Buffalo, New York
HULL NUMBER:	none
LENGTH:	76.9
BREADTH:	18.0
DEPTH:	5.5
GRT:	72.73
REGISTRY NUMBER:	US. 91067
ENGINES:	16" Diameter x 16" Stroke High Pressure Non-Condensing
ENGINE BUILDER:	Sutton Bros. Buffalo 1878

MASSENA at Dundee, Quebec c.1885

MAUCH CHUNK

The 404 foot overall length of the steel steamer MAUCH CHUNK and her sistership WILKESBARRE earned contemporary honors as "the largest package freighters on the Great Lakes". Both vessels were built at Buffalo, New York by the Buffalo Dry Dock Company for the Lehigh Valley Transit Company. MAUCH CHUNK was launched on April 24, 1901.

MAUCH CHUNK and WILKESBARRE were extensive improvements in size and capacity over the Lehigh Valley package freighters of the 1890's. Both ships passed into the fleet of the Great Lakes Transit Corporation in 1919 and, at that time, the MAUCH CHUNK was renamed b) W.J. CONNERS.

IN 1942, W.J. CONNERS was one of several Great Lakes Transit package freighters requisitioned by the U.S. Government for war duty. They left the lakes via the Illinois Waterway and the Mississippi River. Greatly rebuilt from her laker configuration, the W.J. CONNERS served as a Navy transport in the South Pacific theatre. Owned by the U.S. Maritime Commission, she was renamed c)MALACCA STRAITS in 1942, but became d) W.J. CONNERS again in 1943.

In 1947, the steamer was sold as war surplus, her purchaser being the Overlakes Freight Corporation, but she was not returned to the lakes. Instead, she was sold to Haerunger H/F in 1948. Under the name e) HAERUNGER, she continued to operate until sold for scrapping in Europe in 1957.

MAUCH CHUNK upbound in the St. Clair River opposite Marine City

a) MAUCH CHUNK, b) W.J. Conners,
c) Malacca Straits, d) W.J. Conners, e) Haerunger

BUILT:	1901 Buffalo Dry Dock Co. Buffalo, New York
HULL NUMBER:	98
LENGTH:	390.0
BREADTH:	50.5
DEPTH:	26.6
GRT:	4499
REGISTRY NUMBER:	US. 93133
ENGINES:	20", 30", 43", 63" Diameter x 42" Stroke Quadruple Expansion
ENGINE BUILDER:	Detroit Shipbuilding Co., Detroit 1901

MAUCH CHUNK in the ice in Whitefish Bay, Lake Superior in 1911

W.J. CONNERS upbound at Mission Point, St. Marys River in 1921

W.J. CONNERS upbound in the Detroit River, July 28, 1940

W.J. CONNERS in the Atlantic, March 9, 1944

W.J. CONNERS assisted by a tug entering port

MAYFLOWER and PRIMROSE

The steel-hulled, double-ended, sidewheel ferry steamers MAYFLOWER and PRIMROSE were the first vessels built to the order of the Toronto Ferry Company Ltd., upon the incorporation of that firm. They were constructed by the Doty Engine Company at Toronto. MAYFLOWER was launched on May 24, 1890, and christened by Miss Jennie Doty, while PRIMROSE followed into the waters of Toronto Bay on June 28, 1890, sponsored by Miss Mary Williams.

They were built as exact sisterships and were known by many as the "Flowers of the Bay" (even though a number of the Toronto Ferry Company's steamers were named for flowers), and it is fitting that these two vessels are recalled together.

As built, they had elaborately decorated paddleboxes, many panels of stained glass in the main cabins, and handsome, octagonal (or "birdcage") pilothouses on the hurricane deck. They were the first ferries on the bay to boast electric lighting. Although the steamers were double-ended, they originally were loaded through the side gangways. End-loading was commenced later and, from 1906 until 1918, they used upper gangways for loading and unloading via the promenade deck as well as the main.

MAYFLOWER and PRIMROSE were built for the service to Hanlan's Point on the Toronto Islands, where the Toronto Ferry Company maintained a large amusement park. After commissioning the larger BLUEBELL in 1906 and TRILLIUM in 1910, MAYFLOWER and PRIMROSE were used on both the Hanlan's Point and Centre Island routes as traffic demanded.

They operated without major accidents, although on August 13, 1916, PRIMROSE collided with the steamer TURBINIA off the Bay Street Terminal. The masters of both ships were held at fault. TURBINIA'S skipper lost his license for a year, while the ticket of PRIMROSE's master was permanently revoked.

On the August 4, 1924 Civic Holiday, MAYFLOWER and PRIMROSE collided while ferrying holiday crowds back to the city from Centre Island during an evening fog. PRIMROSE was disabled due to damage to her paddlebox, so her sistership took off her passengers and took them to the mainland and then returned to tow the damaged PRIMROSE back to the dock.

About 1925, both MAYFLOWER and PRIMROSE were rebuilt with rather plain, square-ish pilothouses, containing officers' quarters as well as the navigation area. At the same time, the main cabin was rebuilt with window panes of clear glass, and squared paddleboxes replaced the original ornate housings.

Late in 1926, the ferry fleet was purchased by the City of Toronto, which, in 1927, transferred their operation to the Toronto Transportation Commission, the operator of the city's street railways. The T.T.C. refurbished the fleet and upgraded the service provided to the excursionists and Island residents alike.

With their condition greatly deteriorated, and a new diesel ferry SAM McBRIDE expected in service in 1939, MAYFLOWER and PRIMROSE made their last revenue trips on August 30, 1938. Their retirement was much lamented in the local press. Late that year, they were sold to the Russell Construction Company Ltd., of Toronto, and during the following winter they were cut down to barges at Russell's docks in the Keating Channel at Toronto.

MAYFLOWER was renamed b) R.C.C. 26, while PRIMROSE became b) R.C.C. 25, and they were remeasured to dimensions: 132.6 x 28.2 x 6.8 feet; 175 net tons. It was not, however, until 1946 that these changes were reflected in the Canadian shipping register. The two barges, although unusual with their narrow hulls and pointed ends, were used in various construction trades around Lake Ontario until they were scrapped in the mid-1950s.

a) MAYFLOWER, b) R.C.C. 26
a) PRIMROSE, b) R.C.C. 25

BUILT:	1890 Doty Engine Co. Toronto, Ontario
HULL NUMBER:	none
LENGTH:	140.2
BREADTH:	28.2
DEPTH:	6.8
GRT:	189
REGISTRY NUMBER:	MAYFLOWER, C. 94987 PRIMROSE, C. 94990
ENGINES:	25", 25" Diameter x 40" Stroke Diagonal Direct-Acting
ENGINE BUILDER:	Doty Engine Co., Toronto, 1890

MAYFLOWER leaving the islands in Toronto Harbour

PRIMROSE in the early 1890's

PRIMROSE leaving Toronto for the islands

PRIMROSE approaching the City Ferry Docks, June 1, 1927

MELBOURNE

The wooden-hulled, passenger and freight propellor ALMA MUNRO was built in 1873 at Port Dalhousie, Ontario, by Andrews & Son at a cost of $30,000. She was constructed for the Elgin Transportation Company, of Port Stanley, Ontario, which was affiliated with the Dominion Transportation Company, of St. Thomas, Ontario, the North Shore Transportation Company, of Port Stanley, and the London and Port Stanley Railway. The manager of Elgin Transportation was Captain Alex Pollock, who was the first registered owner of the steamer.

ALMA MUNRO first saw service operating in conjunction with the Allan Ocean Steamship Company, of Montreal. Later she joined the fleet of the Merchants Line (a consortium of vessel owners) which operated her between Montreal and various lake ports.

In 1885, ALMA MUNRO was given a substantial rebuild at Kingston, Ontario, by William Power & Company, at which time she was rebuilt to 176.0 x 26.0 x 11.6 feet, which increased her gross tonnage to 895. At this time a Canadian number was assigned - C. 94715. By 1892, she was owned by Graham & Company, St. Catharines, Ontario.

In 1893, the steamer was given a further rebuild at the Cantin Shipyard at Montreal, although there was no change in her dimensions or tonnage. However, the Cantin yard rebuilt her engine, adding an 18 inch diameter cylinder to the existing 36 inch cylinder and thus converting it to a steeple compound type. At this same time, she was transferred to the Melbourne Steamship Company as b) MELBOURNE, which continued to operate in the Merchants Line under the management of G.E. Jaques & Company, Montreal.

MELBOURNE was severely damaged in a fire which occurred while she was moored in the Murray Canal, at the entrance to the Bay of Quinte on Lake Ontario, on September 19, 1905.

After some considerable time, the burned-out hull was towed to Kingston, Ontario, where in 1909 the Davis Dry Dock Company rebuilt the steamer as a single-deck ferry. As constructed, she was 170.4 x 25.6 x 5.6 feet; 225 gross tons, and she was given a new single-cylinder engine, 14 inches in diameter by 18 inches of stroke, which the Davis shipyard built.

In 1910, the steamer was rechristened c) JOHN R. at which time she was given a new registry number, C. 126461. In that year, her owner was the Hamilton Ferry Company, of Hamilton, Ontario, and it is assumed that the vessel saw some service on Hamilton Bay, although no details are available.

Although JOHN R. was still listed in the 1915 Lloyds Register, she was reported as broken up in 1914. However, some sources have indicated that she was reduced to a barge for use during the building of the waterworks intake off Burlington Beach in Lake Ontario, thereafter being discarded in that vicinity.

ALMA MUNRO at her dock

a) Alma Munro, b) MELBOURNE, c) John R.

BUILT:	1873 Andrews & Son Port Dalhousie, Ontario
HULL NUMBER:	none
LENGTH:	136.0
BREADTH:	23.4
DEPTH:	7.5
GRT:	439
REGISTRY NUMBER:	none assigned when built.
ENGINES:	36" Diameter x 30" Stroke Single Cylinder
ENGINE BUILDER:	G.N. Oille, St. Catharines, Ontario 1873

At center in 1900 is MELBOURNE in Toronto behind CAMBRIA. L. to R. are GARDEN CITY, WHITE STAR, OCEAN, CHIPPEWA, TORONTO and an unidentified canaller

MENIHEK LAKE

On a cold January 14, 1959, Collingwood Shipyards Limited launched the steamer MENIHEK LAKE. Her owners were Carryore Limited, a Canadian subsidiary of M.A. Hanna Company of Cleveland, Ohio. She was built to carry iron ore up the St. Lawrence Seaway and was named for a lake in the mining area of Quebec-Labrador upon which the Iron Ore Company of Canada had built a hydro-electric power plant. Hanna was its largest single shareholder.

Lakes' sailors have a habit of assigning nicknames to vessels. Even though her safety record was good, MENIHEK LAKE was sometimes informally known as "maniac lake," apparently only because of a play on words. She did, however, suffer at least one major accident. On October 26, 1977, she struck a lock wall in the St. Lawrence Seaway and sustained $400,000 in damages.

When the recession of the mid-1980s hit the lakes, MENIHEK LAKE, although in excellent condition, had three strikes against her: she was a steamer, she was not of full Seaway dimensions and she was not a self-unloader. She operated briefly in 1984 and then laid up at Hamilton, Ontario. In mid-1985, she was sold to Corostel Trading Ltd., scrap metal brokers. On August 15, she cleared Hamilton under her own power but with a plain black stack, bound for Quebec City. On August 30, along with LEON FALK, JR., she cleared Quebec in tow of the big Canadian tug CAPT. IOANNIS S. The tow arrived off Vigo, Spain on September 25, but local officials would not permit the tug to bring MENIHEK LAKE into port until the following day. After finally making port with MENIHEK LAKE, the tug went back outside, picked up the FALK and delivered her to Gijon, Spain.

The Canadian registry for MENIHEK LAKE was officially closed on October 8, 1985, with the notation "sold Spain". Thus ended the short career of another modern laker.

BUILT:	1959 Collingwood Shipyards Limited, Collingwood, Ontario
HULL NUMBER:	163
LENGTH:	697.4
BREADTH:	75.2
DEPTH:	34.3
GRT:	17023
REGISTRY NUMBER:	C. 188393
ENGINES:	Cross Compound, Double Reduction, Steam Turbine
ENGINE BUILDER:	General Electric Co. 1959

MENIHEK LAKE in the Welland Canal, downbound in 1959

MENIHEK LAKE upbound in the St. Marys River, June 16, 1961

MENIHEK LAKE, CAROL LAKE and LAKE MANITOBA laid up at Hamilton, July 8, 1985

METEOR (1)

METEOR was built by Peck & Masters at Cleveland, Ohio, in 1863 for J.T. Whiting's Pioneer Line of Detroit, Michigan, to run between Cleveland, Detroit and Lake Superior ports. She was a double-decked wooden passenger propellor, and ordinarily carried merchandise upbound and copper and flour down.

On the night of August 9, 1865, METEOR met her running mate, the propellor PEWABIC, off Thunder Bay on Lake Huron around 9:00 p.m. As the two approached, somehow METEOR sheered and struck her sister, sinking the PEWABIC within minutes in 180 feet of water. About one hundred twenty-five people went down with her, and 86 others were saved. METEOR continued on to the Soo in spite of hull damage, and two days later a fire broke out because water leaked into her lime cargo. The ship was scuttled in 30 feet of water to prevent its destruction by fire. It was pumped out a few days later and repaired.

In 1872, METEOR began running in the Union Steamboat Company's Buffalo and Lake Superior Line. Her service was ended abruptly when she burned at Detroit on June 8, 1873, taking two grain elevators with her in the conflagration. The wreck was removed to Belle Isle in 1875 and scuttled. In 1878, what remained of it was taken to the Rouge River boneyard, where the machinery was removed. One engine went into a tug, and the other into the steambarge H. LOUELLA WORTHINGTON.

In the fall of 1881, the METEOR's hulk was bought by J.P. Harrow of Algonac, Michigan, and rebuilt at the Abram Smith shipyard as a three-masted towbarge. Her new dimensions were: 197.7 x 31.2 x 11.3 feet; 549 GRT. She was renamed b) NELSON BLOOM. During the 1880s and 1890s, she was towed by various steamers, but most often by SIBERIA in the 1880s, and ARGO in the 1890s, and after 1900, by the M.T. GREENE. She was wrecked at Algoma Mills, Ontario, on November 14, 1903, but survived to go back into service again. In 1914, she belonged to H.N. Jex of Toledo, Ohio, and in 1919 to Charles W. Harrah, of Detroit. The NELSON BLOOM was reported abandoned in 1925, supposedly at Grayhaven on the upper Detroit River.

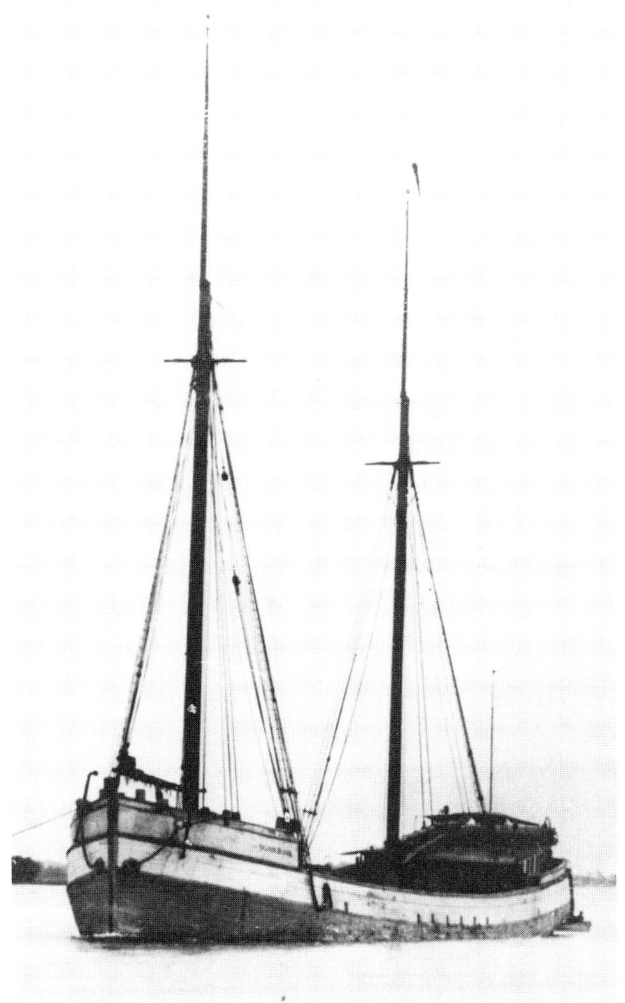

NELSON BLOOM under tow in the St. Clair River

a) METEOR (1), b) Nelson Bloom

BUILT:	1863 Peck & Masters Cleveland, Ohio
HULL NUMBER:	none
LENGTH:	198.5
BREADTH:	30.6
DEPTH:	13.0
GRT:	956.07
REGISTRY NUMBER:	US. 17570
2 ENGINES:	26 1/2" Diameter x 30" Stroke Vertical High Pressure
ENGINE BUILDER:	Cuyahoga Steam Furnace Company, Cleveland, 1863

METEOR at the dock in Munising

METEOR at her dock in Duluth

MIDLAND CITY

The small, sidewheel, passenger steamer MAUD was built on the Clyde at Glasgow, Scotland, in 1870 for Charles F. Gildersleeve, of Kingston, Ontario. The hull was knocked down, shipped across the Atlantic, and assembled in 1871 by George Thurston at the Davis Shipyard at Kingston. The steamer was launched on August 16, 1871, and was christened by Miss Maud Gildersleeve, for whom she was named.

MAUD operated for Gildersleeve on a route from Kingston to ports of the Bay of Quinte, but her speed proved to be unsatisfactory, and in 1872 MAUD was sold to the Folger Brothers for their St. Lawrence Navigation Company. This concern placed MAUD on a route between Kingston and Cape Vincent, New York.

On May 20, 1884, MAUD took part in the funeral of the famous Dileno Dexter Calvin, of Garden Island. Calvin had lived at Clayton, New York, before moving to Garden Island in 1835. MAUD was chosen to carry D.D. Calvin home, and one of the pallbearers who rode the steamer that day was the Rt. Hon. Sir John Alexander Macdonald, Prime Minister of Canada.

During the winter of 1894-1895, MAUD was rebuilt at the Davis Shipyard, at Kingston, and she emerged as 153.2 x 33.0 x 6.6 feet; 553 GRT, with her iron hull sheathed in wood for protection against impact with rocks in the St. Lawrence River rapids. She was renamed b) AMERICA, and for the first time she was given a Registry number, C. 100662.

The enlarged steamer was returned to service for the Folgers' St. Lawrence River Steamboat Company Ltd., of Kingston, operating between Clayton and Montreal. She received minor alterations at Kingston in 1899 which altered her GRT to 521.

During 1912, the St. Lawrence River Steamboat Company was acquired by the Richelieu and Ontario Navigation Company Ltd., of Montreal, to which AMERICA was transferred. In 1913, the R & O itself was swallowed up in the formation of the Canada Transportation Company Ltd., of Montreal, whose name soon was changed to Canada Steamship Lines Ltd. AMERICA operated for C.S.L. through the 1920 season.

In 1921, the steamer was purchased by the Georgian Bay Tourist Company, of Midland, Ontario, which had her refurbished by the Midland Shipbuilding Company Ltd., and renamed her c) MIDLAND CITY. Under the management of Newton K. Wagg, she ran a regular service between Parry Sound and Midland, calling at various hotels and cottage communities en route. On October 27, 1923, she sank at her winter berth at Midland when waves entered via her engine room portholes while her crew was working on her machinery, but she soon was raised by the Burke Towing and Salvage Company Ltd.

Over the winter of 1933-1934, MIDLAND CITY's steam power plant and sidewheels were removed at the Midland shipyard. She was fitted with twin propellers which were powered by two Canadian built Fairbanks-Morse Company diesel engines. Apart from the repowering, the vessel was not altered greatly, but her gross tonnage was increased to 580.

On August 26, 1934, while on a Sunday sightseeing cruise, MIDLAND CITY damaged her bottom on a shoal near Present Island. She was taking water and her crew beached her on a sand bar off Sucker Creek Point, five miles north of Midland. She settled with her stern under water and her bow high in the air, but the passengers were able to walk to shore in the shallow water, and eventually they were returned to Midland by motor launches. The Burke Towing and Salvage Company again was summoned and they refloated MIDLAND CITY on September 6, 1934. She was repaired over the following winter.

In 1949, the ownership of MIDLAND CITY was transferred to the Georgian Bay Tourist and Steamships Ltd., which continued to operate her through the 1953 season. She lay idle in 1954 because she could not be altered to comply with stringent new fire regulations, and her ownership was transferred that year to Murray N. Wagg.

In 1955, MIDLAND CITY was stripped of her machinery and fittings, and was towed out into the bay off Tiffin, just outside Midland Harbour. There she was intentionally burned, after which her hull was towed to an inlet just above the mouth of the Wye River where it was abandoned. The old iron hull lies there still, in some twelve feet of water.

a) Maud, b) America, c) MIDLAND CITY

BUILT:	1870 Glasgow, Scotland Assembled by Davis Shipyard at Kingston, Ontario in 1871
HULL NUMBER:	none
LENGTH:	114.0
BREADTH:	19.0
DEPTH:	6.0
GRT:	293
REGISTRY NUMBER:	none
2 ENGINES:	20", 36" Diameter x 36" Stroke Inclined Tandem Compound
ENGINE BUILDER:	Canadian Engine & Locomotive Co., Kingston 1870

AMERICA in the Thousand Islands

MIDLAND CITY sunk on August 26, 1934

MIDLAND CITY in Georgian Bay

MIDLAND CITY leaving Midland Harbour, August 16, 1949

MOTOR I

The steel motor vessel MOTOR I was built for K. Salveson of Oslo, Norway by the Manitowoc Shipbuilding Company in 1917. Because of the heavy burden of ship construction in European yards during World War I, a few Norwegian ship owners turned to Great Lakes yards for tonnage. MOTOR I was one of the vessels for which contracts were let. She was the same basic size as the steam powered ships being built on the lakes for salt water service, but differed mainly by having her diesel powered machinery installed aft instead of midships as were the steamers.

With the United States entry into the war, MOTOR I was requisitioned by the United States Shipping Board with other ships under construction for a foreign account. After being requisitioned, her name was changed to b) LAKE MOHONK (US. 215702) to conform with the naming policy of having "LAKE" prefix names applied to lake-built vessels.

In 1920, her name was changed to c) ASTMAHCO III to operate as the third unit in the fleet of the Astoria Mahogany Company fleet by that name; then in 1921, to d) ORMIDALE for the Ormidale Shipping Corporation. By 1933, the ship was owned in Buffalo, New York by the Gravel Motorship Corporation when she was purchased by Captain John Roen and Captain Louis Larson of Marinette, Wisconsin. The plan was to operate her under the name of the Motorship Transit Company, carrying bagged sugar and other broker-arranged cargo from Montreal to Great Lakes ports. This did not work out financially as intended. In the spring of 1934, Captain John Roen bought out Captain Larson's interest in the business; Captain Larson continued as master, however. In March of 1934, Captain Roen installed two McMyler cranes on the ship to allow handling of riprap stone and gravel just as his steamer FRED W. GREEN was being used.

In July 1937, Captain Roen sold ORMIDALE to the Old Ben Coal Corporation of New York and she left the lakes for the East Coast. She had several ownership and name changes on the coast. Lisardo Garcia renamed her e) JUPITER in 1938 and A. Garcia & Company, of Nicaragua renamed the vessel f) BLUEFIELDS in 1941.

On July 15, 1942, still under Nicaraguan registry, owned by A.C. Garcia, her end came on a voyage from New York to Havana, Cuba, when she was torpedoed by the German submarine U-576 in position N34º 46'- W 75º 22'. Fortunately, only one life was lost on this, her last voyage.

a) MOTOR I, b) Lake Mohonk, c) Astmahco III, d) Ormidale, e) Jupiter, f) Bluefields

BUILT:	1917 Manitowoc Shipbuilding Co. Manitowoc, Wisconsin
HULL NUMBER:	81
LENGTH:	250.5
BREADTH:	43.5
DEPTH:	20.4
GRT:	1667
REGISTRY:	Norwegian
ENGINES:	Twin 6 Cylinder Diesels 16 1/2" Diameter a 24" Stroke
ENGINE BUILDER:	McIntosh & Seymour 1917

MOTOR I after launching

ASTMAHCO III

ORMIDALE downbound in the St. Marys River

NORCO

The small, single deck, deep sea freighter INCA was built in 1915 for the Clyde Line of New York City, a product of the Great Lakes Engineering Work's Ecorse yard. The Clyde Line had been seeking new tonnage for its growing West Indian service, and found the fresh water shipyard's work to its liking. Also launched by GLEW that year for the same owners were YAQUE (b. DORIS, c. TRAJAN) and YUNA. The former returned to the lakes decades later as TRAJAN, and was then lost during the Second World War. YUNA was much shorter lived in that she was lost off the Bahamas in 1919.

Unlike most of the deep sea ships constructed in lakes yards, INCA found her way back. Purchased from Clyde in 1929 by General Transit Company of Cleveland, Ohio, she served her second owners until 1931, when she was disposed of to the Valley Camp Steamship Company. In 1937, INCA was owned by General Paper Mills, and the following year went to Northern Paper Mills Ltd. of Sault Ste. Marie, Ontario who renamed her b) NORCO, (C. 158168). The latter firm was a subsidiary of the American entity, Northern Paper Company of Green Bay, Wisconsin.

While in the service of Northern Paper, NORCO worked the upper lakes with her consort, the barge NORMIL [a) CITY OF ALPENA, '12, b) CITY OF ALPENA II, '22, c) CITY OF SAUGATUCK, '39, d) SAUGATUCK, '41, e) LEONA], which had been built in 1893 as a passenger vessel. By the late Fifties, NORCO had again changed hands, this time to Kelly Shipping Ltd. who registered her at Montreal. In 1963, she went to her final buyers J.M. Chabot, also of Montreal, who registered her in Nassau, Bahamas.

On April 19, 1964, while engaged in trade in the Caribbean, the venerable NORCO went hard aground on Little Corn Island off the east coast of Nicaragua. Yet it was not until mid-1965 that NORCO was declared a constructive total loss and abandoned.

a) Inca, b) NORCO

BUILT:	1915 Great Lakes Engineering Works Ecorse, Michigan
HULL NUMBER:	149
LENGTH:	246.0
BREADTH:	38.4
DEPTH:	15.5
GRT:	1414
REGISTRY NUMBER:	US. 213730
ENGINES:	17", 28 1/2", 48" Diameter x 36" Stroke Triple Expansion
ENGINE BUILDER:	Shipyard 1915

INCA downbound at Mission Point, St. Marys River

NORCO downbound with pulpwood

NORCO at Light 43, Dondero Ship Canal, St. Lawrence Seaway September 14, 1961

NORMAN

NORMAN unloading at a Lake Erie port

NORMAN, an early steel bulk freighter, was the shortest lived of six identical sisterships built for the Menominee Transit Company in 1890. She was launched on August 30, 1890. The others following NORMAN were BRITON, GERMAN, GRECIAN, ROMAN and SAXON. All six were built at Cleveland, Ohio, by the Globe Iron Works.

The Menominee Transit Company was the transportation unit for the Schlesinger interests and the Chapin Mining Company. The M.A. Hanna Company operated the ships for the owners in the Nineties. In 1901, the five remaining sisterships passed into the Pittsburgh Steamship Company.

NORMAN, however, did not make this last move, having been lost in a collision back in 1895. The small Canadian steam barge JACK, loaded with heavy timber, rammed NORMAN on Lake Huron near Middle Island on May 30, 1895. The NORMAN foundered soon after the collision with the loss of three lives.

One of our illustrations is from a drawing of the ship. The colors of the Menominee ships were reported to have been black hulls with a horizontal white ribbon at the main deck level, natural wood colored cabins, brown or dark red, and black stacks carrying a white shield which had the letter "M" centered on it.

BUILT:	1890 Globe Iron Works Cleveland, Ohio
HULL NUMBER:	36
LENGTH:	296.5
BREADTH:	40.4
DEPTH:	21.0
GRT:	2304.48
REGISTRY NUMBER:	US. 130505
ENGINES:	24", 38", 61" Diameter x 42" Stroke Triple Expansion
ENGINE BUiLDER:	Globe Iron Works, Cleveland 1890

NORMAN a painting by Rev. Edward J. Dowling in 1986

NORMANDIE

The wooden-hulled steam barge NORMANDIE was built in 1894 at Green Bay, Wisconsin by P.F. Thrall for use in the lumber trade for his own company. She plied mostly on Lake Michigan hauling cut timber to the many plants scattered on Lake Michigan and Green Bay.

In 1901, NORMANDIE was sold to Charles G. Foster of Milwaukee, who in turn, sold her to the Michigan, Indiana and Illinois Line in 1906. This much-traveled steam barge was sold to the Morton Salt Company of Chicago, Illinois in 1913. She hauled barreled salt from Michigan ports to Chicago for both these companies.

From 1916 to 1920, NORMANDIE sailed for the Pringle Barge Line and changed her routes to the St. Clair and Detroit Rivers again in the lumber trades. In 1920, she was sold to John R. Lee of Detroit who had her converted to a sand boat complete with self-unloader and renamed b) MARYSVILLE.

During the next eight years, MARYSVILLE was owned first by the Northern Sand and Gravel Company in 1923 and 1924; by Harold Wills of Detroit in 1925 and 1926; by the Lake Gravel Company of Marysville, Michigan in 1926 and by the Service Gravel Company in 1927 and 1928.

The end came to this venerable steam barge on June 25, 1928 in the St. Clair River near the mouth of the Belle River at Marine City, Michigan when she burned and sank. There were no casualties and the vessel was abandoned. The remains of the MARYSVILLE were removed a short time later as her hulk posed a navigational hazard.

NORMANDIE leaving harbor with barreled salt

NORMANDIE in a Milwaukee dry dock

NORMANDIE upbound at Mission Point, St. Marys River in 1917

NORMANDIE at dock

MARYSVILLE at a dock on the St. Clair River in the 1920s

MARYSVILLE after her burning at Marine City

a) NORMANDIE, b) Marysville

BUILT:	1894 P.F. Thrall Green Bay, Wisconsin
HULL NUMBER:	none
LENGTH:	160.0
BREADTH:	35.3
DEPTH:	10.8
GRT:	567
REGISTRY NUMBER:	US. 130655
ENGINES:	20", 40" Diameter x 30" Stroke Fore and Aft Compound
ENGINE BUILDER:	Phoenix Iron Works, Port Huron 1894

NORTH STAR (1)

The Northern Steamship Company of Superior, Wisconsin was the Great Lakes arm of the vast railroad empire of the late James J. Hill - the "Empire Builder". This steamship company would, over the years after 1889, operate a fleet of nine package freighters and two luxurious passenger liners.

The NORTH STAR (1) was one of six similar steel-hulled package freight steamers built in 1889 (launched on February 12, 1889) and 1890 by the Globe Iron Works of Cleveland, Ohio. Her ownership was transferred in 1904 to the Mutual Transit Company of Cleveland. Sailing usually between Duluth, Minnesota and Buffalo, New York, the NORTH STAR saw regular service up to 1908. On November 25th, in that year, NORTH STAR was sunk in a collision with a fellow Northern package freighter, the NORTHERN QUEEN. This accident occurred on Lake Huron a few miles off Port Sanilac, Michigan.

In the year following this loss, the Mutual Transit Company built three new and larger package freighters, one of which took the name of the lost NORTH STAR.

NORTH STAR (1) loading flour at the Eastern Minnesota Flour Sheds, Superior, Wisconsin

BUILT:	1889 Globe Iron Works Cleveland, Ohio
HULL NUMBER:	23
LENGTH:	299.5
BREADTH:	40.8
DEPTH:	21.6
GRT:	2476
REGISTRY NUMBER:	US. 130435
ENGINES:	20", 38", 61" Diameter x 42" Stroke Triple Expansion
ENGINE BUILDER:	Shipyard 1889

NORTH STAR (1) upbound at Mission Point, St. Marys River

OHIO

The wooden-hulled bulk freighter OHIO was built at Huron, Ohio by John F. Squires and launched in April of 1873 for the John Estes Steamship Company of Sandusky, Ohio. In 1891 she was owned by L.P. Mason of Saginaw, Michigan and in 1892, was sold to C.W. Elphicke.

This small steamer had carried a variety of cargoes over the years that she operated. Her last cargo consisted of flour and feed which she loaded at Duluth, Minnesota destined for Ogdensburg, New York. On this downbound trip, the OHIO collided with the schooner IRONTON off Presque Isle, Michigan in Lake Huron and sank in 30 minutes. The date was September 26, 1894. The crew scrambled for the lifeboats and all but five were rescued by the schooner MOONLIGHT, a consort of the steamer CHARLES J. KERSHAW.

BUILT:	1873 John F. Squires Huron, Ohio
HULL NUMBER:	none
LENGTH:	202.2
BREADTH:	35.0
DEPTH:	18.6
GRT:	1101.81
REGISTRY NUMBER:	US. 19438
ENGINES:	unknown
ENGINE BUILDER:	unknown

OHIO on the stocks at Huron, Ohio in 1873

OHIO downbound in the St. Clair River

ONGIARA (1)

The wooden-hulled, double-deck passenger steamer QUEEN CITY (1) was built in 1885 by the famed shipbuilder Melancthon Simpson for the Doty Ferry Company of Toronto. She was operated on the ferry service from the city to the park and summer cottage areas on the Toronto Islands as well as other routes around Toronto Bay and environs. She was a typical steamer of the period with an enclosed cabin on the main deck, and with an ornate, octagonal pilothouse and open promenade on the upper deck.

In 1888, she was sold to the Niagara Navigation Company Ltd. of Toronto, for use as a passenger transfer between Queenston, Lewiston and Niagara-on-the-Lake in connection with the N.N.Co. cross-lake excursion steamers. In 1888, the N.N.Co. was operating the big sidewheelers CHICORA and CIBOLA from Toronto to the ports of the lower Niagara River. CIBOLA burned in 1895, but CHIPPEWA was added in 1893, CORONA in 1896 and CAYUGA in 1907. QUEEN CITY, renamed b) ONGIARA (1), helped with the cross-river transfer of passengers bound to and from the lake steamers. Her name was a variant of Niagara.

ONGIARA was successful in this trade, but by 1912 the scheduling of the company's larger steamers meant that her cross-river services were no longer required. Accordingly, she was sold that year to Captain Patrick J. McSherry of Toronto, who ran her as a tug in various trades around Lake Ontario, although she retained her original cabin configuration. The career of the steamer came to an end when she foundered in Lake Ontario off Bowmanville, east of Toronto, on October 17, 1918.

ONGIARA leaving her dock in the Niagara River

ONGIARA approaching the dock

a) Queen City (1), b) ONGIARA (1)

BUILT:	1885 Melancthon Simpson Toronto, Ontario
HULL NUMBER:	none
LENGTH:	90.5
BREADTH:	18.4
DEPTH:	5.4
GRT:	98
REGISTRY NUMBER:	C. 90562
ENGINES:	14" Diameter x 16" Stroke High Pressure Non-condensing
ENGINE BUILDER:	Doty Engine Co., Toronto 1885

ONTARIO

On the day of Canada's Confederation, July 1, 1867, there were several Great Lakes schooners standing on the stocks ready to be launched into their element. At Goderich, Henry Marlton launched the two-masted schooner ONTARIO. She was to have been named NEW DOMINION but the owners had learned that four other schooners were to be launched that day with this name.

The ONTARIO was engaged in carrying salt, lumber and grain for her owners Horace Horton, William Seymour and Bart Seymour, Jr.

On October 15, 1871, ONTARIO was caught in a storm on Lake Huron. The attempt to reach her home port was a failure as she was driven onto the beach just south of the harbor entrance. Later the efforts of the tugs GEN. U.S. GRANT and PRINCE ALFRED were successful in pulling her off.

She was ashore again in late April of 1882. On the 28th, the tug ERIE BELLE pulled her off the beach north of Goderich.

The great storm of November 11, 1883 caused much damage along the eastern shoreline of Lake Huron. Several ships were driven ashore and wrecked including the ONTARIO. Downbound on Lake Huron with a cargo of lumber, she was driven onto the beach five miles south of Kincardine. The captain swam though the breakers with a line which he then tied to a tree. The remaining crew came ashore on the line, the last man carried the woman cook on his shoulders. The ship was later salvaged. ONTARIO was owned by Joseph Williams of Goderich, at the time of this incident. He had her rebuilt in 1889 with the same dimensions but 210 gross tons.

In 1902, she was owned by Captain Francis Granville and William Spence of Southampton, Ontario. Soon afterwards they dissolved their partnership and William Spence left to sail the schooner WHITE OAK.

In the early morning hours of October 8, 1907, Captain Granville was trying to find the gap in the Long Dock behind Chantry Island at Southampton. He could not know that the schooner ERIE STEWART had crashed into the west dock only a few hours earlier and that one of her masts had fallen across the end of the dock taking the navigation light with it. Since he could not find the gap, Captain Granville turned the ONTARIO and headed for the mouth of the Saugeen River driven by storm winds and rain. She fetched up on the beach near the river mouth.

The schooner was salvaged and taken to Port Arthur, Ontario where the Western Dry Dock Company converted her into a sand dredge for the Ontario Gravel Company. She worked the harbors and small ports along northern Lake Superior until finally abandoned due to age and condition in 1922.

ONTARIO in the St. Clair River

ONTARIO at Kincardine

BUILT:	1867 Henry Marlton Goderich, Ontario
HULL NUMBER:	none
LENGTH:	105.0
BREADTH:	23.0
DEPTH:	9.2
GRT:	186
REGISTRY NUMBER:	C. 77775

ONTARIO on the beach at Southampton in 1908. Tugs JOHN LOGIE, CRAWFORD and A. CHAMBERS

ONTARIO as a sand dredge at Red Rock, Ontario in 1918

OSSIPEE

On September 1, 1914, bids were opened by the United States Treasury Department for the construction of two vessels. The lowest bid was received from the Newport News Shipbuilding and Drydock Company in the sum of $198,000 for each vessel. One of them, Cutter number 26, christened OSSIPEE, was built to replace the Revenue Cutter WOODBURY which was stationed at Portland, Maine.

Launched on the 1st of May, 1915, the OSSIPEE was christened by Miss Sallie Flemming McAdoo. OSSIPEE was designed by the Revenue Service to serve in the North Atlantic as a "derelict destroyer" to render assistance to vessels in distress.

After her commissioning on the 28th of July, 1915, OSSIPEE took up station in New England waters at Portland, Maine. In 1917, OSSIPEE was transferred to the Navy along with five sister cutters as Squadron 2, Division 6, of the Atlantic Fleet under Coast Guard Command. While she was with the Navy, she was outfitted for service escorting convoys around Gibraltar.

In 1919, she was returned to the Coast Guard and again took up station at Portland. During the 1930s, she was involved in efforts to fight shipments of liquor during the Great Depression.

In 1936, OSSIPEE was transferred to the Great Lakes and was stationed at the Soo. During World War II, she was again taken into the Navy and patrolled out of Cleveland, Ohio. After the war ended, the OSSIPEE was decommissioned on December 6, 1945 and declared surplus by the Coast Guard. She was sold on September 18, 1946. For a brief time she was owned by Harold Neff of Cleveland, and the Luria Brothers, of the same city, who had intended to use her. But she was too old and would cost a fortune to operate. They abandoned their plans and sold OSSIPEE for scrap. She ended her days in November of 1948 at the American Ship Building Company yard at Cleveland where she was cut up.

USS OSSIPEE at anchor on Lake Michigan

BUILT:	1915 Newport News Shipbuilding and Drydock Co. Newport News, Virginia
HULL NUMBER:	183
LENGTH:	165.9
BREADTH:	32.0
DEPTH:	11.8
DISPLACEMENT TONNAGE:	964
REGISTRY NUMBER:	USN
ENGINES:	17", 27", 44" Diameter x 30" Stroke Triple Expansion
ENGINE BUILDER:	Shipyard 1914

USS OSSIPEE at anchor

USS PADUCAH (PG-18)

The U.S. Navy gunboat USS PADUCAH (PG-18) operated on the Great Lakes for 18 years, from 1922 to 1940. During this time, the ship was based at Duluth, Minnesota and conducted training cruises for the 9th Naval District, Naval Reservists.

The steel-hulled PADUCAH, built by the Gas Engine & Power Company and the Charles L. Seabury Company of Morris Heights, New York, was launched on October 11, 1904 and placed in commission as PG-18 on September 2, 1905. Early in her career, she joined the Caribbean Squadron in 1906 to protect American lives and interests through patrols and port calls to Caribbean and Central American ports. Considerable hydrographic data was gathered to improve nautical charts of these strategic areas. She patrolled Mexican waters in the aftermath of the Vera Cruz incident through the summer of 1914.

As war clouds formed over Europe, PADUCAH was ordered north to the Portsmouth, New Hampshire, navy yard to prepare for European service during World War I. She sailed from New York on September 29, 1917, reached Gibraltar on October 27, and was based there as a convoy escort to North Africa, Italy, the Azores and Madeira, Portugal. She is credited with attacking and damaging a German submarine. Her ship's logs showed that from July, 1917 through October, 1918, she steamed 41,411 miles, escorted 23 convoys and 75 single ships with only two ship losses.

After the war, PADUCAH left Gibraltar on December 11, 1918, reached Portsmouth on January 7th, and was decommissioned on March 2, 1919. She was recommissioned from August 16, 1920 through September 9, 1921 as AG-7 for additional survey work in the Caribbean for the U.S. Coast and Geodetic Survey.

Her third commissioning came May 2, 1922, when reassignment to Naval Reserve training duty on the Great Lakes saw her underway for a new home base at Duluth, Minnesota, where she arrived on June 20th. For the next 18 years, PADUCAH conducted two-week training cruises throughout the lakes during the summer months in consort with USS DUBUQUE, based at Detroit, the WILMINGTON, at Toledo, WILMETTE, at Chicago and HAWK, relieved by SACRAMENTO, at Michigan City, Indiana. All gunnery exercises of this Inland Navy were conducted on Lake Michigan, as a result of treaty provisions between the United States and Canada.

While berthed at Duluth, PADUCAH was called upon for various ceremonial functions, and occasionally responded to emergency situations. In 1936, she took members of the Minnesota Naval Militia to Isle Royale to assist the Civilian Conservation Corps in fighting a serious forest fire on the island. Another time, the reservists took PADUCAH's boats by truck to perform rescue work on the flooding Mississippi River. In spring and fall, the ship would make weekend "excursions", i.e. training trips, to Isle Royale and the Apostle Islands, where the odd fishing line was wetted.

The ship was hand fired with coal until the early 1930s, when she was converted to oil fired boilers at Superior, Wisconsin. Also in the 1930s, a boat deck was added to provide additional berthing for hammocks and to make a sheltered main deck from the pilot house to the quarterdeck. The two triple expansion engines were quite simple and easy to maintain, and two boilers were arranged fore and aft with a firehold between them. The bunkers were situated outboard, which resulted in lots of shoveling in her coal fired days.

Late in 1940, PADUCAH was recalled to the East Coast to be fitted for war emergency service. Departing Chicago on November 13th for the 3,027 mile, 24-day trip, she arrived at New York on December 7th. Manned by Duluth's Naval Reserve Battalion, the trip involved negotiating 36 locks and winter seas in the Gulf of St. Lawrence and the Atlantic.

Extensive refurbishing was done on the ship at the Brooklyn Navy Yard that winter and, after a short stay at Tomkinsville, Staten Island, PADUCAH moved to Chesapeake Bay where she spent the balance of World War II based at Little Creek, Virginia. There she served as a gunnery training ship for Navy Armed Guard crews, who would man the guns on American merchant vessels. It was said that the ship fired as many, if not more, rounds during the war than any other Navy ship.

Decommissioned by the Navy for the final time on September 7, 1945, PADUCAH was sold on December 19th to Maria Angelo of Miami, Florida, and ultimately was purchased by the Weston Trading Company, a "front" for the Haganah, which was organizing immigration of Jewish refugees into Palestine. This group owned several other ships, including the former east coast passenger ship PRESIDENT WARFIELD (renamed EXODUS) and the ex-USCGC NORTHLAND.

In June, 1947, PADUCAH and NORTHLAND, which had been fitting out on the East Coast, suddenly disappeared, turning up at the French port of Bayonne on July 22. However, the French government announced that it would not give the ships permission to embark refugees at that port. The reason given was that five days earlier, in an infamous post war incident, EXODUS, with 4,554 refugees on board, had been turned around in Palestine's Haifa harbor by British authorities who ruled the immigration illegal and sent them back to the French port from which they sailed.

PADUCAH and NORTHLAND left Bayonne on August 28th, and sailed to the Bulgarian port of Burgas, on the Black Sea. There they embarked 4,000 Jewish survivors of the German concentration camps and sailed south through the Bosporus Strait, ostensibly enroute to Cuba, to avoid being detained in the Strait, but arrived off Tel Aviv on October 2, 1947. The British had been harshly criticized fortime offered little resistance to the ships' arrival.

PADUCAH, which had been renamed b) GEULAH (meaning Redemption) was towed into Haifa harbor and quietly disembarked her 1,385 passengers. The next day NORTHLAND, renamed MEDINA YEHUDATH (Jewish State) landed 2,664 refugees.

The former PADUCAH, now GEULAH, remained in service for a few years as a merchant vessel for the Zim Israel Lines before she was finally scrapped in 1949.

a) PADUCAH, b) Geulah

BUILT:	1905 Gas Engine & Power Co. and Charles L. Seabury Co. Morris Heights, New Jersey
HULL NUMBER:	unknown
LENGTH:	194.0
BREADTH:	35.0
DEPTH:	13.4
DISPLACEMENT TONNAGE:	1084
REGISTRY:	U.S. Navy
ENGINES:	Triple Expansion
ENGINE BUILDER:	unknown 1905

USS PADUCAH (PG-18) as a brand new vessel underway in Long Island Sound, October 7, 1905

USS PADUCAH (PG-18) in dry dock at the Portsmouth, N.H., Navy Yard prior to World War I

USS PADUCAH (PG-18) as she appeared during World War II

GEULAH arriving off Palestine with Jewish immigrants, October 2, 1947

PANOIL (2)

The steel tanker PANOIL (2) was built in 1920 as a) CRUDOIL (1) for the Huasteca Transportation Company of Los Angeles, California by the Alabama and New Orleans Shipbuilding Corporation in Violet, Louisiana. The CRUDOIL was built with two scotch boilers which supplied steam to one turbo generator, which in turn supplied current to two 350 hp electric motors which drove twin propellers.

In 1921, the Staten Island Shipbuilding Company removed the turbo generator and the electric motors, and repowered the vessel with a pair of two-cylinder compound steam engines. In 1925, the vessel was given the name of b) PANOIL (2), and her sistership, Hull number 24, which was launched as PANOIL (1), was given the name CRUDOIL (2).

In 1931, the PANOIL left saltwater and came to the Great Lakes for her new owners the Great Lakes Transport Corporation. PANOIL last ran as a tanker in 1951, and in 1952, she started 29 years of service as a bunker transfer vessel in the Nicholson slip at Ecorse, Michigan. In 1955, she was transferred to the Pure Oil Corporation of Chicago but continued to be a bunkering vessel. She was taken out of Documentation in 1959 but still remained fastened to the Nicholson dock. On September 10, 1981, her end finally came when she was moved by the Gaelic tugs KINSALE and DONEGAL to the South Slip at Nicholson where the vessel was cut up for scrap.

a) Crudoil (1), b) PANOIL (2)

BUILT:	1920 Alabama and New Orleans Shipbuilding Co. Violet, Louisiana
HULL NUMBER:	26
LENGTH:	242.5
BREADTH:	36.9
DEPTH:	10.7
GRT:	1370
REGISTRY NUMBER:	US. 220487
2 ENGINES:	15 1/2", 32 3/16" Diameter x 24" Stroke Fore and Aft Compound
ENGINE BUILDER:	Staten Island Shipbuilding Co., 1921

CRUDOIL (1) at the dock in Toronto

PANOIL (2) downbound in the Detroit River off Belle Isle

PANOIL (2) upbound in the Detroit River

EUGENE W. PARGNY

On January 20, 1917, American Ship Building's Lorain yard launched the steel bulk freighter EUGENE W. PARGNY. The vessel was built for the Pittsburgh Steamship Company and would spend her entire useful lifetime in the service of the United States Steel Corporation. She was named for Eugene William Pargny who was president of the American Sheet & Tin Plate Company and a director of U.S. Steel. When she joined the Pittsburgh Fleet, PARGNY was one of over 100 vessels in the fleet. She served faithfully through two World Wars.

For most of her life, PARGNY was just another of the large number of 600-footers in the Pittsburgh fleet of Tin Stackers. But in 1950, she and her sister, HOMER D. WILLIAMS, were selected for an experiment in repowering. During the winter of 1950-51, American Ship Building's Lorain yard removed the PARGNY's original triple expansion steam engine and installed a 3,500 horsepower diesel engine, with dimensions 21 1/2 inches in diameter by 27 ½ inches stroke, built by the Baldwin, Lima-Hamilton Corporation, thus giving her the honor of being the first diesel-powered Pittsburgher. The following winter, the WILLIAMS was repowered with a steam turbine. Captain Edward C. Baganz sailed both vessels after their conversions and said that there was "no contest"— the PARGNY was faster and more economical to operate. But apparently U.S. Steel officials were not convinced as the next two vessels they repowered, both for the Bradley Fleet, received steam turbines. But, in the long run, PARGNY's experiment had to be ruled successful as every vessel built on the Lakes since 1965 has been diesel-powered.

During spring fit out in 1978, the PARGNY's auxiliary boiler blew so she stayed at the wall all season. She did sail in 1979. Then in 1980, she came out in the spring but quickly laid up in the Tower Avenue slip at Superior, Wisconsin on May 19th, never to sail again. In late 1984, it was reported that the PARGNY had been sold to Shermet Recycling for scrapping at Thunder Bay, Ontario, but this proved to be a false report. On October 28, 1985, the PARGNY was towed to the Azcon/Hyman Michaels scrap dock in Duluth, Minnesota where cutting began on September 7, 1987 and was completed in July of 1988.

EUGENE W. PARGNY upbound into Lake St. Clair

EUGENE W. PARGNY downbound in Lake St. Clair, June 19, 1949

EUGENE W. PARGNY downbound at Mission Point, St. Marys River in 1954

EUGENE W. PARGNY downbound in the St. Clair River, September 1958

BUILT:	1917 American Ship Building Co. Lorain, Ohio
HULL NUMBER:	719
LENGTH:	580.0
BREADTH:	60.0
DEPTH:	32.0
GRT:	7724
REGISTRY NUMBER:	US. 214747
ENGINES:	24 1/2", 41", 65" Diameter x 42" Stroke Triple Expansion
ENGINE BUILDER:	American Ship Building Co., 1917

HENRY PEDWELL

Charles Pedwell and Charles Lemcke of Lion's Head, Ontario, contracted with a Mr. McDonnell of Wallaceburg to have a new tug built at Lion's Head in 1909. The CHARLES LEMCKE was launched into Lion's Head harbor on September 14, 1909. Her engine and boiler came from the tug W.E. GLADSTONE, a) ANN LONG, which had been wrecked in Lion's Head harbor on November 10, 1908.

Pedwell and Lemcke (The Lemcke Tug Company Ltd.) employed their tug in hauling rafts of logs to the sawmills at Wiarton, or towing barges. On occasion, she would haul cargoes of bagged peas or crates of fish packed in ice. She was renamed b) HENRY PEDWELL in 1913.

On August 19, 1915, the PEDWELL burned at Wiarton. John Tackaberry and Wm. Tyndall purchased the sunken hull and machinery in 1916. They had her raised and hauled up onto the marine railway at Wiarton. The hull was rebuilt up to the main deck and launched again September 21, 1916. The PEDWELL was towed to Owen Sound where John Keys completed the rebuild. Mr. Tackaberry ran her along the west shore of Georgian Bay from Owen Sound to Providence Bay on Manitoulin Island.

In the fall of 1925, her hull was punctured in an unique incident. A bull, which had jumped off the loading ramp, holed the PEDWELL while trying to surface. The tug was hauled up on the marine railway at Wiarton to be patched, then sent to the Collingwood Dry Dock for permanent repairs.

HENRY PEDWELL was sold to the Dominion Transportation Company, of Owen Sound, (Booth Fisheries Canada Ltd., managers) in 1927. She sank in Owen Sound Harbour and Mr. Tackaberry bought her again. He had her raised and, in 1930, sent off to the shipyard at Midland, Ontario, where she was widened and her GRT increased to 258. She was given all new cabins and her second engine, a fore and aft compound of 15 inch and 30 inch diameter by 22 inch stroke. This engine had been built in 1894 by the Pontbriand Company Ltd., Sorel, Quebec, and was removed from the steamer ALICE in 1927.

Following the rebuild, she was renamed c) KAGAWONG and chartered to the Owen Sound Transportation Company Ltd. In July and August of 1930, she was the first regular carferry to operate between Tobormory on the Bruce Peninsula and South Baymouth on Manitoulin Island. She could carry up to eight cars per trip.

Later that year, John Tackaberry sold KAGAWONG to Captain R. Vittie and H.W. Harnet, of Southampton, Ontario. However, he had to repossess the ship as a result of non-payment by the purchasers.

KAGAWONG was returned to the Owen Sound to Michaels Bay run. While on this route, she ran aground on Jackson's Shoal, east of Lion's Head, on July 5, 1932. The tug HARRISON was sent to assist her.

Shortly afterwards, she was renamed d) EASTNOR, but on November 18, 1933, she burned at Wiarton. In 1939, the Ross Construction Company, of Kincardine, Ontario, was contracted to remove the hull from Wiarton Harbour.

HENRY PEDWELL at Owen Sound

HENRY PEDWELL at Kincardine

HENRY PEDWELL being rebuilt at Wiarton after 1915 fire

HENRY PEDWELL launching after rebuild in 1916 at Wiarton, she was completed at Owen Sound

a) Charles Lemcke, b) HENRY PEDWELL, c) Kagawong, d) Eastnor

BUILT:	1909 Lion's Head, Ontario
HULL NUMBER:	none
LENGTH:	92.0
BREADTH:	17.6
DEPTH:	9.1
GRT:	101
REGISTRY NUMBER:	C. 126058
ENGINES:	12", 26" Diameter x 16" Stroke Fore and Aft Compound
ENGINE BUILDER:	unknown

PERE MARQUETTE 3

The passenger and freight steamer F. and P.M. No. 3 was launched at Gibraltar, Michigan on March 6, 1887 by the Detroit Dry Dock Company for the Flint and Pere Marquette Railroad Company of East Saginaw, Michigan. Since 1866, the railroad had been extending trackage northwest from Saginaw toward Lake Michigan. It was being extended mainly to bring sawn logs from timber cutting areas to mills along the Saginaw River. By 1874, the rail line had reached Ludington, Michigan, on the shore of Lake Michigan at Pere Marquette Lake. The timber traffic decreased as the trees were exhausted and the railroad began to look for sources of traffic other than timber products. Its gaze turned across the lake to the Wisconsin shore as potential traffic for the line from Ludington to the south and east.

In an effort to acquire traffic from across the lake, the railroad chartered the sidewheel steamer JOHN SHERMAN in 1875 to bring passengers and freight from Sheboygan, Wisconsin, to Ludington, the freight being mostly eastbound grain. In 1876, as traffic increased, the railroad began chartering various vessels from the Goodrich Transportation Company to take care of the increased volume.

In 1882, the railroad decided to acquire its own fleet of breakbulk steamers and had the F. and P.M. No. 1 and F. and P.M. No. 2 built. As a result of further increases in traffic, the fleet expanded with the addition of F. and P.M. No. 3, No. 4 and No. 5. By the late 1890s, cross-lake carferry operations had proven to be a practical proposition at the Straits of Mackinac and cross-lake out of Frankfort, Michigan. As a result of this, and the high cost of freight handling with the breakbulk boats, the decision was made to order a steel-hulled carferry from F.W. Wheeler and Company of West Bay City, Michigan. This carferry was the PERE MARQUETTE and she began operation in February, 1897.

After reorganization of the railroad and a name change to the Pere Marquette Railway Company in 1900, it was decided to rename the breakbulk boats to conform; thus, F. and P.M. No. 3 became b) PERE MARQUETTE 3.

In trying to make the harbor at Ludington on January 17, 1902, PERE MARQUETTE 3 hit the bottom in a heavy Southwest gale, missed the piers and grounded just north on the beach. In order to rest easier, Captain F.A. Dority ordered her sea cocks opened. While lying there, she was severely pounded by the waves and became hogged amidships. The crew and passengers were taken off the stricken vessel by the Coast Guard's breeches buoy. The ship was released eight days later by the tugs W.H. MEYER and JOHN C. MANN. After three months in the shipyard and an expenditure of $40,000, PERE MARQUETTE 3 was back in service.

The successful operation of cross-lake carferries made the breakbulk boats superfluous and they were sold. The PERE MARQUETTE 3 was sold with other boats in 1903 to the Manistee, Ludington and Milwaukee Transportation Company, managed by Gus Kitzinger of Manistee, Michigan. This line's popular name was the "Pere Marquette Line Steamers".

PERE MARQUETTE 3 was used in the passenger and freight trade between Manistee and other Lake Michigan ports, a large percentage of the freight being salt from Manistee. Later in 1903, control of the Pere Marquette Line Steamers was purchased by W.S. Eddy and associates of Saginaw, Michigan. The Eddy group were leading figures in the Michigan Salt Association. In 1904, the line of steamers, including PERE MARQUETTE 3, was reorganized as the Michigan Salt Transportation Company. Through several company ownership changes and reorganizations, Gus Kitzinger remained as manager.

The PERE MARQUETTE 3 continued on the company routes and was also at times chartered to other operators. She was no stranger to late-season operation and had various adventures in Lake Michigan's ice fields and storms. Such was the case on March 8, 1920, when following the carferry PERE MARQUETTE 18 (2), which was breaking a path through the ice from Milwaukee to Ludington. They became stuck in a heavy ice field piled up along the east shore of the lake by westerly winds. PERE MARQUETTE 17 came out from Ludington and attempted to break them out, but became stuck herself. With terrific pressures created by wind shifts and moving ice, PERE MARQUETTE 3 was crushed and settled to the bottom with her upper works being completely destroyed. The two steel-hulled carferries survived the onslaught and were later freed.

The wrecker FAVORITE (2) raised the hull of PERE MARQUETTE 3 on July, 1921. The hull was patched and towed to the dry dock at Manitowoc, Wisconsin. After inspection, it was determined that the damage was beyond economical repair, even for use as a barge. The register was closed and the hull dismantled.

a) F. and P.M. No. 3, b) PERE MARQUETTE 3

BUILT:	1887 Detroit Dry Dock Co. Gibraltar, Michigan	*GRT:*	924.60
		REGISTRY NUMBER:	US. 120677
HULL NUMBER:	77	*ENGINES:*	21", 37" Diameter x 36" Stroke Fore and Aft Compound
LENGTH:	190.0		
BREADTH:	32.8	*ENGINE BUILDER:*	Dry Dock Engine Works (#133), Detroit, 1887
DEPTH:	12.4		

PERE MARQUETTE 3 entering Ludington Harbor

PERE MARQUETTE 3 in the ice

PERE MARQUETTE 3 taking off the crew after stranding on January 17, 1902

PERE MARQUETTE 3 January 17, 1902 stranding after the storm had subsided

PERE MARQUETTE 3 after the disaster of March 8, 1920

PERSIA

The wooden-hulled, passenger and freight propellor PERSIA was built at St. Catharines, Ontario, in 1873 by the famous shipbuilder, Melancthon Simpson. She cost $37,000 to construct and was launched on July 11, of that year. She was christened by Miss Nellie Waud.

PERSIA was built for James Norris, of St. Catharines, and he still was listed as owner in the 1892 register. The steamer's upper works were enlarged in the 1880s, so that her breadth was increased to 26.0 feet and her depth to 12.5 feet; her gross tonnage then was 453. She was rebuilt again in 1887, when steel arch braces were fitted and her gross tonnage increased to 757. The original engine was replaced by a steeple compound power plant with cylinders of 21 inches and 36 inches in diameter and a stroke of 36 inches, which was built in 1873 by the King Iron Works of Buffalo, New York.

Further repair work was carried out on PERSIA in 1890, and at that time she was assigned a registry number, C. 97013, for the first time in her career.

In 1895, PERSIA was owned by Hagarty and Crangle's Toronto and Montreal Steam Navigation Company Ltd., of Toronto. Captain Samuel Crangle and John H.G. Hagarty sold their interests in the company in 1898 to Toronto wharfinger W.A. Geddes and the Jaques interests in Montreal, and ownership of PERSIA was transferred to the Wentworth Transportation Company.

PERSIA received $10,000 fire damage in a blaze which occurred at Toronto on November 28, 1900. In September of 1905, the steamer stranded in the Brockville Narrows section of the St. Lawrence River as a result of poor visibility. She was released by the tug PROCTOR and was able to proceed under her own power. In 1906, the Polson Iron Works Ltd. of Toronto fitted a new steam boiler of 8.6 by 14 feet, which replaced the original firebox boiler.

PERSIA spent most of her life prior to 1907 operating in the consortium, known as the Merchants Line, between Montreal and various lake ports. In 1907 however, she was acquired by the Quebec Navigation Company of Quebec City, for service between Montreal and Quebec. This service did not last long. The steamer was cut down to a barge in 1912 by the Atlas Sand Company of Montreal. As a barge, PERSIA's dimensions were, 141.0 by 25.4 by 10.7 feet; 284 net tons.

The 1914 Canadian register showed that A.A. Laroque, of Sinmac Lines, was manager of PERSIA. The vessel was dropped from the register after 1931, but it is believed that she had been out of service for some period of time before her registry was closed.

PERSIA entering the harbor

BUILT: 1873 Melancthon Simpson
St. Catharines, Ontario
HULL NUMBER: none
LENGTH: 144.0
BREADTH: *23.4*
DEPTH: 7.4
GRT: 347
REGISTRY NUMBER: none
ENGINES: 36" Diameter x 30" Stroke
Low Pressure Single Cylinder
ENGINE BUILDER: Yale & Company, 1873

PERSIA at her dock with the schooner EMERALD at St. Catharines

PEWABIC

Built by Peck & Masters at Cleveland, Ohio, and launched in October of 1863, the PEWABIC was a wooden package freight and passenger steamer built for J.L. Whiting's Pioneer Lake Superior Transit Company of Cleveland. Most of her upper works were completed in early 1864 and she entered service in the spring of that year. Early in 1865, she was readmeasured, correcting earlier mistakes, to 198.0 by 31.0 by 12.0 feet; 979 gross tons.

The end of the Civil War in April 1865 brought with it many changes. Returning troops sought to get transportation back home and the lines that served the Great Lakes at that time were pressed hard to accommodate them. One of these companies was J.L. Whiting's Pioneer Lake Superior Transit Company. The PEWABIC, newest of the fleet, was well equipped to handle returning soldiers as well as excursionists, the more wealthy of whom enjoyed the beautiful and ornate cabins while the rest rode in steerage or with the freight. In 1864, the Whiting fleet had seven steamers but, in 1865, only four remained; DETROIT, MINERAL ROCK, METEOR and PEWABIC. The latter two were involved in a collision on Lake Huron on August 9, 1865, that is still discussed even to this day.

The usual route of the steamers of this line was from Duluth, Minnesota to Buffalo, New York with stops at various ports on Lake Superior, and Lake Huron, and at Detroit and the ports on Lake Erie. The cargoes these vessels carried from the upper lakes were; iron ore from Superior, Wisconsin and Duluth; copper from Ontonagon and Hancock, Michigan; potash from Bayport, Minnesota; fish from Ontonagon and De Tour Village, Michigan; ships knees, the supports which join the decks to the hull of wooden vessels, from Lake Superior forests, and leather rolls from Ontonagon. This is what the cargo of the PEWABIC consisted of at the time of the accident, in addition to the passengers, who numbered 100 to 125 in cabin and steerage, and a crew of about 20. Newspapers of the day printed a list of 75 passengers and 11 crewmen who were rescued.

After loading 202 half-barrels of fish and leaving De Tour Village at 12:45 p.m., the PEWABIC was downbound off Thunder Bay Island Light on Lake Huron at 7:45 p.m. METEOR was upbound with passengers and freight from lower lake ports for Duluth. Because the mate on the PEWABIC mistook the METEOR for another downbound vessel, he signaled the wheelsman to make a starboard turn right across the METEOR's path. The METEOR's bow struck the PEWABIC about midway between her bow and the first port gangway; METEOR had her engines at full astern but the crash was inevitable. Panic ensued on both boats and some of the people on board PEWABIC jumped into the water, rushed to the stern of the sinking vessel or were grabbed by passengers and crewmen on the METEOR which had not yet backed off. Others managed to jump aboard METEOR when she was so close. After the METEOR began to back away, the PEWABIC began her final plunge and the entire hurricane deck was torn loose. People, who were flung into the water as the ship went down, managed to grab onto the floating deck and were later rescued by small boats from the METEOR. Even though the exact number of persons lost will never be known, the total has ranged from 70 to 125 by contemporary newspapers.

The official report of the investigating board placed the blame of the crash on the mate and the master of the PEWABIC, but the tale of this ship was far from over. A series of salvage attempts to recover the valuable cargo of copper ingots were made in 1879, 1880, 1881, 1896, 1917 and 1974. The first few were unsuccessful; the 1917 expedition resulted in one more man lost and did recover part of her cargo. But the 1974 expedition, with its highly technical electronic devices, was a complete success. Most of the steamer's cargo of copper was salvaged and many artifacts from the sunken vessel were brought to the surface.

PEWABIC painting by Norton

BUILT:	1863 Peck & Masters Cleveland, Ohio
HULL NUMBER:	none
LENGTH:	200.24
BREADTH:	31.07
DEPTH:	12.44
GRT:	739
REGISTRY NUMBER:	none
2 ENGINES:	26 1/2" Diameter x 42" Stroke Direct Acting High Pressure
ENGINE BUILDER:	Cuyahoga Steam Boiler Company, 1863

PEWABIC at her dock at Munising

PEWABIC drawing by F.S. Coggins

PIC RIVER

In late 1895, John D. Rockefeller's Bessemer Steamship Company contracted with five lakes' shipyards for 12 large steel vessels (7 steamers and 5 tow barges) of the latest design for 1896 delivery. F.W. Wheeler Company of West Bay City, Michigan was awarded contracts for one of the steamers and two barges. The first of these was launched at 5:00 p.m. on August 27, 1886. "The launch was, to some extent, a private one, tickets of admission being issued to those to whom it was desired to have attend." The new barge was christened JAMES NASMYTH in honor of the Scottish engineer who invented the steam hammer forge. Although designed to be towed by a freighter, the barge had three pole spars upon which were carried four sails. Her pilot house was aft, atop her cabins. She was equipped with a boiler to supply steam to operate her steering engine, auxiliary machinery and a towing machine which was located in a small steel house on her bow.

The new NASMYTH, the largest barge on the lakes, was soon at work under the command of Captain W.J. Hunt. "Beeson's Marine Directory" for 1897, reported that the NASMYTH carried 5,176 net tons of ore—a capacity that could be matched by less than half a dozen lakers at the time. "The Marine Record" for November 26, 1896, reported that the flagship of the Bessemer fleet, SIR HENRY BESSEMER, had been towing the NASMYTH "right along at an average speed better than eleven and one-half miles" per hour. In 1901, the Bessemer boats went into the new Pittsburgh Steamship fleet.

On November 27, 1905, the NASMYTH departed Duluth in tow of the steamer MATAAFA. The pair soon encountered a raging fall gale and, the next morning, the tow turned around and headed for Duluth. When approaching the piers, it became apparent that the steamer could never make it through with the heavily-loaded NASMYTH in tow. So the barge was cast loose to go to anchor and try to ride out the storm in the open lake. MATAAFA struck the pierhead as she tried to enter and was washed into the breakers outside the harbor where nine of her after-end crew perished from exposure. There was much concern for the fate of the crew of the NASMYTH anchored out in a storm that claimed over a dozen vessels on Lake Superior including some of the largest lakers then afloat. But the JAMES NASMYTH, as a testimony to her builders, rode out the storm without damage. Her gross tonnage was changed in 1924 to 3010.

The NASMYTH continued to serve in the large Pittsburgh fleet into the 1930s when the Great Depression and new tonnage made her surplus to their needs. In 1936, she was sold to Duluth's Marine Iron & Shipbuilding Company who soon peddled her to the Pigeon River Timber Company who reflagged her Canadian (C. 158268) and placed her in the lumber and pulpwood trade. In 1937, they renamed her b) MERLE H. She passed through two other owners, Lakehead Transportation Company Ltd. in 1938 and Great lakes Lumber & Shipping Company in 1942. In 1949, she was purchased by the Quebec and Ontario Transportation Company who immediately renamed her c) PIC RIVER in honor of a river on the north shore of Lake Superior where the company had pulp cutting operations. Q & O continued to operate PIC RIVER as a barge, usually pulled by the big tug ROCKY RIVER.

In the fall of 1953, PIC RIVER received a new lease on life at the Port Weller Dry Docks. She emerged the following spring as a self-propelled motor vessel with new cabins. Her new dimensions were, 373.0 by 44.6 by 23.2 feet; 3569 GRT. She had received a rebuilt 6 cylinder Burmeister & Wain diesel engine which came from the Danish passenger vessel ENGLAND (1931) which had been sunk in World War II. Since the engine was the left hand turning engine of a pair that had powered the twin-screw ENGLAND, when PIC RIVER backed, she swung to the right aft instead of to the left as most vessels do.

As a motor vessel, PIC RIVER served Q & O for 26 seasons carrying a wide variety of cargoes. She was a familiar sight in ports from the lower St. Lawrence River to Chicago. But her time ran out after her 83rd season on the lakes. She sailed into Toronto with her last cargo on October 17, 1978. Then on October 25, she tied up in Hamilton at the scrap dock of United Metals, her new and final owners. But they were in no hurry to cut her up! She lay at the dock, unofficially renamed d) PIC R, until 1984, when gradual dismantling of the historic 88-year-old veteran of the lakes began.

PIC RIVER had a twin sister with a remarkably similar career. She also was launched at the Wheeler yard as SIR ISAAC LOTHIAN BELL, for the same owners, a few weeks after the NASMYTH. She was sold out of the Pittsburgh fleet at the same time as the NASMYTH. The BELL became b) BLANCHE H. when the NASMYTH became b) MERLE H., went through the same ownership changes during the 1930s and 1940s, and was renamed c) BLACK RIVER when MERLE H. became c) PIC RIVER. In 1952, she received the ENGLAND's other engine—the right hand turning one. It was not until 1978 that the sisters' paths separated. BLACK RIVER served one more season, 1979, in the Q & O fleet and on October 22, laid up at Marine Salvage Company's Port Colborne scrap slip. But she was not quite finished. She was quickly purchased by the Cayman Shipping Corporation and on November 22, sailed for the Caribbean as d) TUXPANCLIFFE. She sailed intermittently in salt water until sold at a U.S. Marshal's sale at Houston, Texas on September 3, 1983. She was taken to Corpus Christi, Texas and scrapped—apparently about the same time that her twin sister PIC R. was feeling the torch at Hamilton.

a) James Nasmyth, b) Merle H., c) PIC RIVER, d) Pic R.

BUILT:	1896 F.W. Wheeler Co. West Bay City, Michigan
HULL NUMBER:	117
LENGTH:	365.5
BREADTH:	45.8
DEPTH:	23.2
GRT:	3422.64
REGISTRYNUMBER:	US. 77231

JAMES NASMYTH upbound at Mission Point, St. Marys River in 1919

MERLE H. downbound with pulpwood at Mission Point, St. Marys River

PIC RIVER downbound in the St. Clair River, August 6, 1950

PIC RIVER being converted to a motor vessel at Port Weller in 1952

PIC RIVER downbound at Mission Point, St. Marys River

PIC R. awaiting scrap at Hamilton, August 1, 1979

ADM. D.D. PORTER

The ADM. D.D. PORTER was built by Reanie & Archibald at Wilmington, Delaware as a wooden double-decked coastal package freighter for Thomas Clyde of Philadelphia, who chartered her to the U.S. Quartermaster Department for use as a transport and gunboat between 1864 and 1866. She was bought by the Peshtigo Company of Chicago and brought into the lakes in June 1867, where she was converted to a tug to tow lumber barges between Chicago and Green Bay ports.

In March 1870, PORTER was bought by Sol Rumage of Cleveland, who used her for towing log rafts in Lake Huron, Lake Erie and the St. Lawrence River. She was sold by the U.S. Marshal to H.C. Winslow of Buffalo in June 1876, and then to Booth, Jewell and others of Port Robinson, Ontario in February 1877, at which time she was registered in Canada (C. 74376; 152.15 GRT).

She was subsequently owned by McArthur Bros. of Quebec in 1881. The tug was rebuilt at Kingston in 1882 (240.69 GRT) by Powers & Company, and she was given a new 30 by 30 inch low pressure engine by the Davidson & Doran Iron Works also of Kingston. She was used in the Georgian Bay rafting business.

In March 7, 1887, she was sold to Charles M. Garvey of Sarnia and Henry Howard of Port Huron, who sailed her in the Moffatt Tug Line on the Detroit and St. Clair Rivers. She burned at Port Huron November 27, 1888, and subsequently reverted to U.S. registry when she was rebuilt and named b) HOWARD; her new dimensions were, 114.5 x 22.2 x 10.0 feet; 195.48 GRT. Her engine was converted to a steeple compound at the same time (20 and 36 inches diameter by 24 inch stroke). Afterward in 1889, she was operated by the Howard Towing Association.

In 1892, she was bought by A.D. Bennett of Port Huron, who often paired her with the big barges BALTIC and ADRIATIC. In March 1893, she was bought by Walter H. Singer of Duluth. Four years later HOWARD was sold to James Davidson of West Bay City, who ran her in his Michigan Log Towing Company fleet. She sometimes towed the big Davidson barges in the bulk freight trades, and was also fitted up for wrecking purposes. Davidson rebuilt the aging ship at his Bay City yards in 1904.

The tug was stranded on Niagara Reef near Victoria Island in Lake Superior on June 13, 1921. She broke up on the spot.

a) ADM. D.D. PORTER, b) Howard

BUILT:	1864 Reanie & Archibald Wilmington, Delaware
HULL NUMBER:	none
LENGTH:	118.0
BREADTH:	21.5
DEPTH:	8.1
GRT:	111.93
REGISTRY NUMBER:	US. 980
ENGINES:	30" Diameter x 30" Stroke Vertical Low Pressure
ENGINE BUILDER:	Neafie & Archibald, Wilmington, Delaware 1864

HOWARD at her dock in a Lake Huron port

PRESCODOC (2)

PRESCODOC (2) was constructed by Barclay, Curle & Company, and was launched at Whiteinch, Scotland, in April 1929. The vessel was built as a) SIOUX for the St. Lawrence Steamship Company. This Welland, Ontario based firm was a subsidiary of E.G. Crosby & Company of Buffalo, New York. The fleet's ships were painted in the usual livery of gray hull and buff forecastle.

The canaller SIOUX carried grain, and occasionally coal, to St. Lawrence River ports and frequently returned upbound into the lakes with pulpwood.

After a decade of service, SIOUX was deepened from 17.8 to 21.8 feet in 1939, increasing her GRT to 2,140. This work was carried out at the Muir Brothers Drydock at Port Dalhousie, Ontario. It is interesting to note that only her spar deck was raised at that time, with the result that the forecastle head and quarter deck were flush with the spar deck.

A year later, SIOUX was requisitioned by the Canadian government for war service. She was later taken over by the United States Maritime Commission and worked in the East Coast coal trade until 1944.

On her return to the lakes, SIOUX was again a busy ship. In 1945, she hauled 30 cargoes which included twelve loads of grain and ten of coal. She also took five shipments of newsprint out of Trois-Rivieres, Quebec and Thorold for Chicago and three cargoes of steel from Indiana Harbor to Hamilton.

On September 13, 1946, this ship joined the N.M. Paterson & Company Ltd., and was rechristened b) PRESCODOC (2) at Montreal. During 1947, her first full year in Paterson colors, PRESCODOC was employed mostly in the pulpwood trade. She loaded at a variety of small ports in Quebec including Les Mechins, St. Anne de Monts, Petite Vallee and Mont Louis for Port Huron, Michigan. Downbound, PRESCODOC took four loads of salt from Detroit to Port Alfred, Quebec, and also carried many cargoes of coal. PRESCODOC carried a total of 23 cargoes in 1947 and traveled 25,681 miles.

In 1948, PRESCODOC was again rebuilt. This time her forecastle was raised, which increased her gross tonnage to 2,197. Kingposts and derricks were fitted on deck in 1949 to make the steamer more suitable for carrying newsprint, a cargo which she would carry frequently throughout the remaining years of her career.

When the St. Lawrence Seaway opened on April 25, 1959, PRESCODOC was second in line to pass up the waterway, locking through behind the CSL canaller SIMCOE. PRESCODOC survived a few more seasons and, on one occasion in 1961, she carried fourteen open-pit mining trucks from Duluth to Sept-Iles, Quebec for use at Lake Wabush.

PRESCODOC laid up at Cardinal, Ontario after the 1962 season. She was sold to the Western Iron & Metals Company Ltd., and towed to Kingston in July 1963. The tug G.W. ROGERS brought her to Toronto on September 24, 1963. She was scrapped the following year.

SIOUX leaving Lock 7, Welland Canal

SIOUX downbound in Lake St. Clair

PRESCODOC (2) at Cornwall, August 14, 1956

PRESCODOC (2) at Cornwall, April 20, 1957

PRESCODOC (2) downbound in the Detroit River under the Ambassador Bridge

a) Sioux, b) PRESCODOC (2)

BUILT:	1929 Barclay, Curle & Company Whiteinch, Scotland
HULL NUMBER:	632
LENGTH:	252.7
BREADTH:	43.3
DEPTH:	17.8
GRT:	1940
REGISTRY NUMBER:	C. 161516
ENGINES:	15", 25", 40" Diameter x 33" Stroke Triple Expansion
ENGINE BUILDER:	Barclay, Curle & Co., Whiteinch, Scotland 1929

PRESCODOC (2) upbound in the St. Clair River, September 13, 1962

PRINS WILLEM II (2)

The vessels of the Oranje Line began coming to the Great Lakes in 1937. Although this was a Netherlands flag company, and all of their ships deep-sea carriers, the Oranje freighters became very familiar to the Great Lakes ship-watching fraternity.

PRINS WILLEM II (2) was one of the post-war additions to the fleet, and was the second vessel of the Oranje Line to carry this name. (PRINS WILLEM II (1), a steamer, was a war casualty.) She was built at Hardinxveld, the Netherlands, by deMerwede v. Vliet & Company, in 1955. The motorvessel was launched January 29th and, upon commissioning, the general cargo carrier headed for the lakes with a variety of goods.

The Oranje Line ships were designed to operate through the pre-Seaway canals. When ice closed the inland seas, this and other company ships called at Canadian East Coast ports. The Seaway opened in 1959 and, in 1960, PRINS WILLEM II was lengthened from 258 to 295 feet, 10 inches. This reconstruction increased the vessels GRT to 1,965 and allowed her to haul over 3,300 tons deadweight.

During the Seaway years, PRINS WILLEM II made thirty-five trips into the lakes. Her last inland trip under the Oranje Line house flag occurred in 1967, and the ship was sold the following year and renamed b) AMARYLLIS.

She sailed only briefly in this name and became c) GOTHIC PRINCE for a Greek firm, Parnor Shipping Company, in 1969. Then, in 1971, this ship was acquired by Conty Cia. Nav. S.A., also a Greek flag concern, and renamed d) XENY. She made a brief lakes appearance under this name but most of her trading was on the Atlantic or Mediterranean.

On December 2, 1975, XENY caught fire enroute from Port Harcourt, Nigeria, to Rotterdam, The Netherlands. The vessel was abandoned by her crew in position 40.30 N., 11.00 W. XENY was later taken in tow but capsized after being brought into Cadiz Roads on January 1, 1976.

a) PRINS WILLEM II (2), b) Amaryllis, c) Gothic Prince, d) Xeny

BUILT:	1955 deMerwede v. Vliet & Company Hardinxveld, The Netherlands
HULL NUMBER:	532
LENGTH:	258.0
BREADTH:	42.5
DEPTH:	18.1
GRT:	1599
REGISTRY:	The Netherlands
ENGINES:	23.6" Diameter x 35.4" Stroke Four Cylinder Diesel
ENGINE BUILDER:	N.V. Werkspoor, Amsterdam 1955

PRINS WILLEM II (2) at the dock in Erie, Pennsylvania, July 13, 1960

PRINS WILLEM II (2) unloading at Toronto

AMARYLLIS at Malta

GOTHIC PRINCE at Malta

XENY at Malta

PRUDENCE

PRUDENCE was built in 1900 by the famous tug builder John Dialogue, of Camden, New Jersey for F.W. & M.E. Munn of Philadelphia, Pennsylvania. PRUDENCE was built with 750 hp machinery and sailed for the Munns until 1928 when she was sold to the Tug Prudence Company of Philadelphia. In 1930, the James McWilliams Blue Line, of New York City, purchased the PRUDENCE and used her in ocean towing until 1941.

In the year 1941, PRUDENCE was purchased by the Lakehead Transportation Company Ltd., of Fort William, Ontario and rechristened b) LAWRENCE H. SHAW and given the Canadian registry number C. 173278. In 1943, she was incorporated into the Great Lakes Lumber & Shipping Company Ltd., of Fort William to tow timber rafts on Lake Superior. She was in this trade until 1955.

In 1955, she was again given the name c) PRUDENCE by the Hamilton Tugboat Company, of Hamilton, Ontario who purchased her that year. From 1955 until 1957, PRUDENCE operated on the lower lakes. In 1957, PRUDENCE was purchased by Captain Earl McQueen, of Amherstburg, Ontario, for his company, McQueen Marine Limited for which she sailed for three years.

In 1960, Underwater Gas Developers Ltd., of Toronto, purchased the PRUDENCE and stationed her at Erieau, Ontario, in order to tend gas wells in Lake Erie. In 1963, PRUDENCE was sold to Donald Lachine, of Blenheim, Ontario. That year, the tug suffered a fire while she was at Erieau, and her cabins were burned off. Shortly thereafter, the scrapping of the venerable tug began as she was moored under the old coal rig at Erieau. The Canadian registry of PRUDENCE finally was closed on the 19th of December, 1983.

PRUDENCE, an early photo, on the east coast

a) PRUDENCE, b) Lawrence H. Shaw, c) PRUDENCE

BUILT:	1900 John Dialogue Camden, New Jersey
HULL NUMBER:	371
LENGTH:	122.3
BREADTH:	25.0
DEPTH:	14.0
GRT:	292
REGISTRY NUMBER:	US. 150885
ENGINES:	16", 24" 40" Diameter x 28" Stroke Triple Expansion
ENGINE BUILDER:	J.H. Dialogue, 1900

PRUDENCE downbound at Wallaceburg

LAWRENCE H. SHAW and W.E. HUNT at Fort William, October 21, 1954

LAWRENCE H. SHAW at the dock at Owen Sound

QUEDOC (2)

On June 15, 1960, the Davie Shipbuilding yard at Lauzon, Quebec launched the NEW QUEDOC. The owners of the new vessel, N.M. Paterson & Sons Ltd. of Fort William (later Thunder Bay), Ontario, apparently wanted no confusion with the name of their veteran steamer QUEDOC (1) which they had sold the previous year. Thus Paterson added "NEW" to the name of the new vessel which proved to be the last steamer built for Paterson. By 1963, they apparently decided that the "NEW" was no longer necessary so the name was shortened to just b) QUEDOC (2).

QUEDOC served her owners faithfully for 25 seasons; but she did have her share of mishaps. On December 17, 1961, while in winter lay-up at Midland, she sank at her dock because an automatic sea valve was left open. The loss was set at $100,000 but most of this represented damage to her cargo of storage grain. On July 18, 1977, she suffered a cracked bow when she was caught in strong winds and hit a dock at Thunder Bay. On April 10, 1978, she grounded in Lake St. Francis in the St. Lawrence River but was pulled free, apparently undamaged, the following day. On October 11, 1980, she collided with the Greek ship GEORGE L. on Lac St. Louis in the St. Lawrence. QUEDOC came out of this with damage to her bow, forward accommodations and wheelhouse.

In 1984, QUEDOC laid up for the winter at Toronto on December 31. Paterson's early fit-out list for 1985 contained appointments for QUEDOC, but a later revised list omitted the steamer. That year Paterson took delivery of their new, maximum Seaway-size diesel vessel PATERSON (2). This, plus a slowdown in business, spelled the end for three of their smaller post-war steamers—PATERSON (1) of 1953, SENATOR OF CANADA of 1957 and QUEDOC. The latter two boats were sold to Cord Steel of Montreal.

QUEDOC fitted out one more time. On June 20, 1985, she cleared Toronto without the familiar "P" on her stack. Her last voyage under power was only to Quebec City where she remained until, along with SENATOR OF CANADA, she was towed out by the tug CAPT. IOANNIS S. The tow arrived off Curacao, Netherlands Antilles on July 17. Local tugs then towed the two hulks through the narrows and into Curacao's inner harbor. Cutting soon began on SENATOR OF CANADA but QUEDOC did not feel the torch until 1986.

Official Canadian records note simply that QUEDOC's registry was closed on July 30, 1985 as "sold Dutch." But for those who love Lakers there was more to it—a beautiful, post-war steamer had gone long before she was worn out.

NEW QUEDOC downbound in lower Lake Huron, September 14, 1960

QUEDOC (2), October 11, 1980, after the collision with the salt-water vessel GEORGE L. on Lac St. Louis

a) New Quedoc, b) QUEDOC (2)

BUILT:	1960 Davie Shipbuilding Co. Lauzon, Quebec
HULL NUMBER:	624
LENGTH:	590.5
BREADTH:	62.2
DEPTH:	29.3
GRT:	9957
REGISTRY NUMBER:	C. 313931
ENGINES:	Cross compound Steam Turbine, Double Reduction Gear Drive
ENGINE BUILDER:	Parsons Marine Turbine Co. Ltd. 1960

QUEDOC (2) downbound in the St. Clair River, August 30, 1963

QUEDOC (2) at the scrapyard at Curacao, Netherlands Antilles in 1986

RAMAPO

The Great Lakes fleet operated by the Erie Railroad was the Union Steamboat Line, which consisted of several older, wooden-hulled freighters in the coal trade, and four or five iron or steel package freighters. One of the latter was the RAMAPO of 1896.

Built by the Union Dry Dock Company at Buffalo, New York and launched on August 1, 1896, RAMAPO was the first large ship in the fleet. This vessel was unique among package freighters in that her pilot house was positioned on the forecastle deck rather than on the spar deck behind the number one or number two hatch. In 1903, her GRT was changed to 3,314.

In 1911, the ship was renamed b) F.D. UNDERWOOD, honoring Mr. Frederick D. Underwood who was president of the railroad.

In 1916, the UNDERWOOD was transferred to the newly-formed Great Lakes Transit Corporation, along with many of the other lake package freighters. This change was a result of one of the provisions of the Panama Canal Act, which forbade U.S. railroads from operating lake steamships on routes which ran parallel to the rail lines.

F.D. UNDERWOOD continued over her usual route between Buffalo and Chicago until the Depression years, when package freighting on the Great Lakes began to decline. After a few years of lay-up, the vessel was rebuilt in 1930 to the following dimensions: 330.5 x 44.8 x 24.4; 3,270 GRT., deck cranes were installed, and she was chartered briefly to the Gartland Steamship Company, of Chicago. The ship was finally scrapped in 1940 at Hamilton, Ontario, by the Steel Company of Canada.

RAMAPO upbound in the St. Clair River

F.D. UNDERWOOD in the St. Clair River in 1915

a) RAMAPO, b) F.D. Underwood

BUILT: 1896 Union Dry Dock Co.
Buffalo, New York
HULL NUMBER: 78
LENGTH: 319.5
BREADTH: 44.8
DEPTH: 24.4
GRT: 3045
REGISTRY NUMBER: US. 111123
ENGINES: 23", 38", 64" Diameter x 42"
Stroke Triple Expansion
ENGINE BUILDER: King Iron Works, Buffalo 1896

F.D. UNDERWOOD approaching the Locks at the Soo

RED-WHITE AND BLUE

The scow-schooner RED-WHITE AND BLUE was built at Oakley, Michigan by Frank Wallis in 1887. A glance at a map of Michigan will show that Oakley is a very unlikely place for the construction of a lake vessel, even the modest size of the RED-WHITE AND BLUE. Raw material for construction would not have been a problem because of the plenitude of oak available locally. Getting the vessel to lake waters would have presented some problems. The owners, Frank Wallis of Au Gres, Michigan and Sarah A. Dearman of Oakley, solved it by floating the ship down the Shiawassee River via the Saginaw River to the bay.

RED-WHITE AND BLUE was sailed by Captain Wallis and traded around Saginaw Bay ports. Business must have been good, because it was decided that more cargo capacity would be advantageous, and in the fall of 1892, the vessel was taken back up the river system to her birthplace and lengthened from her original 52 feet to 70 feet. Now the sharp bends of the upper Shiawassee must have presented more of a problem to the lengthened ship for her return to Great Lakes waters. The resourceful owners solved it by building a giant sleigh, and towed the boat over the snow to Bay waters. Her new dimensions were: 70.0 x 16.3 x 3.9; 38.78 GRT.

On April 25, 1893, Sarah Dearman sold her half interest in the RED-WHITE AND BLUE to Captain Wallis for three-hundred dollars. In 1895, on October 19, the RED-WHITE AND BLUE washed ashore on Whaleback Shoal on Green Bay, but the vessel was recovered later that year. During the 1900 era, the scow-schooner was usually moored near the Belinda Street Bridge at Bay City, Michigan. In 1911, she grounded near the mouth of the Au Sable River. After failing to refloat her, Captain Wallis decided to sell her "as is, where is".

On July 11, 1911, E.S. and R.G. Colbath became her owners for the consideration of exactly $150.00. The brothers got her afloat and brought her up the river where the balance of her cargo of posts was discharged. She was then used for several trips by the new owners in 1911 to Grace Harbor, the last, apparently on August 21, 1911. Until at least 1919, she was moored in the Au Sable River. No further mention of the little scow-schooner, RED-WHITE AND BLUE has ever been found. One further point of interest was her color scheme, which, as you might guess, was red, white and blue.

BUILT:	1887 Frank Wallis Oakley, Michigan	*BREADTH:*	16.2
HULL NUMBER:	none assigned	*DEPTH:*	3.9
LENGTH:	52.0	*GRT:*	28.32
		REGISTRY NUMBER:	US. 56571

RED-WHITE AND BLUE
in the Saginaw River

RAYMOND H. REISS

EMORY L. FORD was built in 1916 by the American Ship Building Company at Lorain, Ohio for the Franklin Steamship Company, managed by Herbert K. Oakes, and launched on July 15, 1916. During 1932, Bethlehem Transportation Company replaced H.K. Oakes as managers, and in 1940, EMORY L. FORD was transferred to M.A. Hanna management.

In 1944, EMORY L. FORD was sold by the Franklin Steamship Company to the M.A. Hanna Company. While under Hanna ownership, she carried the most valuable cargo ever hauled on the lakes at that time—447,049 tons of flax seed worth $3,000,000. She loaded the flax seed at the Great Northern Elevator at Superior, Wisconsin and delivered it to the Dellwood elevator in Buffalo, New York, spending the winter storing the cargo for Archer, Daniels, and Midland. Flax seeds are relatively small, flat and slimy and, loaded in bulk, are almost water-like. For this reason, the FORD had to be loaded to the hilt to prevent the cargo from shifting.

During the winter of 1957-58, EMORY L. FORD received new tank tops and side tanks, her ballast piping was renewed and numerous shell plates were replaced at the Knudsen Shipyard in Superior. In 1963, EMORY L. FORD was acquired by the Gartland Steamship Company under bare boat charter from Hanna.

In 1965, EMORY L. FORD was purchased by the Reiss Steamship Company and rechristened b) RAYMOND H. REISS. She was named in honor of the chairman of Ronthor-Reiss Corporation of New York and a director of the Reiss Steamship Company.

During the winter of 1965-66, RAYMOND H. REISS was repowered with a new 4320 hp, 16 cylinder Nordberg diesel engine at Fraser Shipyards in Superior. Also added was an 800 hp bow thruster, a controllable pitch propeller, and a new streamlined stack. During her trials, she showed an increase in speed to 15.3 miles per hour from the 11.5 miles per hour accomplished with her original steam engine.

In 1968, RAYMOND H. REISS set the record for the largest coal cargo ever delivered to the port of Ashland, Wisconsin, arriving on September 4, and unloading 14,943 tons.

In 1969, RAYMOND H. REISS was acquired by the American Steamship Company when American purchased the entire 12 boat fleet of the Reiss Steamship Company. In 1971, ownership of the RAYMOND H. REISS was transferred to the Edison Steamship Company, Boland & Cornelius as managers. Again in 1971, the REISS was traded to the American Ship Building Company as partial payment for ROGER M. KYES. American Ship Building transferred ownership of RAYMOND H. REISS to Kinsman Marine Transit Company in 1972. Kinsman Marine Transit then sold her to Cleveland Cliffs Steamship Company also in 1972.

On April 19, 1973, RAYMOND H. REISS lost power in Lake Huron off Harbor Beach and was towed to Port Huron by the tug TABOGA. After engine repairs, she departed for Cleveland on April 22nd.

On August 27, 1974, the engine bed of the REISS collapsed while she was on Lake Huron. She was towed to Nicholson's dock in Ecorse, Michigan where major repairs were completed. The cost of the damage was estimated at $340,000.

In 1980, RAYMOND H. REISS was sold to Marine Salvage of Port Colborne, Ontario. She departed Cleveland under her own power on December 22, 1980, bound for Humberstone (Ramey's Bend), arriving the same day. Her bow and mid-body were scrapped during 1981, while her stern was dismantled in 1982.

a) Emory L. Ford, b) RAYMOND H. REISS

BUILT:	1916 American Ship Building Co. Lorain, Ohio
HULL NUMBER:	715
LENGTH:	580.0
BREADTH:	60.0
DEPTH:	32.0
GRT:	7986
REGISTRY NUMBER:	US. 214318
ENGINES:	24", 41", 65" Diameter x 42" Stroke Triple Expansion
ENGINE BUILDER:	Shipyard 1916

EMORY L. FORD downbound out of Lake St. Clair, July 29, 1939

EMORY L. FORD at the dock at Superior, Wisconsin

RAYMOND H. REISS downbound in the Detroit River, May 30, 1969

RAYMOND H. REISS downbound in the St. Clair River, August 1, 1969

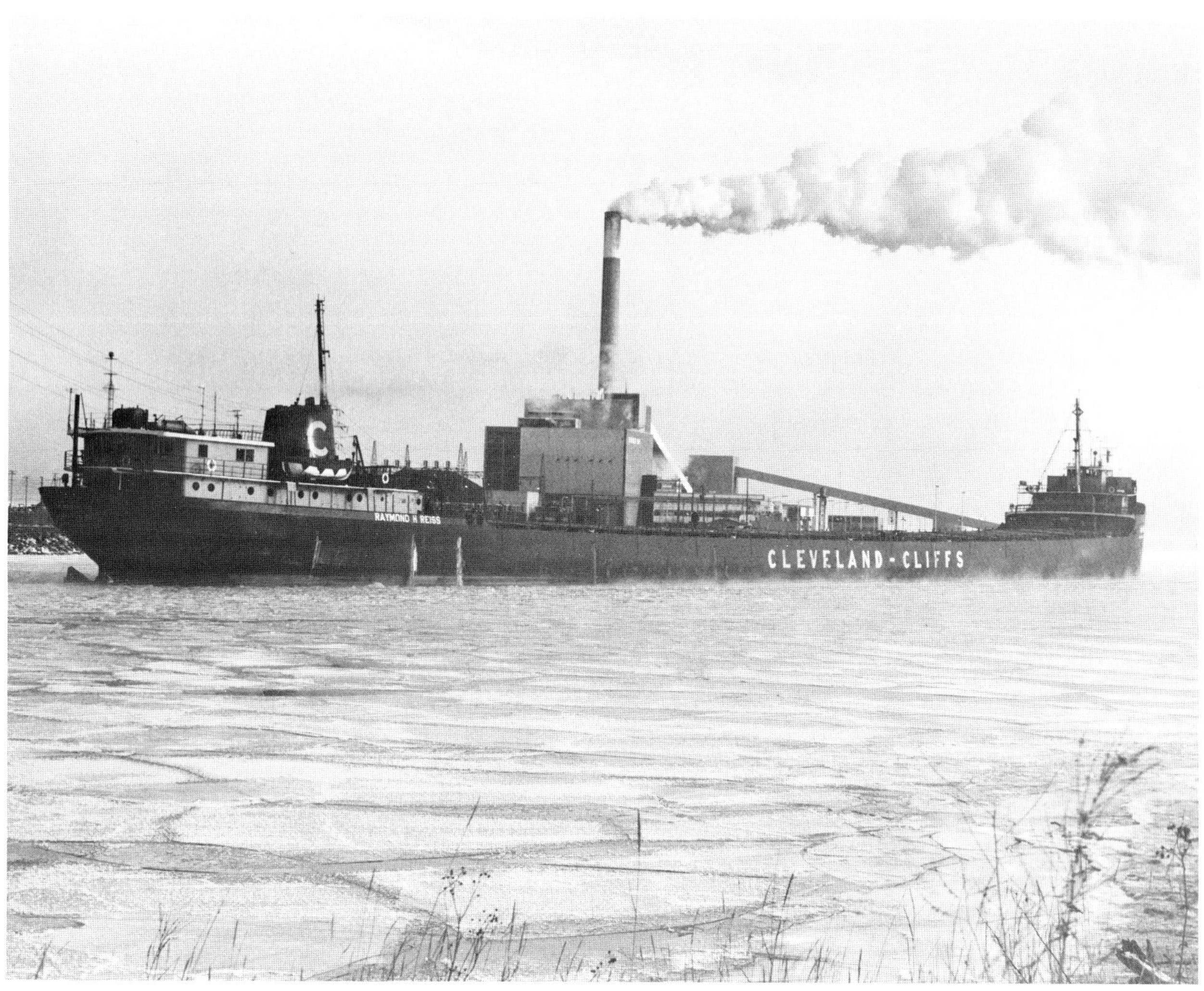

RAYMOND H. REISS in the fog and ice outbound from the Kam River, Thunder Bay in December 1976

RESOLUTE

The little lumber carrier RESOLUTE, built of white oak in 1883 by William Evans, master shipbuilder of the Rathbun shipyard at Deseronto, Ontario, was launched on August 11th. She was propelled by twin screws. The steamer was designed as a "rabbit", that is, she had all her cabins and machinery aft. RESOLUTE and her similar running mate, RELIANCE, originally operated on a tri-weekly service between Deseronto and Oswego hauling lumber southward and returning with coal.

In 1887, RESOLUTE was rebuilt with her length increased to 136.6 feet and a new gross tonnage of 372. It probably was somewhat later that her octagonal pilothouse was moved from the boat deck aft to a position atop the raised forecastle.

Shortly after the turn of the century, RESOLUTE was sold to the Toronto firm of Haney and Miller (Michael J. Haney and Roger Miller, proprietors), for use in the coal and construction material trades into Toronto. She frequently towed one of the company's barges on these trips.

On Wednesday, November 21, 1906, RESOLUTE and her barge, P.B. LOCKE, inbound with coal from Erie, Pennsylvania, attempted to enter Toronto Harbour via the Eastern Gap during a strong southeasterly gale. The steamer did not have sufficient power to risk the dangerous passage, and so the two vessels proceeded westerly to anchor off the Western Gap in the lee of Hanlan's Point. They could not enter the harbor via the Western Gap because RESOLUTE's draft exceeded the depth of water available in the shallow channel. Shortly after they were anchored, the wind calmed somewhat, and Captain Fahey took the steamer and the barge around to the Eastern Gap again, but the vessels still could not negotiate the passage and returned to their anchorage.

During the evening, the wind changed to the south west, and the RESOLUTE and LOCKE found themselves in extreme danger, caught on the lee shore. Captain John Sullivan, who was aboard the RESOLUTE in his capacity as manager of the Haney and Miller fleet, suggested that the steamer, which had begun to take water, should be driven into the Western Gap as far as she would go in an effort to save the crew, but her anchors could not be lifted or slipped. The crew took to the boats but all five men who were in the port boat were lost. The five persons in the starboard boat reached shore safely. When RESOLUTE sank, Captain Sullivan was standing atop the boat deck, attempting to clear the lifeboat falls. The deck broke away from the sinking steamer and it formed a makeshift raft, on which Sullivan was swept through the Western Gap and into the safety of the harbor. For a time, the second engineer shared the raft with Sullivan, but he was washed off and perished. As a result of what came to be known as "Sullivan's Ride", and the testimony which the Captain gave at the inquiry into the wreck, improvements to the Western Gap channel were begun in 1908.

RESOLUTE was raised in October 1907 and was rebuilt at Toronto in 1908 as b) JOHN ROLPH, with a gross tonnage of 421. She was transferred in 1909 to the ownership of Point Anne Quarries Ltd., an enterprise of Haney and Miller in which J.F.M. Stewart was also interested. JOHN ROLPH operated for the company until 1923, when she was laid away in the West Market Street slip at Toronto, where she was allowed to settle into the mud.

As a result of harbor reconstruction, JOHN ROLPH was raised in 1926 and towed to a resting place in the lagoon behind West Island Drive on Hanlan's Point. She lay there for several years until, in the late 1920s, she finally was pumped out, towed out into Lake Ontario, and scuttled in deep water.

a) RESOLUTE, b) John Rolph

BUILT:	1883 Rathbun shipyard Deseronto, Ontario
HULL NUMBER:	none
LENGTH:	126.0
BREADTH:	27.8
DEPTH:	10.3
GRT:	336
REGISTRY NUMBER:	C. 88241
2 ENGINES:	14", 24" Diameter x 16" Stroke Steeple Compound
ENGINE BUILDER:	Thos. Wilson, Dundas, Ontario

RESOLUTE at the dock

JOHN ROLPH at West Market Street, Toronto

T.W. ROBINSON

The steamer T.W. ROBINSON was built by the American Ship Building Company in Lorain, Ohio, for the Bradley Transportation Company and was launched on April 25, 1925. She was named in honor of Mr. Theodore Winthrop Robinson, who was vice-president of the Illinois Steel Company, a subsidiary in the formation of the United States Steel Corporation.

Built as a self-unloader, T.W. ROBINSON was a unique vessel on the Great Lakes when she was launched in 1925. Turbo-electric propulsion was previously unknown to large Great Lakes commercial ships but was successfully used by the U.S. Navy to power its battleships. T.W. ROBINSON also was the first vessel to make extensive use of electric auxiliary machinery, such as winches, galley ranges and forward cabin heating. She was also unique in that she used her main generator to power her self-unloading machinery.

On June 9, 1927, T.W. ROBINSON participated in the formal opening of the new Buffington, Indiana harbor, unloading 12,000 tons of limestone during the official ceremonies.

On May 20, 1939, T.W. ROBINSON arrived in Duluth with an unusual cargo of 9,000 tons of anthracite coal dust which was unloaded at the Hanna-Duluth coal dock. The coal dust was to be shipped by rail, as needed, to the sintering plant of Evergreen Mines Company of Crosby, Minnesota.

After serving the Bradley Transportation Company and the United States Steel Company faithfully for over fifty years, T.W. ROBINSON laid up for the final time on May 23, 1982, in her home port of Rogers City, Michigan. In 1987, the USS Great Lakes Fleet, Inc. received permission from the U.S. Maritime Administration to sell T.W. ROBINSON to Marine Salvage of Port Colborne, Ontario for scrapping.

T.W. ROBINSON was towed from Rogers City on May 2, 1987, under tow of the tug TUSKER, arriving in Port Colborne on May 5th. However, she was not scrapped in Port Colborne, as Marine Salvage resold her to Siderurgica Aconorte S.A. for overseas scrapping.

On July 29, 1987, T.W. ROBINSON departed the Marine Salvage yard in Humberstone under tow of the tugs GLENADA and TUSKER, arriving in Quebec City on August 2nd. The ROBINSON departed Quebec City on August 11th, with U.S. 265808 (ex BENSON FORD) in tow of the Polish tug JANTAR bound for Recife, Brazil. The tow arrived safely at Recife on September 22, 1987.

T.W. ROBINSON downbound in lower Lake Huron, July 21, 1961

BUILT:	1925 American Ship Building Co. Lorain, Ohio
HULL NUMBER:	790
LENGTH:	572.6
BREADTH:	60.2
DEPTH:	29.5
GRT:	7726
REGISTRY NUMBER:	US. 224836
ENGINES:	Steam Turbine/Generator and Electric Drive Motor
ENGINE BUILDER:	General Electric 1925

T.W. ROBINSON in the Welland Canal in tow of the tug TUSKER on the way to scrap

MARQUIS ROEN (1)

In 1921, Captain John Roen and Roy Ranger built the steamer MARQUIS ROEN (1) behind Roen's house on the shore of Round Lake at Charlevoix, Michigan. Captain Roen had set up a saw mill and steam box to cut and form the timbers at the construction site. The boiler and machinery were taken from the FRANK D. PHELPS, which Captain Roen also owned at the time.

The new boat was named for Captain Roen's son. The MARQUIS ROEN was used to carry sawn logs, lumber and pulp wood and to pick up scrap iron and steel from wrecks whenever the opportunity arose. In 1924, Captain Roen purchased the former sailing schooner INTERLAKEN to tow astern of the MARQUIS ROEN. The ROEN with the INTERLAKEN in tow carried many cargoes of pulp wood, logs and lumber from such places as Cedarville, Sugar Island, Hessel and Duck Islands to paper mills and saw mills at Filer City, Alpena, Bay City and Port Huron. Captain Roen sailed as master of the MARQUIS ROEN and his brother-in-law, Henry Isakson, was Chief Engineer.

The ROEN and her consort were kept busy until the depression years when Captain Roen chartered her to W.J. Meacher of Bay City, Michigan. On December 7, 1932, the vessel caught fire at Meacher's dock at Bay City, and before the fire was brought under control, the cabins and after end were destroyed.

After the fire, the MARQUIS ROEN was sold to Harold Neff of Cleveland, Ohio. The hull was repaired only to the main deck after the boiler and machinery were removed and the vessel thereafter was used as a barge. The last known use of the MARQUIS ROEN was in removing the stone piers of the old Court Street bridge in Saginaw, Michigan, prior to the construction of a new bridge in 1938-39.

The ROEN lay idle after that just upstream of the Meacher docks at Bay City, on the east bank of the river. In 1953, the hull was set afire by persons unknown and burned to the water's edge. Until recent years, in periods of high southerly winds when the river level was lowered, the remains still could be seen. The MARQUIS ROEN's final resting place is now part of a marina and her remains have been dispersed.

BUILT:	1921 Captain John Roen/Roy Ranger, Charlevoix, Michigan
HULL NUMBER:	none
LENGTH:	84.0
BREADTH:	24.0
DEPTH:	7.0
GRT:	97
REGISTRY NUMBER:	US. 221243
ENGINES:	12", 36" Diameter x 17" Stroke Fore and Aft Compound from FRANK D. PHELPS
ENGINE BUILDER:	unknown

MARQUIS ROEN (1) upbound at Mission Point, St. Marys River in 1921

MARQUIS ROEN (1) going through a bridge

MARQUIS ROEN (1) laid up at Sturgeon Bay with the barge INTERLAKEN

MARQUIS ROEN (1) abandoned at Bay City c.1952

MARQUIS ROEN (1)'s afterend after the fire at Bay City

MARQUIS ROEN (2)

The self-unloading barge MARQUIS ROEN (2) of the Roen Steamship Company of Sturgeon Bay, Wisconsin, was hailed at the time of her conversion in the mid-1950s as the "Most Versatile Freighter on the Great Lakes", and the variety of cargoes handled and ports-of-call visited in her 20-year stint on the lakes would certainly bear this out.

The life of the vessel began with the launch on May 15, 1900, of the steamer ROBERT W.E. BUNSEN at the Chicago Shipbuilding Company in South Chicago, Illinois. This bulk freighter was built for the Bessemer Steamship Company, which in 1901 merged into U.S. Steel's Pittsburgh Steamship Company, and served for half a century in the iron ore, coal and stone bulk trades. Her big quadruple expansion steam engine and three boilers put her at the business end of a towline hauling the company's barges during a good part of her career. In 1922, her dimensions were changed to: 439.0 x 50.2 x 24.8 and her gross tonnage to 4,473. By the early 1950s, BUNSEN's size and age caught up with her in the day of new 20,000 ton bulkers, and she was laid up Toledo, Ohio.

In December, 1953, the Roen Steamship Company purchased the ship for conversion to a barge for the finished steel products trades. In this conversion, performed at Roen's Sturgeon Bay Shipbuilding & Dry Dock Company yard, the existing spar deck was rebuilt to incorporate a four-foot high trunk which carried rails for deck cranes. Six over-size hatches with special self-sealing steel covers were fitted to enclose three large holds. Two 45 ton electric, fully revolving Clyde cranes with booms 90 feet long were mounted on deck. The ship's engine and boilers were removed and a 100 kw diesel-electric generator set was placed in the former engineering spaces aft to supply electric power. A small oil fired boiler was installed to furnish steam for pumps, deck and steering winches, and heating. Her new GRT was 4,830.

Rechristened b) MARQUIS ROEN (2), in honor of Captain Roen's son, the ship departed Sturgeon Bay on November 20, 1954, bound for Muskegon, Michigan, to load its first cargo, scrap iron for delivery to Lackawanna, New York. During 1955-56, the barge, towed by Roen's big 2,000 hp tug JOHN ROEN IV, was kept busy carrying steel ingots, as much as 8,000 tons per load, from the Soo to Trenton, Michigan, and coils and semi-finished slabs from the Soo to South Chicago.

The versatility of MARQUIS ROEN was further enhanced over the 1956-57 winter at Sturgeon Bay with the installation of a deck conveyor and self-unloading boom. Two movable hoppers were mounted on rails on the starboard side of the spar deck that would receive bulk cargo from the cranes and feed it onto a 310 foot conveyor running the length of the deck. At the forward end, the conveyor discharged into a bucket elevator feeding onto a 180 foot unloading boom. Discharge rates of up to 1,800 tons per hour were possible and bulk cargo could be placed well back on docks. A 100 kw diesel-electric generator set was added to power the conveyor equipment. The boom placed on MARQUIS was a rebuild and earlier had been used on the steamer COL. E.M. YOUNG; it had been removed when that ship was reconverted to the straight-decker SPARKMAN D. FOSTER.

In addition to her ability to carry a wide assortment of cargoes, the MARQUIS ROEN was also a handy vessel for salvage operations. She was involved in lightering cargo from a number of ships, including the ocean ship ZENICA that went aground on Poe's reef, the salty EGLANTINE aground at Marysville and the Canadian laker SILVER ISLE aground at Bar Point in the Detroit River. In these instances, the barge could lighter the ship and then return the cargo back to the ship once it had been refloated (usually with the aid of Roen tugs).

Following the death of Captain John Roen on December 7, 1970, the nonpareil operations of the Roen companies were pared down and in late 1971, the stockholders, who were heirs of John Roen, decided to sell off the equipment as buyers could be found.

MARQUIS ROEN was sold to the Gulf Elevator & Transfer Company of Burnside, Louisiana, on May 31, 1973 for $250,000. She was towed from Sturgeon Bay by the tug JOHN ROEN IV (which had been sold to a New Orleans towing company) via the Welland Canal and St. Lawrence Seaway, to Burnside, which is about 20 miles below Baton Rouge, Louisiana, on the Mississippi River. There she was used for transferring grain and other commodities from river barges to ocean-going ships and vice-versa. Her conveyor equipment had been removed and her 9 1/2 yard buckets replaced with 16 yard clamshells for handling light weight materials.

At present, the MARQUIS ROEN, still carrying this name, is employed on the east coast by USX (formerly U.S. Steel) at their Fairless Works in Pennsylvania. Navios Ships Agencies purchased the barge, which no longer has her cabins but retains her cranes and self-unloading boom, and are using her to unload coke from salties.

a) Robert W.E. Bunsen, b) MARQUIS ROEN (2)

BUILT:	1900 Chicago Shipbuilding Co. South Chicago, Illinois
HULL NUMBER:	40
LENGTH:	439.0
BREADTH:	50.2
DEPTH:	24.8
GRT:	5181
REGISTRY NUMBER:	US. 111294
ENGINES:	20 1/2", 30", 43 1/2", 63" Diameter x 42" Stroke Quadruple Expansion
ENGINE BUILDER:	Shipyard 1900

ROBERT W.E. BUNSEN downbound at Mission Point, St. Marys River in 1907

ROBERT W.E. BUNSEN downbound in Lake St. Clair

ROBERT W.E. BUNSEN downbound in Lake St. Clair, August 25, 1951

ROBERT W.E. BUNSEN downbound in the Detroit River

JOHN ROEN IV bringing MARQUIS ROEN (2) into the Great Northern ore docks, at Allouez, to load her first iron ore cargo on June 30, 1955

MARQUIS ROEN (2) using her 180 foot long conveyor unloading boom to discharge a coal cargo

MARQUIS ROEN (2) downbound in lower Lake Huron, May 26, 1960

MARQUIS ROEN (2) at St. Elmo, Baton Rouge, Louisiana

ROYALTON (1)

The Mathews Steamship Company Ltd., of Toronto, once a major force in Great Lakes shipping, went into bankruptcy and was placed in receivership during the Great Depression. The company's vessels were dispersed and, when the ROYALTON went for scrap in 1980, the last ship of this once great fleet left the lakes.

ROYALTON was built by the Collingwood Shipbuilding Company Ltd. and launched on August 9, 1924. She began service September 1st and served as flagship for the fleet which was owned and operated by A.E. Mathews of Toronto, Ontario. When Mathews was forced out of business in 1932, ROYALTON was operated for the receivers by Toronto Elevators Ltd. On November 24, 1932, ROYALTON laid up at Toronto, and was loaded with newsprint during the winter. This cargo was delivered to Chicago the following spring.

In 1933, ROYALTON was acquired by Captain R. Scott Misener for his Colonial Steamship Company Ltd. of Port Colborne, Ontario. Commencing in 1959, the fleet was known as Scott Misener Steamships Ltd.

ROYALTON hauled ore, grain and coal on the upper lakes for most of her career. Even after the Seaway opened in 1959, this ship seldom visited the St. Lawrence. For example, in 1948 she operated mainly in the grain trades to Georgian Bay ports. In 1950, coal was her main cargo with runs from Lake Erie ports to Depot Harbor, Fort William, Sault Ste. Marie and Midland on Georgian Bay.

In later years, ROYALTON was used mostly in the ore trade. In 1961, over forty of her cargoes were ore out of Depot Harbor for Detroit. By the late 1960s, the ship ran consistently from the Canadian Lakehead ports of Fort William and Port Arthur to Indiana Harbor with ore consigned to the Inland Steel Company.

ROYALTON's career was not without incident. On May 6, 1934, she rescued the powerless freighter TEN in Lake Superior ice and helped her to safety. On June 6, 1958, ROYALTON was in collision in the Welland Canal with the canaller WILLIAM C. WARREN and suffered bow damage. Similar damage occurred on June 25, 1959, as a result of a collision on Lake Huron with the deep-sea freighter MONROVIA. The latter, on her first trip to the lakes, sank with a cargo of steel in her holds.

ROYALTON was rebuilt at Port Weller Dry Docks in 1962. Her original 31 cargo hatches were replaced by 16 new steel hatches serviced by a 5 ton electric crane. Then, in 1971, she was converted to burn oil. Even as late as 1975-76 her after accommodations were improved but the ship was nearing the end of the line.

ROYALTON remained idle in 1978 but saw several months of service in 1979 before going to the wall at Hamilton, Ontario with tailshaft problems.

Sold to Marine Salvage Ltd., ROYALTON was towed out of port on May 18, 1980. She cleared Quebec City on May 1st behind the tug HANSEAT arriving at La Spezia, Italy on June 25, in tandem tow with MARINSAL.

ROYALTON lay at La Spezia for almost a year before cutting on her hull was reported to have begun on September 30, 1981. Soon the last vestige of the Mathews fleet was reduced to scrap.

ROYALTON (1) under construction at Collingwood, August 9, 1924, her launch date

ROYALTON (1) upbound at Mission Point, St. Marys River in 1928

ROYALTON (1) downbound in the St. Marys River, July 23, 1977

ROYALTON (1) downbound in the St. Clair River after her collision with the steamer MONROVIA

ROYALTON (1) being scrapped at La Spezia, Italy

BUILT:	1924 Collingwood Shipbuilding Co., Collingwood, Ontario	*GRT:*	7146
HULL NUMBER:	73	*REGISTRY NUMBER:*	C 151108
LENGTH:	536.6	*ENGINES:*	24 1/2", 41 1/2", 72" Diameter x 48" Stroke Triple Expansion
BREADTH:	58.2	*ENGINE BUILDER:*	Allis-Chalmers, Milwaukee, Wisconsin 1919
DEPTH:	27.2		

USS SACRAMENTO

The USS SACRAMENTO was built by William Cramp and Sons Shipbuilding Company at Philadelphia, Pennsylvania as Gunboat No.19 for the U.S. Navy, and was launched on February 21, 1914. She was placed in commission two months later on April 26, and was assigned to Caribbean waters from 1914 to 1917. Later in 1917, she patrolled off the New England coast, then departed New York on July 22, for Gibraltar to join the U.S. Patrol Force. When she finished this duty, she returned to New Orleans for repairs; then departed from New York, arriving at Murmansk, Russia to join the U.S. Naval Forces, Northern Russia on May 22, 1919. The SACRAMENTO was there but a short time and returned to Hampton Roads, Virginia via Norway, Britain and France on February 15, 1920.

USS SACRAMENTO was reclassified PG-19 on July 17, 1920 and was assigned to Caribbean waters again. She departed Charleston, South Carolina on June 12, 1922 for service with the Asiatic Fleet, where she served for many years. On January 12, 1939, she departed Cavite, Philippine Islands for New York via the Mediterranean. Re-assigned to the Ninth Naval District on the Great Lakes November 20, 1939, SACRAMENTO was in use on the lakes as a training ship until late in 1940. Although she sailed just a short time on fresh water, she created a lasting impression on the men who served her. Due to the world situation at the time, she was taken off the lakes for more ocean service.

On December 7, 1941, the SACRAMENTO was at Pearl Harbor during the Japanese attacks but survived without damage, a lucky vessel like the MAKAWELI which was also undamaged. She patrolled the Hawaiian sea frontier until September 27, 1942. After this duty, SACRAMENTO served as tender for P.T. boats at Palmyra Island. In November 1942, she arrived at San Diego, California where she trained gun crews and patrolled out of San Francisco through March of 1945.

The ship was decommissioned at Suisun Bay, California on February 6, 1946, and transferred to the War Shipping Administration for disposal. She was sold to Italian owners on August 23, 1947, renamed b) FERMINA and converted for mercantile use. Like other old soldiers and sailors, she "just faded away". No further records have been found after 1948.

a) USS SACRAMENTO (Gunboat #19), b) Fermina

BUILT:	1914 William Cramp and Sons Shipbuilding Co. Philadelphia, Pennsylvania
HULL NUMBER:	unknown
LENGTH:	226.2
BREADTH:	40.8
DEPTH:	12.5
DISPLACEMENT TONNAGE:	1425
REGISTRY:	U.S. NAVY
ENGINES:	Triple Expansion
ENGINE BUILDER:	William Cramp & Sons, 1914

USS SACRAMENTO on tour of the Great Lakes

HUNTER SAVIDGE

The graceful schooner HUNTER SAVIDGE was built in 1879 at Grand Haven, Michigan by Duncan Robertson, master shipbuilder for the Grand Haven Ship Building Company. She was constructed to the order of the firm Cutler & Savidge, and was launched on August 21st of that year. The vessel was named after a prominent lumber man and, with her fine lines and abundance of canvas, had a reputation for beauty and speed.

The SAVIDGE remained under the ownership of Cutler & Savidge until 1890, when she was listed as being owned by John Muellerweiss of Alpena, Michigan. It was during this ownership that the schooner was lost.

On August 20th, 1899, while on a trip light from Sarnia, Ontario, to Alpena under the command of Captain Fred Sharpsteen, the schooner lay becalmed on Lake Huron in thick hazy weather. Around 4:00 p.m., a strong gust of wind came up without warning and struck her sails. Not being underway, the vessel could not stand the force of the wind. Within ten seconds, the SAVIDGE capsized on her beam ends in 200 feet of water, 7 1/2 miles east by south off Point Aux Barques, Michigan.

On board the schooner, in addition to a crew of eight, were Mary Muellerweiss and Henrietta Muellerweiss, the owner's wife and small daughter. Also aboard was Captain Sharpsteen's wife, Rosa. The three were along for a pleasure trip and were trapped in the vessel's cabin at the time of the capsizing; they were unable, due to the suddenness of the wind gust, to get out in time and were drowned.The crew, who were all on deck at the time were carried under and two were lost

The whole incident was seen by the upbound steamer ALEX McVITTIE, which rescued the survivors and then transferred them to the downbound steamer H.E. RUNNELS, which brought them to the Sand Beach Lifesaving Station.

Soon after the accident became known, the tug FRANK W. was sent to search for wreckage and bodies and return them to Alpena for burial. The captain of the tug, with the help of two lifesaving crews, was unable to find any trace of the wreck.

The captain of the McVITTIE came under criticism from the citizens of Alpena for not searching for bodies or towing the schooner into shallower waters. It was said that, should he ever have visited that city, he would be required to explain his actions, as the citizens regarded them as cowardly or brutal.

On the 26th of August, the fish tug MARTIN was reported to have found some wreckage floating on the lake but little else. No trace of the schooner or of the bodies was ever found.

The exact location of the wreck was unknown for 89 years until, on August 13th, 1988, divers found a large structural member of a ship on which was a name board inscribed "HUNTER SAVIDGE".

HUNTER SAVIDGE just prior to launch, August 21, 1879

HUNTER SAVIDGE at the dock at Milwaukee

BUILT:	1879 Duncan Robertson Grand Haven, Michigan
HULL NUMBER:	none
LENGTH:	117.0
BREADTH:	26.6
DEPTH:	8.2
GRT:	152.14
REGISTRY NUMBER:	US. 95569

HUNTER SAVIDGE downbound in the St. Clair River

J.F. SCHOELLKOPF JR.

The steamer HUGH KENNEDY was built by the American Ship Building Company in Lorain, Ohio for the Buffalo Steamship Company. She was launched on January 26, 1907, and sailed for Buffalo Steamship until 1922, when she was sold to the American Steamship Company.

In 1933, HUGH KENNEDY was renamed b) J.F. SCHOELLKOPF JR., in honor of Mr. Jacob Frederick Schoellkopf, Jr., president of Niagara Shares Corporation and a member of the board of directors of the American Steamship Company. Also in 1933, she was converted to a self-unloader by the American Ship Building Company at Lorain. Her new dimensions were: 531.2 x 56.2 x 27.2 feet; 7,301 gross tons.

In 1950, J.F. SCHOELLKOPF JR. was repowered with a 3500 hp Skinner Unaflow steam engine, which had four equally sized cylinder diameters of 28 inches and a 42 inch stroke. New tank tops were installed in April, 1960.

On October 5, 1967, after delivering a cargo of limestone to Saginaw, Michigan, the SCHOELLKOPF JR. was downbound in the Saginaw River when her steering mechanism failed, which caused her to ram into the west fixed span of the Zilwaukee Bridge. Although damage to the SCHOELLKOPF was minor, the bridge was not so fortunate. Both southbound lanes of Interstate 75 were closed for several days while repairs were completed.

In 1973, J.F. SCHOELLKOPF JR. was acquired by the Erie Sand Steamship Company to operate in the lower lake stone trade, principally from the quarry at Marblehead, Ohio. In March of 1975, she was converted from coal to oil burning by the Oldman Boiler Works in Buffalo, New York.

J.F. SCHOELLKOPF JR. laid up in Erie, Pennsylvania for the last time in December, 1979. In 1980, she was sold by Erie Sand to Marine Salvage Ltd. in Canada, who resold her to C.N. Santa Maria.

On May 2, 1980, the SCHOELLKOPF was towed out of Erie by the tugs STORMONT and ARGUE MARTIN, arriving at Humberstone in the Welland Canal the next day. On June 17, the SCHOELLKOPF departed Humberstone under tow of CATHY McALLISTER and HELEN M. McALLISTER, arriving at Quebec City in late June. On June 27th, J.F. SCHOELLKOPF JR. was towed out of Quebec City bound for La Spezia, Italy. Scrapping operations began at La Spezia on July 29, 1980.

HUGH KENNEDY upbound leaving the Locks at the Soo in 1924

J.F. SCHOELLKOPF JR. downbound at Mission Point, St. Marys River in 1930

a) Hugh Kennedy, b) J.F. SCHOELLKOPF JR.

BUILT:	1907 American Ship Building Co. Lorain, Ohio
HULL NUMBER:	349
LENGTH:	532.0
BREADTH:	56.0
DEPTH:	31.0
GRT:	7064
REGISTRY NUMBER:	US. 203906
ENGINES:	23", 38", 63" Diameter x 42" Stroke Triple Expansion
ENGINE BUILDER:	Shipyard 1907

J.F. SCHOELLKOPF JR. downbound in the St. Clair River opposite Port Huron, June 9, 1960

J.F. SCHOELLKOPF JR. downbound in lower Lake Huron, June 12, 1979

J.F. SCHOELLKOPF JR. outbound from Erie to Genoa, Italy for scrap in tow of STORMONT and ARGUE MARTIN, May 2, 1980

SENATOR OF CANADA

SENATOR OF CANADA upbound in the St. Marys River, August 15, 1960

In 1956, Collingwood Shipyards Ltd. was given an order to construct a straight-deck bulk carrier for N.M. Paterson & Sons Ltd. Given the name SENATOR OF CANADA, the steamer slid from the launching ways on the 30th of May, 1957. The ship was named for Norman McLeod Paterson, founder of the Paterson fleet who later became a member of the Canadian Senate.

The SENATOR OF CANADA led a relatively uneventful life. She usually was in the grain trade down the Seaway, with a back-haul of iron ore for mills in the United States. In 1984, SENATOR OF CANADA laid up at Toronto for the last time.

In April of 1985, Paterson decided that the handsome steamer's services would no longer be needed so she was put into permanent lay-up. Late in June 1985, SENATOR OF CANADA and QUEDOC (2), which also had been laid up at Toronto, headed down the Seaway to Quebec City. Upon arrival at Quebec City, SENATOR OF CANADA and QUEDOC were made up in tandem tow, bound for Caracas, Venezuela where they arrived on the 18th of July, 1985, for scrapping.

BUILT:	1957 Collingwood Shipyards Ltd. Collingwood, Ontario
HULL NUMBER:	159
LENGTH:	590.5
BREADTH:	62.2
DEPTH:	29.3
GRT:	9958
REGISTRY NUMBER:	C. 188389
ENGINES:	Cross Compound Steam Turbine
ENGINE BUILDER:	Westinghouse Electric Company 1957

SENATOR OF CANADA downbound in the St. Marys River

SHENANGO No.1

The wooden-hulled carferry SHENANGO No.1 was built at Toledo, Ohio by the Craig Shipbuilding Company and launched August 5, 1895 for John Shaw, manager for the United States & Ontario Steam Navigation Company. In 1903, she and her sister vessel SHENANGO No.2 were sold to the Marquette & Bessemer Dock & Navigation Company.

Both vessels had an unusual feature - a bow engine and propeller, which later was adopted by most carferries operating on the lakes. The railroad cars ferried across Lake Erie from Conneaut, Ohio to Port Dover, Ontario were loaded with coal for the industries at Hamilton, Ontario. After much dredging at the harbor in Port Dover, the company decided to abandon this port because a carferry could not enter with a full load without grounding.

The company was plagued with problems from the start. The two wooden ferries were almost useless in severe ice conditions. Each ferry was stuck in the ice a number of times and, even though designed by Frank Kirby and possessing three engines, they were not powerful enough to carry on. Port Dover was dropped from the route and Port Stanley and Erieau, Ontario were substituted on the north shore. Conneaut on the south shore remained the terminus.

Captain John McLeod sailed the SHENANGO No.1 out of Conneaut on New Year's Day in 1904. She docked at Rondeau, Ontario but on the return trip, was caught in the ice again and could only get inside the Conneaut breakwall. She was still stuck in the ice when she caught fire in the engine room on March 11, 1904. The vessel was completely destroyed by the fire and one oiler's life was lost.

BUILT:	1895 Craig Shipbuilding Co. Toledo, Ohio
HULL NUMBER:	68
LENGTH:	282.6
BREADTH:	53.0
DEPTH:	19.4
GRT:	1941
REGISTRY NUMBER:	US. 116688
3 ENGINES:	20", 40" Diameter x 36" Stroke (Forward Engine) 23", 46" Diameter x 36" Stroke (Aft Engines) Fore and Aft Compounds
ENGINE BUILDER:	Frontier Iron Works 1895

SHENANGO No.1 inbound Cleveland Harbor, August 1902

SHENANGO No.1 right, SHENANGO No.2 left, backing through the ice

SHENANGO No.1 in dry dock

SHENANGO No.1 burning at Conneaut, March 11, 1904

SILVERDALE

GLENEAGLES was constructed in 1925 by the Midland Shipbuilding Company at Midland, Ontario for James Playfair's Great Lakes Transportation Company, (Glen Line). She was designed primarily for grain service and incorporated 12 foot hatches on 18 foot centers which, at that time, marked a departure from normal shipyard practices. The name GLENEAGLES was reportedly derived from the Gaelic "Glen Eaglais" meaning glen of the church, and was also the name of a narrow picturesque glen in Perthshire, Scotland.

GLENEAGLES was purchased by the Canada Steamship Lines in 1926. In 1948, she was outfitted with radar by Midland Shipyards. In 1963, GLENEAGLES was converted to a self-unloader at the Port Arthur Shipbuilding Company at Port Arthur, Ontario. Upon completion, GLENEAGLES became the largest self-unloader under Canadian registry. Her new gross tonnage was 8,582.

In 1964, GLENEAGLES was transferred to the Canada Steamship Lines affiliate Ocean Lines Limited, of Hamilton, Bermuda. On April 3, 1964, she arrived at the Chicago & North Western ore dock in Escanaba, Michigan opening the 1964 season at that port.

In 1965, GLENEAGLES both opened and closed the season at Depot Harbor, Ontario. Arriving on May 10, she loaded 12,509 gross tons of ore pellets bound for Great Lakes Steel in Detroit. On December 16, she loaded 10,517 gross tons of ore bound for the Hanna Furnace plant in Detroit.

In 1973, GLENEAGLES was placed under the ownership of another Canada Steamship Lines affiliate, Pipeline Tankers Limited.

On April 14, 1977, GLENEAGLES was loading at the CSL stone dock in Humberstone. Her boom had been swung out over the side during the loading procedure, but was brought inboard to allow passage of a vessel. When the boom was swung back out, it dropped to the deck, breaking into two sections. After fishing out part of the boom from the canal, she proceeded to the Stone Dock in Port Colborne for repairs.

In 1978, GLENEAGLES was sold to Westdale Shipping Ltd. and was renamed b) SILVERDALE. She was acquired primarily to service the needs of the Ontario Stone Company of Cleveland, Ohio. Also purchased by Westdale in the deal was the Century Stone Dock in Humberstone.

In 1983, SILVERDALE laid up in Windsor, Ontario for the last time. During February 1984, Westdale Shipping Limited went into bankruptcy and SILVERDALE was sold to M & M Metals of Hamilton, Ontario for scrapping. On June 2, 1984, SILVERDALE was moved from her berth at the Consol Coal Dock in Windsor by the tugs PRESCOTONT, GOTHAM and MANCO, approximately 1 1/2 miles up to the Sterling Fuels slip. Scrapping operations on SILVERDALE began shortly thereafter.

GLENEAGLES launching, August 26, 1925

GLENEAGLES at an ore dock at Superior, Wisconsin

GLENEAGLES downbound at Mission Point, St. Marys River, August 13, 1964

GLENEAGLES downbound in the St. Clair River, May 30, 1965

SILVERDALE upbound at the Homer Bridge, Welland Canal, April 15, 1981

a) Gleneagles, b) SILVERDALE

BUILT:	1925 Midland Shipbuilding Co. Midland, Ontario
HULL NUMBER:	14
LENGTH:	582.0
BREADTH:	60.2
DEPTH:	28.2
GRT:	8233
REGISTRY NUMBER:	C. 152643
ENGINES:	24 1/2", 41 1/2", 72" Diameter x 48" Stroke Triple Expansion
ENGINE BUILDER:	Hooven, Owens, Rentschler, Hamilton 1918 Installed 1925

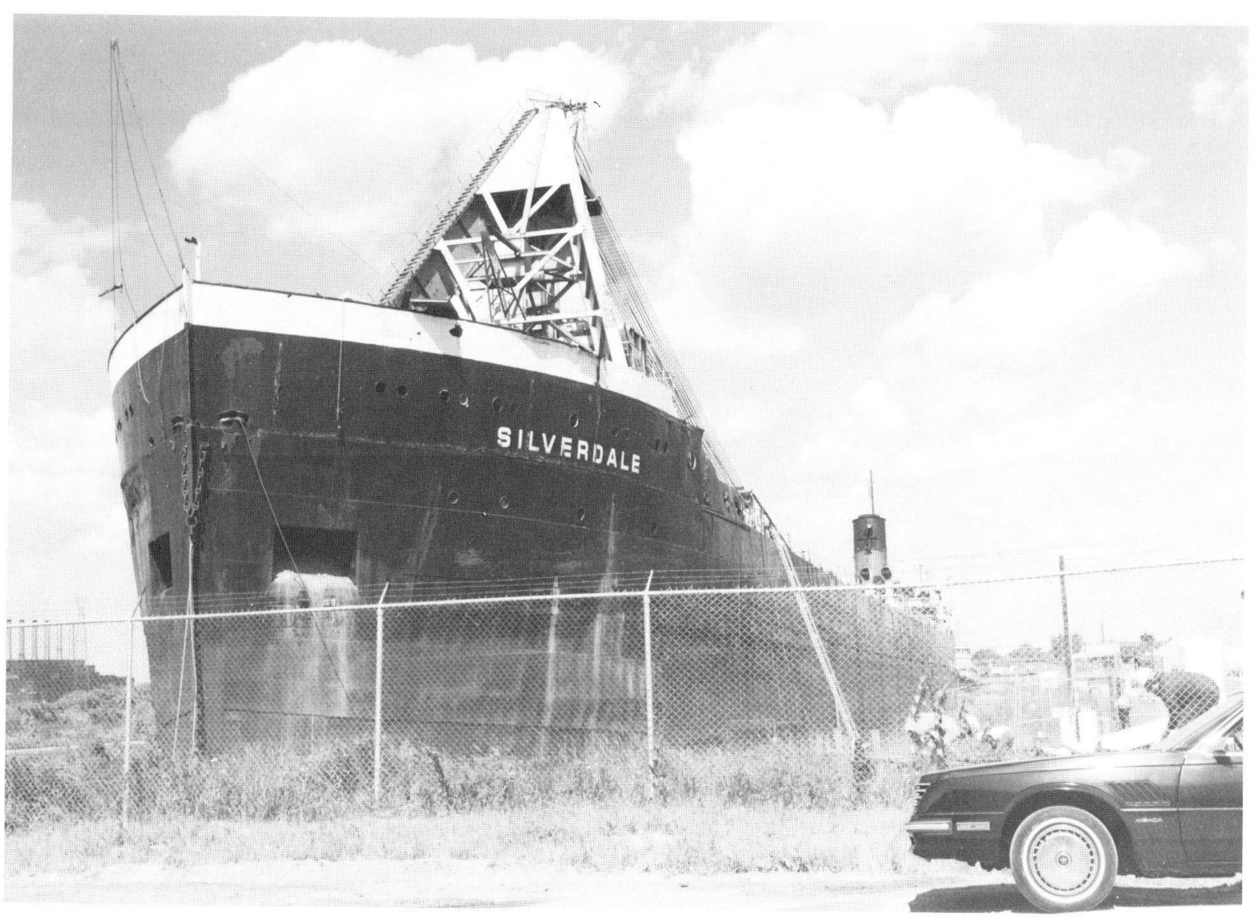

SILVERDALE being scrapped at Windsor, June 25, 1984

C.G.S. SIMCOE (1)

The Canadian Coast Guard ship SIMCOE was launched in March of 1909 at Newcastle-on-Tyne, England by Swan, Hunter and Wigham Richardson Ltd. The Canadian Department of Marine and Fisheries took delivery of the new ship and stationed her at its Parry Sound Agency. This was the first Department of Marine ship built for permanent service on the Great Lakes.

SIMCOE ferried lightkeepers and supplies to lighthouses on the Canadian side of the upper Great Lakes and Georgian Bay. She also placed and removed channel markers each season.

In 1917, it was decided to send her to the east coast of Canada to replace the C.G.S. DOLLARD, which was considered underpowered for work on the Bay of Fundy. Accordingly, in the fall of 1917, SIMCOE left the lakes and proceeded to Quebec City. She then operated along the lower St. Lawrence River for a few weeks before going on to the east coast.

Early in December, SIMCOE departed Sydney, Nova Scotia with coal and supplies for Bird Rocks. She then had orders to pick up the Magdalen buoys and it is believed that she may have had some on board when lost. On December 7, 1917, the day after the great Halifax Explosion, the wireless operator at Grindstone in the Magdalen Islands copied this message: *SOS SINKING CONDITION SW MAGDALEN ISLANDS OR BY FEW MILES EXACT POSITION NOT OBTAINABLE SHOULD JUDGE ABOUT TEN MILES SOUTHWEST MAGDALEN ISLANDS NOW CLEARING AWAY BOATS HEAVY SEAS RUNNING SOS.*

This was the last heard of C.G.S. SIMCOE. Very heavy seas were running at the time of the disaster, with high winds and heavy snow. The C.G.S. ARANMORE searched for four days but found no trace. The only object ever recovered from the steamer was a lifering found on the beach at Sable Island in 1922.

BUILT:	1909 Swan, Hunter and Wigham Richardson Ltd., Newcastle-on-Tyne, United Kingdom
HULL NUMBER:	unknown
LENGTH:	180.0
BREADTH:	35.2
DEPTH:	15.5
GRT:	913
REGISTRY NUMBER:	C. 125456
TWIN ENGINES:	13 1/2", 22", 36" Diameter x 27" Stroke Triple Expansion
ENGINE BUILDER:	Shipyard 1909

SIMCOE (1) during trials in 1909

SIMCOE (1) at the dock in Kincardine

SIMCOE (1) at a dock in Georgian Bay

SINGAPORE

The wooden-hulled schooner SINGAPORE was built at Kingston, Ontario by William Power in 1878. Mr. Power and his partner operated her mainly on Lake Ontario.

By 1892, she was owned by Gunn and Company. Elizabeth Thompson, of Toronto, was her registered owner in 1894. The schooner was sold to S.C. Malcolmson, of Hamilton, in 1895. He owned her through the season of 1899, and by 1901, Captain James C. Sutherland, of Goderich, was master and owner. Captain Sutherland commanded several schooners before investing his life savings in the SINGAPORE.

On September 15, 1904, SINGAPORE was downbound on Lake Huron with a load of pine lumber from Blind River for Sarnia. Captain Sutherland's wife was the cook and her brother's four children were on board for the trip. They had intended to leave the children at Goderich while the schooner proceeded for Sarnia, but the vessel was caught in heavy weather and never reached Goderich.

SINGAPORE began to leak and soon became waterlogged. The waves carried away the yawl boat and shifted the deck cargo. The crew hung in the foremast rigging, while Mrs. Sutherland and the children stood on the after cabin roof. The poop deck was often swamped and Captain Sutherland was up to his waist in water at times.

The children had to be lashed to the rigging in order to keep them from being swept overboard. One child was injured as she was being pulled up from the cabin gangway. She and the Captain had been washed into the spinning steering wheel by a wave. Months later, she was to die as a result of these injuries.

Captain Sutherland steered for Kincardine as the SINGAPORE wallowed in the big waves. Right at the end of the piers, she hit bottom and lost headway. The current and waves pushed her past the end of the south pier and she pounded across the bottom and onto the beach south of the harbor.

The Kincardine lifeboat, manned by Tom McGraw and six volunteers, was successful in removing the entire crew and the children from the wrecked schooner. The waves quickly battered the SINGAPORE into pieces. There was no insurance on her and Captain Sutherland lost everything as he abandoned his schooner on the beach.

SINGAPORE almost at the piers at Kincardine

SINGAPORE hitting the bottom

SINGAPORE gradually breaking up

SINGAPORE being washed ashore

SINGAPORE on the beach

BUILT:	1878 William Power Kingston, Ontario
HULL NUMBER:	none
LENGTH:	106.0
BREADTH:	25.4
DEPTH:	9.9
GRT:	186
REGISTRY NUMBER:	C. 77629

SKYLARK

SKYLARK was a small passenger and freight propellor built at Detroit by Stewart McDonald in 1864. Although she was reportedly built for Traverse Bay service, she served almost everywhere else on the upper Lakes. At first she ran largely on Lake Huron between Saginaw Bay and Alpena, Michigan. She was given enlarged cabins in 1866 (134.88 GRT), and shifted to Lake Michigan routes between Chicago and western Michigan ports. Official records show that the little steamer changed owners as frequently as she changed routes, and interestingly, she changed silhouettes nearly as often. The following owners of the SKYLARK and the years are enumerated to give an idea of the many and various forms she took in the thirty years of her existence: J.T. Whiting of Detroit 1864; L.L. McKnight of Detroit 1865; J.E. Stevens of St. Joseph, Michigan in 1866...passenger vessel of 90.18 GRT; Thomas L. Parker of Chicago in 1869.

On February 1, 1871, the SKYLARK was purchased from Thomas L. Parker by the Goodrich Transportation Company for the sole purpose of using her machinery in a new steamer. During the season of 1871, SKYLARK was used between Chicago, Illinois, Kenosha, Wisconsin, Racine and Milwaukee. She rendered valuable service during the Chicago fire when she rescued all the company records, the families of Captain Goodrich's staff, office furniture, and many trapped passengers. At the end of the season, the SKYLARK was laid up at Manitowoc, Wisconsin and her engines removed to be placed in the new OCONTO being built by Rand during the winter of 1871-1872.

W.A. and F.J. Preston of Grand Haven, Michigan took over in 1873. The ship was first a barge and later that year rebuilt as a steambarge; 127.64 GRT with an engine from the tug L.H. BOOLE of 1858 (122.3 x 23.2 x 8.7); H.W. Williams of Benton Harbor, Michigan purchased the SKYLARK in 1878 and had her lengthened 20 feet at St. Joseph in 1879 (260.93 GRT). Graham & Morton Transportation Company bought her in 1880. SKYLARK was cut down to a lumber steamer (130 GRT) in 1882. She was again made a three-masted schooner and renamed b) BERRIEN in 1883, (144.93 GRT), but then re-engined a third time in 1885 (114 GRT) as a steambarge. Her third and forth engines are of unknown description. An 1887 newspaper article indicated that the ship "never lost a man nor made a cent, but on the contrary played no small part in impairing the fortunes of several of her numerous owners." In 1887, S.B. Barker of Chicago became her owner and early in 1893, George G. Robinson also of Chicago took over. Her last owner was Fowler J. Preston of Chicago.

The old ship was reported dismantled in 1894. The Benton Harbor Daily Palladium said at the time "scarcely a stick of her original hull has been left after the numerous rebuildings..."

SKYLARK at Alpena in 1865, the schooner is unidentified

SKYLARK at the dock

Passenger steamer SKYLARK of Detroit in 1865 on which many of the earliest settlers came to Alpena

a) SKYLARK, b) Berrien

BUILT:	1864 Stewart McDonald Detroit, Michigan
HULL NUMBER:	none
LENGTH:	100.0
BREADTH:	19.4
DEPTH:	7.6
GRT:	134 88/95
REGISTRY NUMBER:	US. 22554
ENGINES:	16", 16" Diameter x 20" Stroke Two Cylinder High Pressure
ENGINE BUILDER:	Jackson & Wiley, Detroit 1864

WILLIAM P. SNYDER JR.

On January 27, 1912, the Great Lakes Engineering Works' Ecorse yard launched the steel bulk freighter WILLIAM P. SNYDER JR. for the Shenango Steamship and Transportation Company, a subsidiary of the Shenango Furnace Company. She was named for William Penn Snyder, Jr. who had joined Shenango the previous year. Since the WILLIAM P. SNYDER was already sailing the lakes, the new boat was always referred to as the "SNYDER JUNIOR." She was a duplicate of her sister COL. JAMES M. SCHOONMAKER which had been built the previous year. At the time, the pair were not only the largest lakers but also the largest vessels in the world devoted exclusively to carrying freight.

SNYDER JR. cleared Ecorse on her maiden voyage on April 27, 1912, and before the season was over, had set a speed record for lakers when she arrived at Ashtabula, Ohio just 73 hours after she had cleared Duluth, Minnesota—an average speed of 12 miles per hour in spite of delays at the Soo and in the rivers.

Nineteen thirteen was an extraordinary year for the SNYDER JR. On June 15, while upbound in a fog with coal, she collided with the steamer JESSE SPALDING, downbound with ore, off Lake Superior's Keweenaw Point. Both vessels survived but damages to the SPALDING amounted to $10,000 and the SNYDER JR. received $3,000 worth of repairs at Superior by the time she departed on June 27. On her next trip to Lake Superior she set a new record for grain when she departed Duluth on July 10 with 464,000 bushels of wheat—enough to make 30 million loaves of bread! Later the same month, she broke the Lake Superior ore record when she loaded 12,362 tons at Duluth. Then on August 2, she set a Lake Erie coal record when she cleared Lorain, Ohio with 14,243 net tons.

In 1950, WILLIAM P. SNYDER JR.'s original quadruple expansion steam engine was replaced by a 5-cylinder Unaflow steam engine (28 inch diameter by 36 inch stroke) built by the Skinner Engine Company of Erie, Pennsylvania.

The SNYDER JR. operated in the Shenango fleet through the 1965 season. For 1966, she was under charter to the Interlake Steamship Company who purchased her at the end of the season. In November of 1970, she went to Manitowoc, Wisconsin for dry docking and boiler automation and when she came off the dock in December, she was owned by the Cleveland Cliffs Iron Company, coming out in their colors the following spring.

On December 17, 1980, the SNYDER JR. laid up at Ashtabula amid reports that she was to be cut up there. But, on December 14, 1981, she was towed to Toledo, Ohio. In 1983, it was reported that she and several other Cliffs boats had been sold to American Bulk Shipping of Los Angeles, California but apparently in the years that followed the new owners defaulted and Cliffs got the boats back. Finally, in mid-1986, Cliffs sold the SNYDER JR. to Port Colborne Marine Terminals, Inc. for scrap. On June 17, 1987, she arrived at Port Colborne in tow of the tugs THUNDER CAPE and MICHAEL D. MISNER. At that port, International Marine Salvage soon began cutting and, by early 1988, WILLIAM P. SNYDER JR. was only a memory.

The "Shenango Sisters" were two of the more historic steamers that sailed the lakes. Their elaborate passenger cabins were unique. While it is unfortunate that the SNYDER JR. was cut up, we can take solace that much of her woodwork was salvaged by Detroit's Dossin Great Lakes Museum and that her identical sister, WILLIS B. BOYER, (ex COL. JAMES M. SCHOONMAKER) is being preserved as a museum vessel at Toledo.

WILLIAM P. SNYDER JR. upbound at Mission Point, August 15, 1957

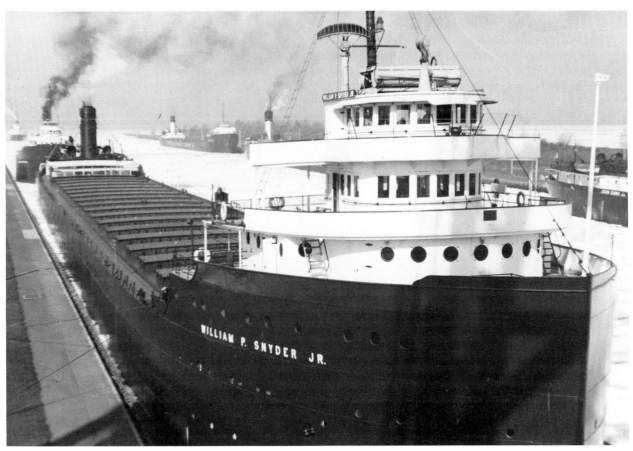

WILLIAM P. SNYDER JR. downbound in the ice, waiting for passage through the Locks

WILLIAM P. SNYDER JR. downbound in the St. Clair River

WILLIAM P. SNYDER JR. downbound in the Detroit River, Livingstone Channel, May 30, 1969

BUILT: 1912 Great Lakes Engineering Works
Ecorse, Michigan
HULL NUMBER: 83
LENGTH: 590.0
BREADTH: 64.2
DEPTH: 34.2
GRT: 8603
REGISTRY NUMBER: US. 209662
ENGINES: 22 3/4", 33 1/4", 48", 69"
Diameter x 42" Stroke
Quadruple Expansion
ENGINE BUILDER: Shipyard 1912

WILLIAM P. SNYDER JR. upbound in the St. Marys River, July 29, 1974

WILLIAM P. SNYDER JR. at Port Colborne, June 20, 1987. ARTHUR B. HOMER astern

SOLVEIG

The pulpwood barge SOLVEIG, of the Roen Steamship Company, of Sturgeon Bay, Wisconsin, had its beginnings as a large landing ship of the U.S. Navy. Laid down on February 8, 1944, at the Bethlehem Shipbuilding Company at Quincy, Massachusetts, the ship was launched five weeks later on March 11th, and commissioned one month later on April 12th, as Landing Ship, Tank (LST) 1006.

During World War II, LST-1006 was assigned to the Asiatic-Pacific theater. She participated in the Philippines operations - the Leyte landings in October, 1944, and the Zambales-Subic Bay landings in January, 1945, and then moved north to take part in the Okinawa assault and occupation April-June, 1945. The ship earned three battle stars for WWII service.

Following the war, LST-1006 performed occupation duty in the Far East and saw service in China until late March, 1946. She returned to the States and was decommissioned on July 26, 1946, and stricken from the Navy list on August 28th. LST-1006 was sold in 1946 for private operation to the Construction Power & Merchandising Company and was enrolled under Official Number US. 261849. She was sold to the Stanolind Oil & Gas Company in 1947.

In 1951, Captain John Roen needed more pulpwood carrying capacity for his fleet, so he purchased the LST-1006, which was then lying at Beaumont, Texas. He had her sailed under her own power to New Orleans and towed up the Mississippi River to Lockport, Illinois. There her superstructure was removed and Roen tugs moved her into the Great Lakes at Chicago and on to Sturgeon Bay. Work started immediately to convert the ship to a barge. Her diesel engines were removed to be used later on Roen's tugs JOHN ROEN V and JOHN PURVES. The landing ship bow doors were welded shut, and the ship's spar deck was modified by providing ten 20 by 20 foot hatches and installing on deck a 25 ton diesel traveling crane with a 75 foot boom. Renamed b) SOLVEIG, for Captain Roen's wife, the barge was ready for service in the spring of 1952.

SOLVEIG carried most of her cargo below deck although pulpwood and lumber piles extended above the spar deck. Since she had only one cargo hold with large hatches, she was not difficult to load or unload. During her dozen years under Roen colors, SOLVEIG primarily carried pulpwood, but also had other cargoes on occasion such as wood pulp in bales, calcium chloride, soda ash, raw sulfur from South Chicago to paper plants at Marinette, DePere and Green Bay, and even a few loads of iron ore. Her first iron ore cargo of 4,535 tons was loaded at the D.M. & I.R., docks in Duluth in October, 1952, destined for Republic Steel in Cleveland.

SOLVEIG was also involved in several salvage operations including lightering the OREFAX which had run aground on Point aux Barques in Lake Huron.

The 1970s brought an end to the unique operations of the Roen Steamship Company following the death of Captain Roen on December 7, 1970. Cargoes for the company's vessels were dwindling, and the stockholders, who were the heirs of John Roen, decided late in 1971to sell off major pieces of equipment as purchasers could be found.

Thus, in 1971 the SOLVEIG was sold to Robert Krause, of Kewaunee, Wisconsin, for $25,000 for scrap and by 1974 dismantling was completed.

LST-1006 in the Pacific Theater during World War II

SOLVEIG upbound in the Detroit River

SOLVEIG loading a full cargo of pulpwood from the boom pond at Port Arthur, Ontario in June, 1958

a) USS LST-1006, b) SOLVEIG

BUILT:	1944 Bethlehem Shipbuilding Co. Quincy, Massachusetts
HULL NUMBER:	unknown
LENGTH:	316.0
BREADTH:	50.0
DEPTH:	11.4
DISPLACEMENT TONNAGE:	1625
REGISTRY:	U.S. NAVY
2 ENGINES:	8 ¾" Diameter x 10 ½" Stroke Diesel
ENGINE BUILDER:	General Motors Corporation

SOLVEIG being scrapped at Kewaunee, July 15, 1974

SOO RIVER TRADER

Eight vessels have carried the name of Samuel Mather in Great Lakes history. The fourth ship to honor the Cleveland industrialist was launched at Wyandotte, Michigan, by the Detroit Shipbuilding Company on July 28, 1906.

The steel-hulled bulk carrier SAMUEL MATHER entered service for the Masaba Steamship Company and became part of the Interlake Steamship Company upon its formation in 1913. SAMUEL MATHER carried ore downbound with upbound cargoes of coal. In 1925, the vessel was renamed b) PATHFINDER (2) and her work for the Pickands, Mather fleet continued until she was laid up at Superior, Wisconsin on June 20, 1960.

The vessel remained idle until sold to Upper Lakes Shipping Ltd., of Toronto, on June 26, 1964. She made one trip for them as PATHFINDER, registered at London, England, before being renamed c) GODERICH (2) and brought into Canadian registry with official number C. 306336.

GODERICH received the boilers from PORTADOC in 1967 and was converted to burn oil rather than coal over the winter of 1972-73.

GODERICH occasionally visited her namesake port on Lake Huron where she might call to unload grain or to load salt. In 1977, during the 150th anniversary of the town of Goderich, the ship carried the "Jubilee 3" crest on her bow.

In the spring of 1980, GODERICH was sold to the Soo River Company and was upbound in the Welland Canal on her first trip on April 27, 1980. After the maiden voyage, the ship was renamed d) SOO RIVER TRADER. She operated primarily in the grain trade, however, she brought the first shipment of bulk cement to open the $18 million St. Lawrence Cement distribution dock at Duluth on May 1, 1982. Her cement cargo had been loaded at Clarkson, Ontario.

When the Soo River Company went into receivership and ceased operations in 1982, all of its ships were purchased by the P & H Shipping Division of Parrish & Heimbecker Ltd. The new owner renamed her e) PINEGLEN but she had only a few months of work remaining. The vessel laid up at Toronto after the 1982 season, and never operated again. She cleared Toronto on September 27, 1984, under tow of the tugs GLENEVIS and GLENSIDE and they arrived at Port Maitland, Ontario two days later. The steamer's name was shortened to f) NEGLEN to reserve the former name for a future member of the fleet. Then the old laker was broken up for scrap.

SAMUEL MATHER (4) upbound at Mission Point, St. Marys River in 1919

PATHFINDER (2) upbound in the St. Clair River, July 14, 1951

GODERICH (2) downbound in the Detroit River, May 16, 1969

GODERICH (2) upbound below Lock 2, Welland Canal, May 28, 1977 with her Jubilee 3 anniversary crest

SOO RIVER TRADER upbound in the St. Marys River, July 19, 1980

a) Samuel Mather (4), b) Pathfinder (2), c) Goderich (2), d) SOO RIVER TRADER, e) Pineglen, f) Neglen

BUILT:	1906 Detroit Shipbuilding Co. Wyandotte, Michigan
HULL NUMBER:	165
LENGTH:	530.0
BREADTH:	60.2
DEPTH:	32.2
GRT:	6751
REGISTRY NUMBER:	US. 203407
ENGINES:	23 1/2", 38", 63" Diameter x 42" Stroke Triple Expansion
ENGINE BUILDER:	Shipyard, Detroit 1906

PINEGLEN in tow of GLENEVIS in the Welland Canal, September 28, 1984

SPRUCEGLEN

The WILLIAM K. FIELD was built as the flagship of the Reiss Steamship Company by the Toledo Shipbuilding Company and was launched January 24, 1924. She was designed with a triple-deck forward cabin, the extra deck designated for passenger accommodations.

The steamer's name was changed to b) REISS BROTHERS in 1934. She was repowered with a DeLaval steam turbine at Toledo, Ohio, in 1957, and was equipped with a bow-thruster during the winter of 1964-65. In 1969, management of the Reiss fleet was taken over by Boland & Cornelius of Buffalo, New York. In 1970, the vessel was renamed c) GEORGE D. GOBLE and a year later, she was sold to the Edison Steamship Company, Boland & Cornelius, managers.

GEORGE D. GOBLE was sold to the Kinsman Marine Transit Company of Cleveland, Ohio in 1972, and in 1975, her ownership was transferred to the affiliated S & E Shipping Corporation. On July 21, 1975, the GOBLE arrived at Lorain, Ohio with an unusual deck cargo loaded at American Ship Building Company's yard at South Chicago, Illinois. She was carrying the deckhouses for two Interlake Steamship Company thousand-foot self-unloaders being built at AmShip's Lorain yard. These vessels were completed as the JAMES R. BARKER and MESABI MINER.

In 1980, GEORGE D. GOBLE was brought into Canadian Registry after being sold to Pierson Steamships Ltd. She was renamed d) ROBERT S. PIERSON (C. 391528) and served as the flagship of Pierson's Soo River Company. The Pierson fleet went into receivership on August 6, 1982 and the fleet was subsequently bought by P & H Shipping Division, Parrish & Heimbecker, Limited which renamed the ROBERT S. PIERSON as e) SPRUCEGLEN.

She had the distinction of being the last coal-fired Canadian Great Lakes steamer, but P & H ran the vessel only until the end of the 1982 season. She suffered structural damage to her hull that autumn, and she was laid up at Goderich, Ontario. She was sold to Goderich Elevator & Transit Company Ltd. and served as grain storage hull.

In mid-September, 1983, her bow-thruster was removed and it was refitted with the usable thruster parts from ELMGLEN (1) and placed in WILLOWGLEN. On June 14, 1985, SPRUCEGLEN was towed from Goderich by the tug THUNDER CAPE en route to the scrapyard of Shearmet-Recycling at Thunder Bay, Ontario. Her dismantling was completed by the Lakehead Scrap Metal Company, successor to Shearmet.

WILLIAM K. FIELD downbound at Mission Point, St. Marys River in 1925

REISS BROTHERS downbound in the St. Clair River May 29, 1960

GOERGE D. GOBLE downbound at Mission Point, St. Marys River July 1971

GEORGE D. GOBLE downbound in Lake St. Clair May 28, 1973

ROBERT S. PIERSON downbound in the St. Clair River September 6, 1980

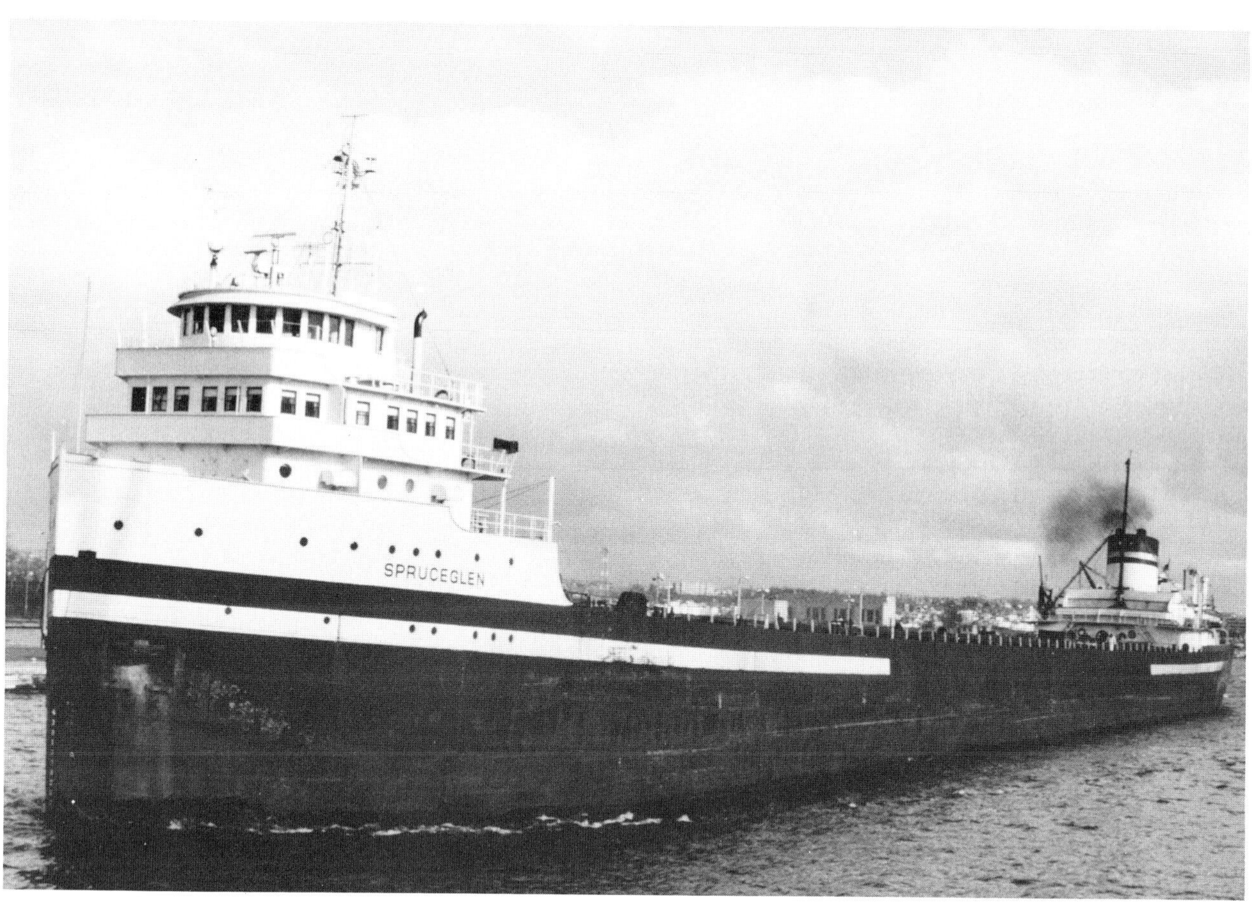

SPRUCEGLEN upbound at he Soo

a) William K. Field, b) Reiss Brothers, c) George D. Goble, d) Robert S. Pierson, e) SPRUCEGLEN

BUILT:	1924 Toledo Shipbuilding Co., Toledo, Ohio
HULL NUMBER:	176
LENGTH:	588.0
BREADTH:	60.3
DEPTH:	27.7
GRT:	8195
REGISTRYNUMBER:	US. 233607
ENGINES:	25 1/5", 41", 67" Diameter x 42" Stroke Triple Expansion
ENGINE BUILDER:	Shipyard 1924

STARBELLE

The steel-hulled tanker IMPEROYAL was built to the order of the Imperial Oil Company Ltd., of Toronto, Ontario, and was launched during April of 1913 by the Greenock & Grangemouth Dockyard Company Ltd. at Grangemouth, Scotland. The tanker trade on the Great Lakes was still in its infancy at that time, and IMPEROYAL was typical of the early Canadian tankers. She had a trunk deck, her bridge structure was set amidships and she carried a very tall stack aft.

IMPEROYAL crossed the North Atlantic under her own power and entered lake service during the summer of 1913, and ran for her first owner for forty years. In line with a general renaming of the Imperial Oil fleet vessels, she became b) IMPERIAL COBOURG in 1947.

IMPERIAL COBOURG was retired at the close of the 1952 season, and she was sold to Powell Transports Ltd., of Winnipeg, Manitoba. During 1953, she was rebuilt as a bulk carrier in the shipyard at Port Dalhousie, Ontario. During reconstruction, her pilothouse was relocated aft, her depth was altered to 19.4 feet and her GRT was increased to 2,274. Before she entered service, she was rechristened c) STARBELLE.

Along with the former package freighter STARBUCK, the STARBELLE operated for Powell Transports in the Canadian grain trade, although occasionally she did carry other cargoes. On December 9, 1960, she was caught in a late season storm on Lake superior, and suffered cracks to her deck and sides. Despite this severe damage, she reached port safely and the necessary repairs were completed during the following winter by Collingwood Shipyards Ltd.

The aging STARBELLE was retired at the end of the 1962 season and was laid up at Fort William, Ontario. She was sold in 1963 to High & Heavy Rigging Ltd. and was to be converted to a derrick and lightering barge. Work on cutting her down to a barge was begun but the decision then was made to scrap the hull instead, and STARBELLE was scrapped during 1963-1964 in the Kaministiquia River at Fort William by the Lakehead Scrap Metal Company.

a) Imperoyal, b) Imperial Cobourg, c) STARBELLE

BUILT:	1913 Greenock & Grangemouth Dockyard Co. Grangemouth, Scotland
HULL NUMBER:	351
LENGTH:	249.5
BREADTH:	43.1
DEPTH:	19.7
GRT:	2253
REGISTRY NUMBER:	C. 135209
ENGINES:	21", 34 3/8", 56" Diameter x 36" Stroke Triple Expansion
ENGINE BUILDER:	Cooper & Greig, Dundee, Scotland 1913

IMPEROYAL downbound in the St. Marys River

IMPERIAL COBOURG downbound in the Detroit River under the Ambassador Bridge

STARBELLE being rebuilt at Port Dalhousie, May 24, 1953

STARBELLE upbound in the Detroit River at Windsor, October 4, 1953

STARBELLE downbound in the St. Clair River

STARBELLE being dismantled at Fort William in 1963

SUMATRA

The wooden-hulled schooner SUMATRA was built at Black River (Lorain), Ohio by Quayle & Peck for the Cleveland Transportation Company in 1874.

On the night of September 6, 1883, SUMATRA was at anchor off Marquette, Michigan when the seas drove her ashore as she dragged her anchor. The steamer SPARTA and two tugs tried to release her but to no avail. Then four steamers and the tugs pulled on her. The SUMATRA moved only eight feet at the bow. Cables parted frequently with the CONTINENTAL losing hers three times. The four vessels and tugs finally gave up. She was finally freed on Tuesday October 2nd by Captain McKay. He used 45 jack-screws to lift her off the beach after many hours of work. The SUMATRA was towed to Port Huron, Michigan for repairs and returned to service.

In 1889, she was sold to the Ohio Transportation Company and in 1892 to the Mills Transportation Company. On September 30, 1896 the SUMATRA foundered in Milwaukee Bay, Lake Michigan in a severe storm. She carried a cargo of steel rails and was towed by the steamer B.W. ARNOLD. Four lives were lost in the foundering.

BUILT:	1874 Quayle & Peck Black River, Ohio (Lorain)
HULL NUMBER:	none
LENGTH:	204.1
BREADTH:	34.0
DEPTH:	14.2
GRT:	845.34
REGISTRY NUMBER:	US. 115240

SUMATRA ashore at Marquette, September 6, 1883

SYLVANIA

The steel bulk freighter SYLVANIA was built by the West Bay City Shipbuilding Company for the Duluth Steamship Company managed by G.A. Tomlinson and was launched on March 18, 1905. SYLVANIA had many accidents in her life and her first year was no exception. In June of 1905, she collided with the steamer SIR HENRY BESSEMER off Whitefish Point on Lake Superior putting an 80 foot hole in the BESSEMER. SYLVANIA was repaired at the Craig Shipbuilding Company at Toledo, Ohio.

In 1914, she was renamed b) D.M. PHILBIN and was renamed c) SYLVANIA again in 1929.

In 1958, SYLVANIA was lengthened and converted to a self-unloader by the Manitowoc Shipbuilding Company. This was a prime reason in insuring her longevity. Her new dimensions were: 552.0 x 54.0 x 26.7 feet; 7,352 gross tons.

On June 1, 1967, SYLVANIA was unloading her cargo at the Peerless Cement Company at Port Huron, Michigan. The CSL steamer RENVOYLE had been discharging her cargo at the sheds on Point Edward immediately across from the Peerless Cement dock. The RENVOYLE began her turn-around in the narrow St. Clair River, when the current caught her and she began to swerve into the opposite bank of the river. She struck the SYLVANIA and punched a hole in her side. SYLVANIA, still tied up to the dock, began to list to starboard and sank in a few minutes. There was no loss of life but both steamers were heavily damaged. SYLVANIA was subsequently raised and towed to the AmShip yard at Lorain, Ohio where she was repaired. The RENVOYLE, however, was not as fortunate. Although she did not sink, RENVOYLE was so severely damaged that repairs were deemed inadvisable and she was sold for scrap at Ashtabula, Ohio.

In 1971, SYLVANIA was sold to the Columbia Transportation Division, Oglebay Norton Company, who had chartered the vessel since 1969. In 1977, SYLVANIA was relegated to the Lake Erie coal run in which she ended her days. Her final trip was made on May 10, 1980. In her career SYLVANIA had carried over 20 million tons of cargo. On October 31, 1983, SYLVANIA departed Toledo in tow of the tug OHIO for Ashtabula where she arrived the next day for scrapping. Her final remains were put to the torch in 1984. Thus ended 78 years of service and the making some 30 million dollars for her various owners.

SYLVANIA being repaired at Toledo after the collision with SIR HENRY BESSEMER

D.M. PHILBIN entering Duluth Harbor in the ice

a) SYLVANIA, b) D.M. Philbin, c) SYLVANIA

BUILT:	1905 West Bay City Shipbuilding Co., West Bay City, Michigan
HULL NUMBER:	613
LENGTH:	504.0
BREADTH:	54.0
DEPTH:	26.7
GRT:	6272
REGISTRY NUMBER:	US. 201840
ENGINES:	23 1/2", 38", 62" Diameter x 42" Stroke Triple Expansion
ENGINE BUILDER:	Detroit Shipbuilding Co. 1905

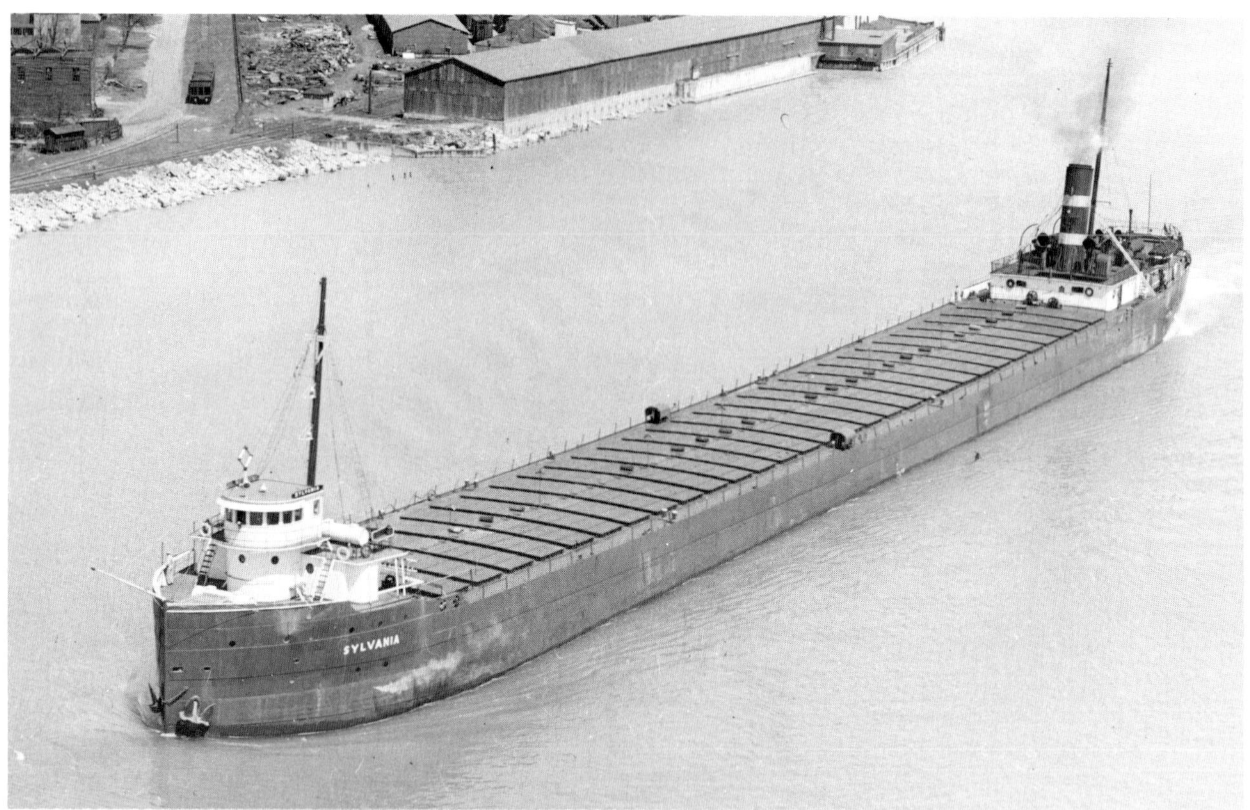

SYLVANIA downbound in the St. Clair River under the Blue Water Bridge

SYLVANIA downbound in lower Lake Huron, May 19, 1960

SYLVANIA sunk at Port Huron after the collision with RENVOYLE, June 2, 1967

SYLVANIA upbound in the Detroit River

BEN E. TATE

On Saturday June 28, 1902, the American Ship Building Company launched a steel bulk freighter at their South Chicago yard. At the launch Miss Maud Carter, daughter of C.H. Carter, the general manager of the Erie Steamship Company, christened the vessel PANAY. Contemporary accounts said that the Erie Steamship Company was to be her owner but official records show her owner as E.D. Carter until 1915. In that year she passed to the Paisley Steamship Company which was managed by the Cleveland-Cliffs Iron Company.

On November 12, 1919, the PANAY, upbound on Lake Superior for Duluth, Minnesota in rough weather, was one of the last vessels to see the downbound JOHN OWEN which, apparently later the same day, disappeared with all hands.

During the winter of 1927-28, the PANAY was renamed b) WILLIAM NELSON. In 1929, Paisley transferred her management to the Valley Camp Steamship Company. Then during the winter of 1929-30, the steamer was taken to the Leathem D. Smith Dock Company at Sturgeon Bay, Wisconsin and converted to a scraper-type self-unloader. No change in her official tonnage resulted from the conversion.

In September of 1930, her first season as a self-unloader, the NELSON was involved in one of the classic rescues on the Lakes. During the night of September 25-26, in mid-Lake Michigan, a gale tore away all of the sails of the last lakes-built sailing vessel still in commercial operation, the 55 year-old schooner OUR SON, leaving her helpless. Because of high seas it was impossible to launch her yawl so her 73 year-old master, Captain Fred Nelson and his crew of five, without a radio, were at the mercy of the Lake. Also because of the storm, all other commercial shipping was hugging Lake Michigan's west shore, far from the foundering schooner. To the north at dawn on the 26th, the WILLIAM NELSON came out of the Straits of Mackinac bound for Chicago with sand. For some unknown reason, her skipper, Captain Charles H. Mohr, elected to run down the storm-tossed eastern shore instead of seeking the lee of the west side of the lake. South of Ludington, again for unknown reasons, Captain Mohr changed course and headed directly into the seas, straight across the Lake. The NELSON took a real beating, suffering damage to her cabins, but she plowed on. Thus it was about 3 p.m. that the NELSON came upon OUR SON. The high seas precluded the NELSON's lifeboats being launched but her radio summoned the big carferry PERE MARQUETTE NO. 22. Just as smoke from the ferry was sighted, Captain Mohr decided that he could wait no longer and he ordered storm oil spread on the seas. Then he headed the NELSON straight for OUR SON, bringing her along side the schooner for a few brief seconds—just long enough for all six crewmen from OUR SON to leap aboard the steamer. The NELSON arrived safely at South Chicago on the afternoon of September 27th, greeted by a cheering crowd. The OUR SON sank soon after the rescue. Captain Mohr was later awarded a Congressional Medal for what was termed "One of the most daring pieces of expert seamanship in the history of navigation."

In 1935, the Paisley Steamship Company was reorganized as the J.A. Paisley Steamship Company of Delaware. In the same year, the Valley Camp boats passed to the management of Oglebay Norton and Company. The following year, she was renamed c) BEN E. TATE in honor of Benjamin Ethan Tate, a director of several coal companies that provided cargoes for the vessel. In 1940, the TATE's gross registered tonnage was increased slightly to 3,954 tons. It was not until 1954 that the J.A. Paisley Steamship Company sold her to Columbia, and she was painted in Columbia colors.

No appointments were announced for BEN E. TATE in 1968 and, before the year was over, she was sold to Marine Salvage Ltd. of Port Colborne, Ontario into whose scrapyard she was towed by the tugs OKLAHOMA and LAURENCE C. TURNER on December 3, 1968. On May 19, 1969, the tugs ROBERT B. NO. 1 and JERRY G. departed Port Colborne with her. Two months later on July 12th, she arrived for scrapping at Bilbao, Spain, along with the laker DONNACONA a) W. GRANT MORDEN, in tow of the Dutch tug MISSISSIPPI.

a) Panay, b) William Nelson, c) BEN E. TATE

BUILT:	1902 American Ship Building Co. South Chicago, Illinois
HULL NUMBER:	56
LENGTH:	356.0
BREADTH:	50.0
DEPTH:	24.0
GRT:	3811
REGISTRY NUMBER:	US. 150959
ENGINES:	20", 33 1/2", 55" Diameter x 40" Stroke Triple Expansion
ENGINE BUILDER:	Chicago Shipbuilding Co., 1902

PANAY at the dock at Cleveland

WILLIAM NELSON downbound at Mission Point, St. Marys River in 1929

WILLIAM NELSON downbound leaving the Soo Locks

WILLIAM NELSON at far left coming to the rescue of the OUR SON in Lake Michigan, September 26, 1930

BEN E. TATE upbound in the Detroit River, August 8, 1940

BEN E. TATE downbound in lower Lake Huron, June 1, 1960

W. P. THEW

The wooden steam barge W. P. THEW was built in 1884 by H. D. Root of Lorain, Ohio for Captain Richard Thew and was named in honor of his father William P. Thew. She was launched on March 15th.

Several modifications were made to the steamer during the years that Captain Thew owned her. In 1886, she was lengthened to 132.5 feet and, in 1888, a second deck was added to improve her carrying capacity, which increased her GRT to 403. However, this deck appears to have been removed around 1893, at which time her GRT was reduced to 206. Sometime during the 1880's, she was given a steeple compound engine, with cylinders of 14 and 28 inches in diameter and a stroke of 20 inches; this machinery having been built by the same builder, Sutton Brothers of Buffalo, New York in 1884.

The steamer remained under Thew's ownership until 1895, when she was listed as being owned by W. H. Barriss, of Cleveland, Ohio. The vessel was transferred in 1896, probably as a result of a mortgage default, to the ownership of Marine Bank of Cleveland. In 1898, she was owned by Shannon & Garey, of Saginaw, Michigan, and used in their lumber operations. The THEW's ownership changed again in 1904, when she was owned by Hugh R. Havey, of Detroit, Michigan.

The W. P. THEW had her share of misfortunes during her twenty-five year career. The first incident occurred in June of 1894, when the steamer was moored at the lumber piles at Bay City, Michigan. The lumber caught fire and the blaze spread to the vessel, burning her almost to the waters edge. The owner had the THEW rebuilt and then returned her to service.

On June 22, 1909, the THEW's career came to an end when she was sunk in a collision with the freighter WILLIAM LIVINGSTONE off Thunder Bay Island, Lake Huron.

W. P. THEW downbound in the St. Marys River in 1905

BUILT:	1884 H. D. Root Lorain, Ohio
HULL NUMBER:	none
LENGTH:	107.1
BREADTH:	23.4
DEPTH:	8.5
GRT:	139
REGISTRY NUMBER:	US. 81024
1st ENGINE:	18" Diameter x 20" Stroke High Pressure Non-condensing (A rebuild)
ENGINE BUILDER:	Sutton Brothers, Buffalo

W. P. THEW sheltering at Harbor Beach, Michigan

A. TREMBLAY

Perhaps the most unique vessels found on the St. Lawrence were the goelettes, the small, wooden-hulled, diesel powered freighters usually constructed in tiny lower riverside communities by local workmen. These ships were indigenous to the Province of Quebec.

A. TREMBLAY was even more unique in that she was powered by a steam engine, whereas most of the newly built hulls or those converted from sail were diesel powered. While most sources indicate that A. TREMBLAY was built as a sailing vessel prior to 1912, and converted to steam in 1916 at Matane, Quebec, there is at least one source which feels that the conversion itself took place in 1912, for either A. Tremblay of Matane, or for the Price Lumber Company.

Chartered during World War I by the Clarke Steamship Company of Montreal, A. TREMBLAY traded on their Quebec, Gaspe coast and Newfoundland services. She continued in their service until 1921 or 1922. The period 1922-1925 was perhaps even more demanding, in that she spent much of her time hauling coal from Sydney Mines, Nova Scotia to ports on the south shore and the Gulf of St. Lawrence.

By the mid-Twenties, the lure of the illicit became too great. Her owners pressed A. TREMBLAY into the rum-running trades from 1925 to 1929, and it can be assumed that there was little or no red ink in the ledger of the owners. This idyll came to an abrupt end in early May 1929 when A. TREMBLAY, ghosting quietly into Godbout with a cargo of booze, had her lines taken by some friendly fellows, who turned out to be RCMP constables. Placed under guard, the ship crossed to Matane where unloading took place prior to being laid up at Lauzon, Quebec.

By late in World War II, the search for civilian tonnage had become a desperate one. The hulk of A. TREMBLAY was acquired by Jean Tremblay of Tadoussac, who incorporated only her bottom in the newly built MONT BLANC (C. 173945).

A. TREMBLAY at Matane, Quebec c.1927

BUILT:	1916 Matane, Quebec	*GRT:*	245
HULL NUMBER:	none	*REGISTRY NUMBER:*	C. 138262
LENGTH:	111.5	*ENGINES:*	12", 24" Diameter x 15" Stroke Two-Cylinder Compound
BREADTH:	28.2		
DEPTH:	10.4	*ENGINE BUILDER:*	F.H. Dralet & Co., Quebec

BYRON TRERICE

In 1882 Dresden, Ontario lumberman, Captain Alexander Trerice contracted with William R. Peck of Wallaceburg, Ontario to build a fast, large capacity, shallow draft vessel to be used as a night boat in the river trade between Dresden, Wallaceburg and Detroit. The steamer would also make occasional stops at Baby's Point and Port Lambton, Ontario.

The steamer was designed by Captain Allen Kirby and was constructed at Dresden during the winter of 1881-1882 from materials obtained in the area. The engine, also a local product, was built by Charles Wesley Wees, also of Dresden. Since she would be carrying some passengers, the vessel was equipped with staterooms, which opened onto her upper deck, leaving the main deck and hold open for carrying many different types of freight. The vessel was valued at $24,000. Alex Trerice named the vessel BYRON TRERICE in honor of his son.

In the spring of 1882, she made a trial run to Wallaceburg. The local newspaper was very enthusiastic about her, stating that "she proved herself complete in every particular. Her engines worked without jar and she sailed through the water so steadily that not the slightest move was perceptible." This comment is a bit contradictory but no doubt what they wished to convey was that she had great stability. The new steamer made her maiden voyage to Detroit on Saturday July 8, 1882, with several passengers and a cargo of sixty cords of cordwood. Her first skipper was Captain Asa Ribble.

For reasons of economy, the TRERICE would tow two or three barges, and, when returning to Dresden, would drop the tow allowing the tug MYRTLE to take the barges up river to Molly Creek for loading; the procedure was reversed when the cargo was loaded, as there was no turning basin at Dresden. The steamer always began the season as soon as the ice went out of the Sydenham River, however, on the first few trips she would carry enough provisions on board to last a week in the event that she became trapped in the ice along her route. One of her frequent return cargoes was fifty or sixty barrels of whiskey taken aboard at Walkerville, Ontario. The whiskey posed a bit of a problem for the TRERICE. It was suspected that some of the crewmen in the "graveyard watch" were sampling the whiskey so the distillery solved the problem by inviting the crew to bring their own jug ashore for filling. There was a grand rush and, after that, there were no more complaints about losses in transit.

In 1883, her passenger cabins were extended her full length, and she devoted the rest of her short life in the passenger trade. Her GRT was now 200.

In 1888, the steamer was sold to John S. Nesbit of Sarnia, Ontario who operated her until 1890, when the TRERICE was sold to Captain W.D. McRae of Wallaceburg. In 1892, the BYRON TRERICE saw service on the open lake, when she was placed on the Cleveland, Ohio to Rondeau, Ontario run under the command of the owner's brother, Captain David McRae.

On September 13, 1893, the steamer encountered a severe storm on Lake Erie, and, out of concern for the vessel's safety, the captain put into Leamington, Ontario for shelter. The vessel tied up at the Wigle Dock for the evening to wait out the storm.

It was fortunate that the busiest part of the tourist season was over and there were only a few passengers aboard, because, shortly after dark the BYRON TRERICE caught fire, and soon became a raging inferno fanned by the winds. In the excitement, the cook, Miss Fennacy, jumped overboard to escape the flames and was drowned. The cook was not the only casualty. It was also reported that two crewmen were burned to death. Captain Walter Power, who was the mate at the time, broke his ankle when he jumped onto the dock. Hundreds of spectators gathered at the scene, but little could be done due to the intensity of the fire. The TRERICE continued to burn through the night and, by morning, she had burned to the waters edge. After the fire had burned itself out, there was nothing left to salvage.

Such was the unfortunate end of one of the most popular and best known steamboats on the Sydenham River, and until the day she burned, was a credit to her builders and to Captain Trerice.

BUILT:	1882 William R. Peck Dresden, Ontario
HULL NUMBER:	none
LENGTH:	102.0
BREADTH:	26.0
DEPTH:	9.0
GRT:	268
REGISTRY NUMBER:	C. 83028
ENGINES:	20" Diameter x 24" Stroke High Pressure Non-Condensing
ENGINE BUILDER:	Charles Wesley Wees, Dresden 1882

BYRON TRERICE at Dresden, Ontario

BYRON TRERICE after conversion to a passenger vessel Hamilton, Ohio, 1918

A.C. VAN RAALTE

The 100-foot A.C. VAN RAALTE was a wooden passenger and freight propellor built in 1867 by Hitchcock & Gibson at Buffalo, New York for John T. Edwards of St. Joseph, Michigan. She was designed for the route between Chicago, Holland and St. Joseph, and operated in Edwards & Stevens' Lake Michigan Transportation Line along with four other similar craft. Woltman and Kraai of Holland, Michigan owned her in 1870.

In 1871, she was sold to F.M. Knapp and J.I. Case of Racine, Wisconsin and others in Charlevoix and Northport, Michigan, and she subsequently ran on Little Traverse Bay. J.M. Jones of Detroit owned her in 1872, while Fox and Ross from Petoskey, Michigan were the owners in 1874. In the fall of 1880, she went to the Smith Brothers of Cheboygan, Michigan, who appear to have run her between Cheboygan and the Sault. They housed-in her lower deck and enlarged her passenger cabins in 1883. Her engine was then replaced by a steeple compound; 15 and 30 inches diameter by 20 inch stroke by Sheriffs Mfg. Company of Milwaukee, Wisconsin. Two years later she was switched to a route between Petoskey and Manistee, Michigan for Charles H. Caskey and J. M. Burbeck of Harbor Springs, Michigan, after which she was sailed on Muskegon Lake in 1888 by Captain A.C. Majo of Muskegon, Michigan, running as a day excursion boat.

In 1890, the little steamer was condemned for passenger use. She was sold to the Garden City Sand Company of Chicago, who removed most of her cabins and converted her to a work tug or lighter, 103.82 GRT. She was used for dock contracting work around Chicago for the next several seasons. John and William Ross of Chicago became her owners in 1895.

In the summer of 1898, the VAN RAALTE was acquired by C.R. Leihy of Bayfield, Wisconsin, who rebuilt her as a single-decked tug; 87.0 x 19.6 x 6.8 feet; 97.31 GRT. He employed her in rafting work. In April 1901, she was bought by the John Schroeder Lumber Company of Ashland, Wisconsin who also used her in the rafting business in western Lake Superior. Schroeder renamed her b) ASHLAND in 1903. Following the Depression, the lumber business had all but disappeared, and the tug was idle most of the time. She was finally laid up around 1935 and the 70 year old hull was dismantled on the Ashland waterfront in 1937.

A.C. VAN RAALTE as a passenger steamer on Lake Michigan

ASHLAND after being renamed

a) A.C. VAN RAALTE, b) Ashland

BUILT: 1867 Hitchcock & Gibson
Buffalo, New York
HULL NUMBER: none
LENGTH: 96.4
BREADTH: 23.0
DEPTH: 8.6
GRT: 176.63
REGISTRY NUMBER: US. 1496
ENGINES: 20" Diameter x 24" Stroke
High Pressure Non-Condensing
ENGINE BUILDER: Farrar & Traffts, Buffalo 1867

VIKING

VIKING was one of a small number of steel hulls built originally for the lumber trade on the Great Lakes and, like most of the steel lumber hookers, VIKING ended her days in the sand trade. The reasons behind this frequent transfer of trades were evident; the lumber trade declined soon after the vessels were built, and these ships, although often still relatively new hulls, were too small for other bulk trades. Dredging and the movement of sand were ideal uses for these ships.

VIKING was built at Buffalo, New York in 1889 by the Union Dry Dock Company for the Gilchrist lumber interests of Alpena, Michigan. Her original registered owner was F.W. Gilchrist, and in 1903, she was transferred to F.R. Gilchrist. In 1904, her ownership was taken over by the Merida Steamship Company, and she passed to the Petrol Traffic Company in 1915. All of these owners were Gilchrist affiliations.

The steamer remained with the various Gilchrist fleets until 1918, but in that year she passed into the Canadian register (C. 141661), owned by A.E. Mathews, of Toronto, Ontario. When registered in Canada, she was listed as 217.0 x 36.7 x 14.7 feet; 1231 GRT. She was renamed b) CYLATON in 1918, which name was changed (or corrected) to c) CLINTON in 1920. In 1921, her ownership was transferred to the Mathews Steamship Company Ltd., of Toronto.

Back in United States registry in 1925 and given her original name and U.S. registry number again, d) VIKING was purchased by the Seneca Washed Sand Corporation of Buffalo. Refitted as a sand sucker, VIKING served her last owners until 1935, when the vessel was scrapped. Despite very humble work, VIKING's forty-five years on fresh water marked her as a superior hull.

a) VIKING, b) Cylaton, c) Clinton, d) VIKING

BUILT:	1889 Union Dry Dock Co. Buffalo, New York
HULL NUMBER:	49
LENGTH:	217.4
BREADTH:	37.1
DEPTH:	15.0
GRT:	1117
REGISTRY NUMBER:	US. 161612
ENGINES:	21", 42" Diameter x 42" Stroke Fore and Aft Compound
ENGINE BUILDER:	S.F. Hodge & Co., Detroit 1889

VIKING downbound in the St. Clair River as a lumber hooker

VIKING downbound at Mission Point, St. Marys River

VIKING at the dock unloading coal

CYLATON at her dock

CLINTON in the Welland Canal

ENDERS M. VOORHEES

The ENDERS M. VOORHEES was one of five "AA-Super Class" bulk freighters built in 1942. Great Lakes Engineering Works built three of the five vessels. The VOORHEES was the second one G.L.E.W. built and she was launched April 11, 1942. She cleared River Rouge, Michigan, July 29, 1942, to begin her career with the Pittsburgh Steamship Company.

The VOORHEES had a serious mishap on November 14, 1942, in Lake Superior. During a storm, she was simultaneously struck by waves at both ends of the ship and a serious crack developed in her hull. The Pittsburgh steamer NORMAN B. REAM came to her rescue. The REAM released her "storm-oil" to calm the seas while the crew of the VOORHEES ran cables around the ship and made them fast with the ship's winches to help hold her together. The VOORHEES was then escorted to the Soo by the REAM. A crew member was quoted in the newspaper at the time that, "the hatches were the only thing that held us together". The VOORHEES sailed back to the Great Lakes Engineering Works for repairs. Extra strengthening straps were installed on the VOORHEES and subsequently on all of her four sisters.

On July 11, 1943, the VOORHEES had the honor of opening the new MacArthur Lock at the Soo. In 1950, she was involved in a collision during a snow storm in the Straits of Mackinac with the ELTON HOYT II. Both vessel received bow damage.

In 1952, her ownership was transferred to the United States Steel Corporation. On Tuesday, April 12, 1955, she opened the second century of navigation through the St. Marys Falls Ship Canal while upbound from Monroe, Michigan to Duluth, Minnesota. In a colorful ceremony, the VOORHEES entered the fourth lock to open officially the 1955 shipping season. On hand to greet her were civic and military leaders from Sault Ste. Marie, Michigan and Ontario, and all parts of Chippewa County. The Soo High School Band played and soldiers from the 8th AA Battalion walked their posts as the ceremonies got underway.

In the winter of 1973, her boilers were converted to oil-firing at the Bay Shipbuilding Company, Sturgeon Bay, Wisconsin. The VOORHEES participated in United States Steel's all-winter navigation season in 1974-75. She arrived in Milwaukee, Wisconsin for lay-up on March 25th and fitted out for the 1975 season on April 24th. On November 20, 1978, she delivered 17,800 tons of iron ore to Lorain, Ohio. This included the 100 millionth ton of ore produced by the U.S. Steel Minnesota operations Minntac Plant.

On April 27, 1980, after loading pellets in Duluth, theVOORHEES stopped at the Seaway Dock to load a large wooden stairway (three sections) on deck which was taken to the AmShip yard at Lorain. It was used for an open house on the newly built EDWIN H. GOTT in 1979 and was also used for christening the EDGAR B. SPEER. The steps were designed by Marine Consultants and built by G & W Industries of Cleveland, Ohio. They were first used for christening the JAMES R. BARKER in 1976, then they were taken to Duluth on the THOMAS WILSON (3) for use in christening the MESABI MINER.

On June 5, 1981, United States Steel announced the formation of a new subsidiary, USS Great Lakes Fleet, Inc., which was intended to contract with commercial shippers for the cartage of bulk cargoes on the Lakes and Seaway trades. All of the U.S. Steel vessels were transferred to the new subsidiary at that time.

The ENDERS M. VOORHEES laid up for the last time at Duluth on December 26, 1981. During May, 1986, her bowthruster was removed through a large hole cut in her starboard side. It was taken out in one piece and hull plates were welded back into place; the machinery was installed as a stern-thruster on the fleet's JOHN G. MUNSON during the winter of 1986.

On July 12, 1986, a severe thunderstorm hit Duluth-Superior. At the Hallett Dock #5 in West Duluth the VOORHEES, A.H. FERBERT and IRVING S. OLDS pulled the bollards out of the dock but the ships remained chained together as they tore off a number of chutes on the ore dock, blew across St. Louis Bay and grounded in Superior. They were towed back to West Duluth the next day.

On August 22, 1987, the tug AVENGER IV departed Duluth with the VOORHEES in tow and they locked through the Soo on August 24th. The tow passed through the St. Lambert Lock in the Seaway on September 2nd, a few hours before the THOMAS W. LAMONT, the first time two scrap tows had passed through the Lock on the same day. The VOORHEES arrived in Quebec City on September 3, 1987, towed by AVENGER IV and GLENBROOK.

On September 15, 1987, the VOORHEES and the THOMAS W. LAMONT departed Quebec City under tow of the tug IRVING CEDAR and arrived at Algeciras, Spain, on October 24, 1987. On January 24, 1988, while under tow of tug EVEREST, the VOORHEES encountered force 9 winds, parted her towline and went aground and subsequently broke in two at Profitis Elais, Kythnos Island (Thermia) in the Cyclades between the Mirto and Aegean Seas. She was on her way to Turkey for scrapping at the time. Both sections were later retrieved and arrived at Aliaga, Turkey on August 23, 1989 where they were to be dismantled by Kalka Vanlar Gemi Sokum Ticaret A.S.

BUILT:	1942 Great Lakes Engineering Works, River Rouge, Michigan
HULL NUMBER:	288
LENGTH:	622.6
BREADTH:	67.0
DEPTH:	30.3
GRT:	10294
REGISTRY NUMBER:	US. 242023
ENGINES:	Cross Compound Steam Turbine
ENGINE BUILDER:	DeLaval 1942

ENDERS M. VOORHEES downbound at Mission Point, St. Marys River

ENDERS M. VOORHEES upbound at Mission Point, St. Marys River, June 18, 1953

ENDERS M. VOORHEES on her way to scrap, August 26, 1987

ENDERS M. VOORHEES in tow of the tugs AVENGER IV and WILLIAM A. WHITNEY under the Ambassador Bridge

WAHNAPITAE

The C. Beck Manufacturing Company Ltd., of Penetanguishene, Ontario, required a steady supply of logs for its mill. Accordingly, the company had the wooden-hulled tug WAHNAPITAE built in 1904. She was intended to bring log rafts from the North Channel ports of Thessalon, French River and Little Current to Penetanguishene.

In 1920, the owners sent her to the shipyard at Midland, Ontario where she was completely rebuilt and enlarged. Emerging with a length of 107 feet and GRT of 191, she was then more suited to carry loads of supplies north-bound in addition to towing log rafts.

At 3 a.m. on June 7, 1921, she struck a rock near Burinot Island, 12 miles west of Little Current. She sank in 40 minutes, which interval allowed the crew to escape safely in two small boats. After borrowing a gas-powered launch at Clapperton Island, the crew returned to Little Current, where the tug CHARLTON was engaged to attempt to salvage WAHNAPITAE. Using an "alligator" salvaging outfit proved futile, so the effort was discontinued and the tug FAVORITE (2) was called down from the Soo. FAVORITE brought two divers with her to the scene of the wreck. One of the divers was drowned during the efforts to raise WAHNAPITAE. The FAVORITE then abandoned the salvage effort.

On August 15, 1921, the Georgian Bay Shipping and Wrecking Company Ltd. succeeded in bringing the wreck to the surface and taking it to Midland. WAHNAPITAE had a large hole in her bow, but repairs were completed by the end of August.

In 1929, she was sold to Keenan Wooden Ware, of Owen Sound. She towed the barge DAN PROCTOR with cargoes of lumber for several years. Keenan sold her to the J.J. McFadden Lumber Company Ltd., of Blind River, Ontario in 1937. In 1940, McFadden sold her to Sorel Harbour Tugs Ltd., and the new owners then renamed her b) DICK T. She was wrecked in the Chaudiere Basin, St. Lawrence River in 1941.

WAHNAPITAE at her dock in Georgian Bay

WAHNAPITAE - another view

a) WAHNAPITAE, B) Dick T.

BUILT:	1904 Penetanguishene, Ontario
HULL NUMBER:	none
LENGTH:	91.0
BREADTH:	18.6
DEPTH:	10.2
GRT:	153
REGISTRY NUMBER:	C. 116754
ENGINES:	unknown
ENGINE BUILDER:	unknown

WESTMOUNT (1)

The steel-hulled, canal-sized, bulk carrier WESTMOUNT (1) was launched during 1903 by G.S. Swan & Hunter Ltd. at Wallsend-on-Tyne, England, having been built to the order of the Montreal Transportation Company Ltd., Montreal, Quebec. She and her sistership, FAIRMOUNT (1), were two of the most handsome canallers ever built, and the lines of their hulls were of classic design.

The only major misfortune suffered by WESTMOUNT during her years of lake service came on October 20, 1905, when the steamer, towing the big M.T.Co. schooner-barge MINNEDOSA, encountered heavy weather on Lake Huron. The elements proved to be too much for the wooden-hulled MINNEDOSA, and she foundered. The steamer was not damaged.

WESTMOUNT operated primarily in the grain trade until the demand for tonnage to assist in the war effort took her to salt water in 1915. The steamer had been sold that year to the Inter-American Steamship Company Ltd., Toronto, and in 1916 she was renamed b) WETHERSFIELD. In 1918, her ownership was transferred to the Canadian Maritime Company Ltd., Montreal, and in 1920 she was sold to E. J. Heinz (London) Limited, Montreal.

WETHERSFIELD was sold in 1922 to the former Hamilton entrepreneur, A. B. Mackay, who at that time was a resident of the Isle of Wight. He appears to have acquired her for resale purposes only, and she did not return to the lakes under his ownership.

In 1923, the steamer was sold to Arnold Bernstein, of Hamburg, Germany, who renamed her c) MAX BERNSTEIN and kept her in deep-sea service. She was rechristened d) FORDSON I in 1926 and was converted to carry automobiles, trucks and tractors with the addition of a raised shelter deck. Bernstein renamed her e) TRACTOR in 1927, and under his name she did trade back into the lakes in 1928 and again in 1932.

TRACTOR was sold in 1937 to Egon Oldendorff, of Lubeck, Germany, and she was renamed f) LUDOLF OLDENDORFF that same year. She never again returned to the lake waters for which she had been built. Her career ended on October 9, 1944, when she was bombed and sunk by British aircraft at Egersund, Norway.

WESTMOUNT (1) in old Welland Ship Canal

a) WESTMOUNT (1), b) Wethersfield, c) Max Bernstein, d) Fordson I, e) Tractor, f) Ludolf Oldendorff

BUILT:	1903 G.S. Swan & Hunter Ltd. Wallsend-on-Tyne, England
HULL NUMBER:	287
LENGTH:	248.7
BREADTH:	42.0
DEPTH:	20.6
GRT:	1875
REGISTRY NUMBER:	C. 114445
ENGINES:	21", 35", 58" Diameter x 39" Stroke Triple Expansion
ENGINE BUILDER:	North Eastern Marine Engineering Co. Ltd., Newcastle, England 1903

TRACTOR leaving the canals

THOMAS WILSON (3)

THOMAS WILSON (3) was one of sixteen "Maritime Class" freighters built for lakes trading during World War II. Of the L6-S-A1 type, she was launched on November 14, 1942, at the American Ship Building Company yard in Lorain, Ohio, and was delivered on May 13, 1943, as the first of the class to enter service.

This vessel was constructed for the United States Maritime Commission. They traded her to the Wilson Transit Company in exchange for the obsolete steamers A.W. OSBORNE and CAPTAIN THOMAS WILSON, later KICKAPOO.

THOMAS WILSON was intended for the ore trade. Approximately 80% of her cargoes during her Wilson years were iron ore. Lesser amounts of coal, grain and stone were also handled. Over half of her ore moved out of Allouez, Wisconsin, for the docks at Ashtabula, Ohio.

This steamer was acquired by the Kinsman Marine Transit Company when Wilson ceased operations in 1972. Her stay in Kinsman colors was brief as a result of U.S. Government divestiture requirements regarding Kinsman's purchase of the Wilson fleet. In 1974, she joined the Columbia Transportation fleet but remained on charter to Kinsman for a year.

The THOMAS WILSON had a Lentz-Poppet double compound engine, the first and one of the few to be used on the Lakes. This machinery was the source of continual problems and was one of the reasons for the disposal of the vessel. Her water tube boilers were originally coal-fired but she was converted to burn oil over the winter of 1976-77. THOMAS WILSON burned in the range of 7,000 gallons per day and, during her final season, she consumed 1,557 tons of fuel. This amounted to a cost of about $2,000 per day.

This ship sat out the occasional season. She was idle at Superior for 1961 and Toledo for 1975. She resumed trading in 1976 and ran aground in the St. Marys River late in the year. The December 13 accident required lightering before THOMAS WILSON would float free.

THOMAS WILSON operated until December 16, 1979, when she tied up at Toledo. During that final year, the vessel carried only thirty cargoes and all were ore. Fourteen originated at Silver Bay, Minnesota and ten at Duluth. Toledo, Conneaut and Cleveland were the recipients of most of the shipments.

This steamer was sold to the Corostel Trading Company for scrap in 1987. The tugs TUSKER and THUNDER CAPE moved THOMAS WILSON down the Welland Canal on October 4, 1987. After a time at Lauzon, Quebec, she left on December 21 behind the tug OSA RAVENSTURM. The reported designation was Kaosiung, Taiwan, and THOMAS WILSON was in tandem tow with her former fleetmate ASHLAND.

THOMAS WILSON never arrived. On December 30 she broke loose in position N34º 08'-W61º 36' while northeast of Bermuda. The tug gave chase and closed to within seven miles at which time THOMAS WILSON's image disappeared from the radar screen as the ship plunged to the bottom of the Atlantic.

THOMAS WILSON downbound in the St. Marys River August 17, 1960

THOMAS WILSON upbound the St. Clair River May 27, 1974

THOMAS WILSON upbound the St. Marys River July 21, 1976

BUILT:	1942-43 American Ship Building Co. Lorain, Ohio
HULL NUMBER:	826
LENGTH:	604.8
BREADTH:	60.2
DEPTH:	30.2
GRT:	8758
REGISTRY NUMBER:	US. 243357
ENGINES:	50", 22 5/8", 22 5/8", 50" Diameter x 48" Stroke 4 cyl Lentz Poppet Double Compound
ENGINE BUILDER:	Shipyard 1943

THOMAS WILSON at Port Colborne October 3, 1987 in tow of THUNDER CAPE on her way to scrap

WISSAHICKON (2)

Wissahickon is the name of a small river or creek which flows through the city of Philadelphia. Two ships, both owned by the Pennsylvania Railroad's Erie and Western Transportation Company, carried this name. Early in its existence, the "Anchor Line", as this fleet was popularly known, adopted the policy of naming its ships after the rivers of the State of Pennsylvania.

This steel-hulled, package freighter was Anchor Line's second WISSAHICKON, built at Buffalo, New York in 1907 and launched on July 11th of that year. In size and appearance, this ship was nearly identical to DELAWARE (1905), MUNCY (1902), ALLEGHENY (1910) and CONEMAUGH (1910). As did the other Anchor Liners, WISSAHICKON carried the attractive colors of green and white hull, white houses and bright red stack.

WISSAHICKON and the other ships of this fleet were transferred to the Great Lakes Transit Corporation in 1916. She was readmeasured in 1924 (4,253 GRT). The WISSAHICKON was renamed b) DANIEL WILLARD in 1925.

Greatly rebuilt, the vessel left the Great Lakes via the Illinois and Mississippi Rivers for salt water after her requisition by the U.S. War Shipping Administration in 1942.

In 1947, the ship was sold as war surplus to Panamanian owners, Cia Panamena de Nav. "Santa Maria" and was renamed c) ANNE MARIE. This veteran of 48 years sailing was sold for scrap in 1955.

a) WISSAHICKON (2), b) Daniel Willard, c) Anne Marie

BUILT:	1907 Buffalo Dry Dock Co. Buffalo, New York
HULL NUMBER:	210
LENGTH:	350.0
BREADTH:	46.0
DEPTH:	30.9
GRT:	4062
REGISTRY NUMBER:	US. 204416
ENGINES:	19", 27", 40", 58" Diameter x 42" Stroke Quadruple Expansion
ENGINE BUILDER:	Detroit Shipbuilding Co., Detroit 1907

WISSAHICKON downbound the St. Clair River opposite Marine City

WISSAHICKON downbound at Mission Point, St. Marys River in the fog

DANIEL WILLARD upbound at Mission Point, St. Marys river in 1928

WISSAHICKON in the dry dock at Buffalo in 1917

VESSEL INDEX

A

B

C

D

E

F

N

O

T

U

V

W

X

Y

Z